THE SPLENDOR OF FAITH

DATE DUE

Demco, Inc. 38-293

The Splendor of Faith

The Theological Vision of Pope John Paul II

AVERY DULLES, S.J.

A Herder & Herder Book
The Crossroad Publishing Company
New York

The Crossroad Publishing Company
370 Lexington Avenue, New York, NY 10017

Printed in the United States of America

Library of Congress Cataloging-in-Publication Data

Dulles, Avery Robert, 1918–
    The splendor of faith : the theological vision of Pope John Paul
II / Avery Dulles.
      p.   cm.
    Includes bibliographical references.
    ISBN 0-8245-1792-X (pbk.)
    1. John Paul II, Pope, 1920– . 2. Catholic Church—Doctrine.
I. Title.
    BX1368.5.D85   1999
    230'.2'092—dc21   99-11634
                                                         CIP

2   3   4   5   6   7   8   9   10   04   03   02   00

Nihil Obstat: Francis J. McAree, S.T.D., Censor Librorum
Imprimatur: + Patrick Sheridan, D.D., Vicar General,
   Archdiocese of New York
Date: January 4, 1999

Contents

Preface

∞

THIS BOOK HAS ITS ORIGINS in a course I taught as visiting scholar at St. Joseph's Seminary, Yonkers, New York, in the fall semester, 1996. At the end of the semester, several students suggested that I should publish the lectures as a book. I did not act immediately on the suggestion, but in the next few years I reworked and updated the lectures until I felt that I had the makings of a book.

Over the past decade I have devoted many lectures and articles to the work of John Paul II, and in composing this book I have not hesitated to incorporate passages from some of these previous pieces. In particular I have drawn on those enumerated in the list of acknowledgments that immediately follows this preface. I am grateful to the publishers of these journals and symposia for permission to reprint substantial portions of these articles.

As this work goes to press, I am conscious that it has many limitations. As a general survey of the pope's thinking on a vast range of topics, it cannot pretend to take the place of specialized studies that would show the development and content of the pope's thinking on particular subjects in greater detail. To avoid being taken too far afield, I have generally refrained from discussing movements and authors with whom the pope might be brought into comparison. Since he himself rarely refers to his theological allies and adversaries, I have thought it best not to speculate on the possible sources of the pope's thought and on positions he might be intending to criticize. In particular, it would be unfitting to engage in controversial arguments, since in doing so I would have to depart from the pope's own style of discourse. While he is firm, he is never polemical. He believes that a serene exposition of the truth is its best defense.

A difficulty arises from the fact that the pope is continuing to publish significant documents. I have been able to take account of his major writings through the year 1998, including his great encyclical on "Faith and Reason," released on October 15. The year 1999 has already seen the appearance of several important new documents of which no cognizance could be taken in this work. In Mexico City on January 22 he promulgated his post-synodal apostolic exhortation on "The Church in America," which gives many important pastoral applications of his previous teaching on Christian spirituality, the Church, and social justice. Documents such as this seem to suggest that John Paul II has substantially completed the corpus of his doctrinal teaching and that the remainder of his pontificate will be devoted to bringing it to bear on current situations in the Church and the world. But even if new and surprising documents are still in the offing, the kind of overview I have given may provide a helpful framework for understanding these future writings.

When I expressed hesitations about bringing out this book prematurely, the publisher convinced me that the time is ripe for this type of synthesis, and that further developments in John Paul II's teaching could be incorporated, as necessary, in subsequent revised editions.

As an author, I have profited immensely from studying the thought of the present pope. I can only hope that I have managed to communicate some of the deep faith and wisdom that permeate his writings. The splendor of the Catholic faith finds a magnificent expression not only in the words but in the very person of this extraordinary successor of Saint Peter. His deep humanism, his keen sense of the exigencies of our times, and his mastery of the Christian heritage have made him, in the view of many competent observers, the preeminent religious and moral leader of the world in our day. It is a privilege to have a part in disseminating his theological vision.

In closing I wish to express my indebtedness to Dr. James Le Grys of Crossroad Publishing Company for his constant encouragement, to Professor Mary F. Rousseau of Marquette University for her helpful comments on the first draft of this book, and to my faithful assistant, Dr. Anne-Marie Kirmse, O.P., for her unfailing advice on matters that include, but go far beyond, the merely technical and stylistic.

February 22, 1999   Avery Dulles, S.J.
Feast of the Chair of St. Peter   Fordham University
                                                        New York, N.Y.

Acknowledgments

IN QUOTATIONS FROM SCRIPTURE I have generally followed the Revised Standard Version (Oxford University Press, 1962), but in cases where Scripture is being quoted in other documents I have retained the translation in those documents.

In quotations from the documents of Vatican II I have followed by preference the version for which Walter M. Abbott served as general editor and by Joseph Gallagher as translation editor, *The Documents of Vatican II* (America Press, 1966).

For the works of John Paul II, I have followed the translations cited in the respective footnotes.

I have reprinted, with permission from the respective publishers and editors, portions of the following articles and talks of my own:

"John Paul II and the New Evangelization," *America* 166 (February 1, 1992): 52–59, 69–72.

"The Prophetic Humanism of John Paul II," *America* 169 (1993): 6–11.

"John Paul II and the New Millennium," *America* 173 (December 9, 1995): 9–15.

"Mary at the Dawn of the New Millennium," *America* 178 (January 31/February 7, 1998): 8–10, 12–16, 18–19.

"Truth as the Ground of Freedom: A Theme from John Paul II," published as an "Occasional Paper" by the Acton Institute, Grand Rapids, Michigan, 1995.

"John Paul II Theologian," *Communio* 24 (Winter 1997): 713–27.

"John Paul II as a Theologian of Culture," *Logos* 1 (Summer 1997): 19–33.

"The Ecclesiology of John Paul II," in *The Gift of the Church: Essays in Ecclesiology in Honor of Patrick Granfield,* edited by Peter C. Phan (Collegeville, Minn: Liturgical Press, 1999).

Abbreviations

Documents of Vatican II

AG   *Ad gentes.* Decree on the Church's Missionary Activity

DH   *Dignitatis humanae.* Declaration on Religious Freedom

DV   *Dei Verbum.* Dogmatic Constitution on Divine Revelation

GS   *Gaudium et spes.* Pastoral Constitution on the Church in the Modern World

LG   *Lumen gentium.* Dogmatic Constitution on the Church

NA   *Nostra aetate.* Declaration on the Relationship of the Church to Non-Christian Religions

PO   *Presbyterorum ordinis.* Decree on the Ministry and Life of Priests

SC   *Sacrosanctum concilium.* Constitution on the Sacred Liturgy

UR   *Unitatis redintegratio.* Decree on Ecumenism

Encyclicals of John Paul II

CA   *Centesimus annus.* 1991

DM   *Dives in misericordia.* 1980

D&V   *Dominum et vivificantem.* 1986

EV   *Evangelium vitae.* 1995

FR   *Fides et ratio.* 1998

LE   *Laborem exercens.* 1981

RH   *Redemptor hominis.* 1979

RMat   *Redemptoris mater.* 1987

RMis   *Redemptoris missio.* 1990

SA   *Slavorum apostoli.* 1985

SRS   *Sollicitudo rei socialis.* 1987

UUS   *Ut unum sint.* 1995

VS   *Veritatis splendor.* 1993

Other Writings of John Paul II

Church   *The Church: Mystery, Sacrament, Community. Catechesis on the Creed*, vol. 4. Boston: Pauline Books & Media, 1998

CL   Apostolic Exhortation *Christifideles laici*, 1988

CT   Apostolic Exhortation *Catechesi tradendae*, 1979

CTH   *Crossing the Threshold of Hope*. New York: Alfred A. Knopf, 1994

DC   Letter to Bishops, *Dominicae cenae*, 1980

DD   Apostolic Letter *Dies Domini*, 1998

EA   Apostolic Exhortation *Ecclesia in Africa*, 1995

FC   Apostolic Exhortation *Familiaris consortio*, 1981

GM   *Gift and Mystery: On the Fiftieth Anniversary of My Priestly Ordination.* New York: Doubleday, 1996

God   *God, Father and Creator. Catechesis on the Creed*, vol. 1. Boston: Pauline Books & Media, 1996

Jesus   *Jesus, Son and Savior. Catechesis on the Creed*, vol. 2. Boston: Pauline Books & Media, 1996

MD   Apostolic Letter *Mulieris dignitatem*, 1988

OS   Apostolic Letter *Ordinatio sacerdotalis*, 1994

PDV   Apostolic Exhortation *Pastores dabo vobis*, 1992

RP   Apostolic Exhortation *Reconciliatio et paenitentia*, 1984

SCdn   *Sign of Contradiction*. New York: Seabury/Crossroad, 1979

SD   Apostolic Letter *Salvifici doloris*, 1984

Spirit   *The Spirit, Giver of Life and Love. Catechesis on the Creed*, vol. 3. Boston: Pauline Books & Media, 1996

SR   *Sources of Renewal: The Implementation of Vatican II*. San Francisco: Harper & Row, 1979

TB   *Theology of the Body: Human Love in the Divine Plan*. Boston: Pauline Books & Media, 1997

TMA   Apostolic Letter *Tertio millennio adveniente*, 1994

VC   Apostolic Exhortation, *Vita consecrata*, 1995

Other Abbreviations

AS   *Acta synodalia Concilii Vaticani Secundi*. Vatican City, 1970–78

DS   *Enchiridion symbolorum, definitionum et declarationum de rebus fidei et morum*, ed. H. Denzinger, rev. A. Schönmetzer, 36th ed. (Freiburg: Herder, 1976)

PG   *Patrologiae cursus completus*. Series graeca. Edited by J.-P. Migne. Paris, 1857ff.

ST   Thomas Aquinas, *Summa theologiae*

CHAPTER 1

Karol Wojtyła
as a Theologian

WOJTYŁA AS A THEOLOGIAN

SOME MIGHT QUESTION whether John Paul II should be ranked among the the-ologians. Since the age of thirty-eight he has been a bishop, and for the past twenty years pope, heavily charged with pastoral and administrative responsibil-ities. As a pastoral leader he has sought to express, defend, and promote the teach-ing of the Church, but he has rarely engaged in the kinds of academic research and speculation that are expected of university professors. Should not theology be defined rather in terms of the work of professors who freely probe the sources and develop their theories even when such pursuits bring them into conflict with offi-cial Church teaching? Can a pastor claim to be a theologian?

These questions, though they might seem to undermine the very purpose of this book, are not unanswerable. In the first place, we may recall that Karol Wojtyła did pursue academic studies to the extent of earning doctorates both in theology and in Christian ethics. He taught for some years on seminary and uni-versity faculties and published more than three hundred articles in scholarly jour-nals, especially in the field of moral theology. At Vatican II he played a significant role in supporting the major renewal of Catholic doctrine effected by the council. His appointment as a bishop should not disqualify him any more than it disqual-ifies Gregory of Nyssa and John Chrysostom, Hilary and Ambrose, Augustine and Anselm, and other doctors of the Church who taught from episcopal chairs. If the papal office excluded its occupants from the theological confraternity, one would have to delete Leo the Great and Gregory the Great from the roster of theologians. It may be time for us to recognize again what was obvious to earlier generations, viz., that theology is not the special preserve of professors.

Among the Catholic theologians of the second half of this century, John Paul II holds a place of special eminence. Perhaps more than any other single individ-ual he has succeeded in comprehensively restating the contours of Catholic faith

1

in the light of Vatican II and in relation to postconciliar developments in the Church and in the world. With his keen interest in contemporary culture, philosophy, economics, and international affairs, he has been able to give fresh relevance to the Catholic tradition. Avoiding the pitfalls of compromise and polemics, he has offered a serene and balanced presentation of what Catholics may and should believe on a multitude of questions. No private theologian, however brilliant, speaks with comparable authority.

To present the theology of John Paul II is a challenge. For one thing, he has written, and continues to write, so extensively on so many different topics that the material vastly exceeds what most students, including the present author, have been able to digest. My objective is the relatively modest one of gathering up the essentials of his teaching on strictly theological questions. This book is no substitute for detailed studies of the pope's teaching on specific themes.

As a pastoral leader, the pope is more concerned with presenting normative Catholic doctrine and giving pastoral exhortation than with pursuing the fine points of speculation. But his remarkable formative experiences and powers of insight give freshness and power to all that he writes. To indicate his distinctive contribution I shall try to pick out his more personal insights rather than recapitulate his complete teaching.

It is admittedly difficult to be sure whether works published in the pope's name were actually written by him. In preparing encyclicals and other official documents he unquestionably makes use of assistants who are responsible for many of the footnotes and no doubt for parts of the actual text. But we can find much that is distinctive to the pope, especially if we use as clues what he published before he became pope, when he was working as a private theologian, and his "unofficial" writings as pope, such as the interview *Crossing the Threshold of Hope* and his reflections on the fiftieth anniversary of his priestly ordination, *Gift and Mystery*.[1] Many of his official writings as pope, notably his first encyclical, *Redemptor hominis*, are so personal in tone that they cannot plausibly be ascribed to another hand.

THEOLOGICAL FORMATION

For the purposes of the present monograph it will not be necessary to give a detailed account of the biography of John Paul II.[2] We shall not be concerned with

---

[1] John Paul II, *Crossing the Threshold of Hope*, ed. Vittorio Messori (New York: Alfred A. Knopf, 1994); *Gift and Mystery: On the Fiftieth Anniversary of My Priestly Ordination* (New York: Doubleday, 1996).

[2] Tad Szulc, *Pope John Paul II: The Biography* (New York: Scribner, 1995) and Jonathan Kwitny, *Man of the Century: The Life and Times of Pope John Paul II* (New York: Henry Holt, 1997) are the most complete biographies to date, but both neglect his theological activities.

Wojtyła the actor, poet, sportsman, and linguist, though all of these interests have probably affected his theology in one way or another. Nor shall we attempt to investigate his political influence, vast though this has been, or even his pastoral ministry as bishop and pope, although some aspects of his theology touch closely on his concerns as a pastor. But a few indications of his formation and ministry are indispensable to set his theology in proper context.

Born in Wadowice, Poland, on May 18, 1920, Karol Wojtyła lost his mother when he was eight, his only brother when he was twelve, and his father when he was twenty. As a Pole living through the horrors of the Nazi occupation, the devastation of World War II, and the harsh domination of the Soviet Union, the young Wojtyła acquired great powers of endurance. His piety and faith were tried by fire and purified.

One early influence that should be mentioned is that of Jan Tyranowski, a remarkable layman who was a tailor in Kraków. As a young man, Tyranowski had been a leader in Catholic Action and in the Marian Sodality. During the Nazi occupation he organized from the parish a kind of informal academy, of which Wojtyła was a member. Tyranowski trained the group in ascetical and mystical theology in the tradition of Adolphe Tanquerey's textbooks, and inspired some of his followers to peruse the mystical works of St. John of the Cross and St. Teresa of Avila. Tyranowski also organized a "living rosary" of young men who turned in prayer to the Blessed Virgin to save Poland from its perils. As a leader of one of the fifteen "chaplets" (corresponding to the fifteen mysteries of the rosary) Wojtyła met for an hour every week with Tyranowski to consult about his life of prayer. Tyranowski seems to have been an authentic mystic, and he gave Wojtyła a lasting respect for Carmelite spirituality. Wojtyła at one point considered becoming a Carmelite.

After his first year at the Jagiellonian University of Kraków (1938–1939) Karol Wojtyła's course of study was interrupted by the war. He labored for two years in a stone quarry connected with the Solvay chemical plant and in 1942 secretly entered an underground seminary organized by the future Cardinal Adam Stefan Sapieha. After completing the prescribed course of study, partly at the Jagiellonian University, he was ordained a priest on November 1, 1946. Two weeks later Cardinal Sapieha sent him to Rome to study with the Dominicans at the Angelicum for a doctorate in theology. His dissertation was on the theology of faith of John of the Cross.[3] While fully accepting the idea of faith as an assent to revealed truths, John of the Cross, as interpreted by Wojtyła, held that for union with God it was necessary for faith to be vivified by charity, which effects a transformation through participation in the divine life. The spirit adheres to God in darkness, without support of any proper representation. In an appendix to the dis-

---

[3] Karol Wojtyła, *Faith according to Saint John of the Cross* (San Francisco: Ignatius, 1981).

sertation Wojtyła tried to show that John of the Cross's teaching on faith agreed with that of Thomas Aquinas, a point that some scholars had contested.

In the interval between his two years in Rome, Father Wojtyła was directed by Cardinal Sapieha to spend his summer holiday of 1947 visiting France, Belgium, and Holland. In Paris, where he lived at the Polish seminary, he made contact with the worker-priest movement (which interested him as a former worker-seminarian) and studied the issues raised by Fathers Henri Godin and Yvan Daniel in their book *La France, pays de mission?*[4] He visited the vibrant parish run by the Abbé Michonneau in the outskirts of Paris and studied other efforts to win the working classes back to the Church. He then traveled to Belgium, where he met Canon Joseph Cardijn, who had founded the Young Christian Workers (*Jocistes*) to bring the working people to the practice of the faith. Cardijn, he found, was critical of the worker-priest movement in France. He felt that priests should present themselves distinctly as priests and not "go secular" in their effort to reach out to workers. While reserving judgment on the new experiments being conducted in France, Wojtyła admired the zealous efforts of the priests to reclaim the masses from secularism and disbelief and expressed the hope that the faith in Poland would not be eroded by a split from culture such as had occurred in France.[5] Before returning to Rome Wojtyła also spent some time at Ars, where he deepened his devotion to St. Jean Vianney, the great apostle of the confessional.

After defending his dissertation in July 1948, Father Wojtyła returned to Poland, where he was initially assigned to parish duties in a small country parish. A year later he was transferred to a parish in Kraków, where he was given special responsibility for working with university students. Two years after that, in 1951, he was sent back to the Jagiellonian University to study for a second doctorate, this time in philosophy. He wrote on the ethics of a German phenomenologist, Max Scheler, who had tried to build an ethical system on the basis of a personally experienced hierarchy of values. Relying heavily on feeling and emotion, Scheler rejected the role of authority. Wojtyła found some merit in Scheler's personalism, but he believed that this ultimately called for a personal relationship to God and reverence for Jesus as a commanding moral authority.

After teaching briefly at the seminary faculty at Kraków (1953–1954), Father Wojtyła joined the philosophy faculty of the Catholic University of Lublin. He published many journal articles in the next few years and established himself as one of the leaders of "Lublin Thomism," a personalist interpretation of Thomas

---

[4] Henri Godin and Yvan Daniel, *La France, pays de mission?* (Paris: Union Générale d'Éditions, 1943).

[5] For his reflections on the apostolic movements in France in 1947, see his article "Mission de France," originally published in *Tygodnik Powszechny*, no. 9 (1949) and republished in French translation in Karol Wojtyła, *En Esprit et en Vérité* (Paris: Centurion, 1980), 9–17.

Aquinas influenced by French philosophers such as Maurice Blondel, Emmanuel Mounier, and Gabriel Marcel.[6]

On July 4, 1958, Pius XII named Wojtyła auxiliary bishop of Kraków. Consecrated on September 28, he was compelled to relinquish his full-time academic career. As bishop he continued to work closely with youth groups, and it was partly out of that experience that he developed the ideas for his next book, *Love and Responsibility* (Lublin, 1960).[7] In this volume he set sexual activity within the larger framework of a theology of interpersonal love. The symbolism of sexual intercourse, he maintained, required that the act take place within marriage and be open to the possibility of procreation.

INVOLVEMENT IN VATICAN II

Already as a young bishop Wojtyła submitted numerous suggestions to the antepreparatory commission for the agenda of the coming council.[8] In a nine-point memorandum he singled out, in the first place, the importance of proposing Christian personalism as an antidote to contemporary materialism in its various forms (scientific, positivist, and dialectical). The human person, created in the image and likeness of God and called to share eternally in the inner life of the tri-une God, stands above all visible creation. Christian personalism, he said, should be the foundation of all ethics.

As a second point Bishop Wojtyła spoke of ecumenism. Christians separated from the Catholic Church, he said, are not outside the Body of Christ, which is one, even though wounded by heresy and schism. The council should emphasize factors that unite Christians, thus contributing to a union of hearts that could eventually lead to doctrinal consideration.

Wojtyła's third point was to foster the lay apostolate without confusing the roles of clergy and laity. In his remaining six points he dealt with the formation of future priests, clerical celibacy, the intellectual standards of seminaries, the role of vowed religious in the Church, the reform of the liturgy, and the updating of canon law. In all his main points he anticipated what Vatican II would actually declare.

By the time of his appointment as archbishop of Kraków (January 13, 1964)

---

[6] For a collection of these philosophical pieces, see Karol Wojtyła, *Person and Community: Selected Essays* (New York: Peter Lang, 1993).

[7] Revised English translation: Karol Wojtyła (John Paul II), *Love and Responsibility* (New York: Farrar, Straus, & Giroux, 1981).

[8] These suggestions are printed in *Acta Synodalia Series I (Antepreparatoria)* (Vatican City: Libreria Editrice Vaticana, 1970), II/2, 741–48.

the council had gone through its first two sessions, and Wojtyła was heavily involved in its work. As a member of the drafting committee for the Pastoral Constitution on the Church in the Modern World he contributed to the section dealing with the role of the Church in relation to the world (part I, chapter 4).

The *Acta Synodalia* of the council contain some twenty-three of Wojtyła's interventions, several of them in the name of the whole Polish episcopate, some in writing, and eight orally delivered.[9] In terms of their subject matter the interventions can be listed as follows:

On the Sacred Liturgy (#1). Bishop Wojtyła insists that Christian initiation should be understood not simply as baptism but as including the catechumenate. Baptism itself is not a sufficient introduction to the Christian life.

On the Sources of Revelation (#2). The real source of revelation is neither Scripture nor tradition but God himself, who speaks through both these channels.

On the Media of Social Communication (#3). Communication, Wojtyła holds, should be seen not simply as a means of entertainment and gratification, as in a consumerist culture, but for the true development of the human person.

On the Church (##4, 5, 7, 8). The main goal of the Church is sanctification. The teaching office is subordinate to this goal. The chapter on the People of God should precede that on the hierarchy, which is an instrument for the common good of the whole people of God. The evangelical counsels of chastity, poverty, and obedience should be so explained that they are seen as having significance for all Christians, not just for consecrated religious.

On the Blessed Virgin Mary (##4, 6, 9). It is a mistake, says Bishop Wojtyła, to put this chapter at the end of the Constitution on the Church, where it appears as a mere appendix. As mother, Mary built up Christ's physical body, and now she performs the same office toward the Church. Thus, this chapter should come immediately after the first, in which the Mystery of the Church is described.

On the Lay Apostolate (##13, 14; cf. 5). The exhortation to engage in apostolic activities should be focused not just on associations but on individual persons, who must give an example of living the faith. The apostolate is a service not just to the Church but also to humanity. Lay people have an apostolate both within the Church and from Church to the world.

On Religious Freedom (##10, 11, 12, 18, 19). The schema deals mainly with immunity from coercion, presenting a negative and partial conception of freedom,

---

[9] See the tabulation in the appendix to this chapter.

especially inadequate for interchurch relations. Mere tolerance is too static; it cannot serve as a principle of growth, which involves unity in the truth. More should be said about the power of truth to give freedom. Christian freedom is grounded in the word of God and in the grace that liberates from sin and its consequences. The council should proclaim the Christian doctrine of freedom on the basis of revelation rather than give a lesson in political philosophy. Finally it should be said that religious freedom is limited not only by positive law but by the moral law itself.

On the Church in the Modern World (ordered by topics).

(a) *General Observations* (##15, 20). The tone of the document should not be authoritarian, but should indicate that Catholics join with the rest of humanity in seeking true and just solutions to the problems of human life. Starting from experience, the document should show how the truth embodied in divine and natural law respects and enhances human values. Speaking pastorally to the world, the Church should keep the focus on eternal salvation, which transcends immanent worldly finality. The work of creation should be seen as being completed by God's redemptive act in the cross of Christ, which profoundly alters the condition of all human beings. In the light of Christ the Church knows the integral truth about man.

(b) *Atheism* (#20). The dialogue with atheism should begin with the study of the human person and should show that the vocation of the person cannot be fulfilled except with the help of God the Redeemer. A clear distinction should be made between atheism stemming from personal conviction and that imposed by state propaganda.

(c) *Marriage and the Family* (##17, 21). Marriage should be seen as a school of love and charity. The mutual fidelity of the spouses mirrors the union between Christ and the Church. Scientific knowledge about fertility can serve virtue and be consonant with human dignity and responsibility in family planning.

(c) *Culture* (##16, 22). It needs to be emphasized that one's human dignity consists more in what one is than in what one does. Contemporary culture is threatened by utilitarianism. Culture is founded upon wisdom, without which truth, beauty, goodness cannot stand or progress. The study of ontology is particularly important because it enables people to contemplate created things in relation to God as their first cause.

(d) *The Economy* (##17, 22). The rights of private property and private ownership of the means of production should be affirmed against state socialism. Cognizance should be taken of the distinctive character and value of women's work.

On Priests (#23). More should be said about the interior life and sanctification of priests and about their conscious participation in the priesthood of Christ. They must help one another through fraternal union and cooperation. In contemporary ministry it is particularly important to emphasize the mercy of God.

These and other themes from the council interventions of Wojtyła are of special interest because they foreshadow ideas that he will develop in his teaching as cardinal and as pope.

POSTCONCILIAR ACTIVITY

On June 26, 1967, Paul VI bestowed the cardinalate on Archbishop Wojtyła. As one of Poland's two cardinal-archbishops he was heavily involved in all the synods of bishops from 1967 to 1977. Although designated to take part in the first synod (1967), he did not actually attend because he felt obliged to protest the Polish government's refusal to permit Cardinal Wyszynski to participate. At the synod of 1969 he proposed his views on papal primacy and episcopal collegiality; in 1971 he contributed to the documents on the ministerial priesthood and on world justice; in 1974 he played an important role in the discussion of evangelization; and in 1977 he took an active part in the debates on catechetics.

As a member of the papal "birth control" commission Wojtyła, following the positions taken in *Love and Responsibility*, opposed any change in Church doctrine on this point. It is certain that his influence made an impact on Paul VI; some maintain that he was one of the drafters of the encyclical *Humanae vitae* (1968).[10]

In 1969 he published the first edition of his *Acting Person*, a work of philosophical anthropology written in dialogue with Marxism.[11] He emphasizes that human beings freely determine what they in time become. By human action we make ourselves to be what we are. Against Marxist materialism and determinism this work strongly affirms the transcendence of the person as attested by freedom, responsibility, and loyalty to truth. Wojtyła understood this philosophy of the person to be in full accord with Vatican II.

The English translation, published in 1979, is very hard to read. According to some commentators the translator has injected much of her own thought into the translation, which is presented as an update of the original. The new edition removes many classical Thomistic notions found in the Polish text and delves more deeply into contemporary phenomenology. It is regrettable that we do not have an exact translation of the Polish original.[12]

---

[10] Szulc, *Pope John Paul II*, 253–55; cf. Kwitny, *Man of the Century*, 219.

[11] Cardinal Karol Wojtyła, *The Acting Person* (Dordrecht, Holland: D. Reidel, 1979), "translated and revised from the 1969 Polish edition, *Osoba i czyn*. This definitive text of the work established in collaboration with the author by Anna-Teresa Tymieniecka."

[12] See the comments of George H. Williams, *The Mind of John Paul II* (New York: Seabury,

Cardinal Wojtyła's next work, *Sources of Renewal* (Polish original 1972),[13] is based on conferences he gave to implement Vatican II pastorally in the archdiocese of Kraków, which was at the time holding a diocesan synod. Wojtyła in this work keeps a double focus: on the Church in itself and on the Church in the modern world. The fundamental question to be answered by the council, he says, was the existential one: *"Ecclesia, quid dicis de teipsa?"* ("Church, what do you say of yourself?"). The Church, as it travels down the road of history, participates in the consciousness of Christ and shares in his mission. The consciousness of the Church unfolds historically, somewhat as does the world itself. Vatican II, in the estimation of Wojtyła, calls for a fundamental shift of consciousness in the Church as a whole, leading to a more dialogical posture, as it enters into conversation with all groups of people, believers and unbelievers. The mission of the Church is to make all men and women conscious of the communion into which the triune God intends them to enter. Revelation is an invitation to salvation through communion with God.

In 1976 Cardinal Wojtyła was invited to give the Lenten retreat to the pope and the papal curia. As his theme he chose *Sign of Contradiction*,[14] since he wished to emphasize the need for the Church to stand up in opposition to materialism and secularism in their various forms, whether Marxist or capitalist. The word of God, he holds, encounters an anti-word; the truth of God struggles against the lies of Satan; the obedience of Jesus pays the price for human disobedience. In the course of the retreat the cardinal praised Paul VI for having taken a firm stand against contraception in *Humanae vitae*.

Since his election as pope on October 16, 1978, John Paul II has been almost incredibly productive. In the midst of all his apostolic journeys and pastoral visitations he has found time to compose (as of this writing) thirteen encyclicals and eight post-synodal apostolic exhortations. Most of these twenty-one documents are practically book-length.

1981), 197–201; also those of Kenneth L. Schmitz, *At the Center of the Human Drama: The Philosophical Anthropology of Karol Wojtyła/Pope John Paul II* (Washington, D.C.: Catholic University of America Press, 1993), 58–59. Further discussion will be found in Rocco Buttiglione, *Karol Wojtyła: The Thought of the Man Who Became John Paul II* (Grand Rapids, Mich.: Eerdmans, 1997), 117–18.

[13] Karol Wojtyła, *Sources of Renewal: The Implementation of Vatican II* (San Francisco: Harper & Row, 1980).

[14] Karol Wojtyła, *Sign of Contradiction* (New York: Seabury/Crossroad, 1979), translated from the Italian original of 1977.

THE ENCYCLICALS

The thirteen encyclicals issued between 1979 and 1998, inclusively, represent what may be called the core of John Paul II's teaching as pope.[15] The doctrinal assertions in these encyclicals exemplify what may be called the ordinary papal magisterium, but the encyclicals also contain many personal reflections and hortatory remarks. It is helpful to distinguish between different classes of encyclicals, some being primarily doctrinal (those on Christ, God the Father, the Holy Spirit, the Virgin Mary, and faith and reason), some containing moral teaching (*Veritatis splendor* and *Evangelium vitae*), some setting forth social teaching (*Laborem exercens*, *Sollicitudo rei socialis*, and *Centesimus annus*), and some primarily pastoral (those on missiology, ecumenism, and Slavic Europe).

The first encyclical, *Redemptor hominis* (1979), might be called the programmatic document of the pontificate. Primarily christological, it sounds a number of themes that will be pursued in other documents and shows how these are connected with the central idea of human dignity founded upon the gifts of creation and redemption. It presents human dignity and liberation as the central focus of the Church's proclamation. The realization that we are so loved by God that he gave his only Son to be our redeemer should fill us with gratitude, hope, and courage, expelling all fear and despondency.

Dives in Misericordia, the second encyclical (1980), deals with the mercy of God the Father and with the requirement that justice in human relations be crowned by mercy and forgiveness. These first two encyclicals, dealing with the Son and the Father, are rounded out by the fifth, *Dominum et vivificantem* (1986), which deals with the Holy Spirit as the gift of the Father and the Son. These three encyclicals together constitute a trinitarian triptych.

Three further encyclicals deal with the social teaching of the Church—*Laborem exercens* (1981), *Sollicitudo rei socialis* (1987), and *Centesimus annus* (1991). *Laborem exercens* deals with work and the economy; *Sollicitudo* with international development; and *Centesimus annus* with capitalism, socialism, and the question of culture. In *Centesimus annus*, written to commemorate the centenary of Leo XIII's *Rerum novarum*, the pope supports the free-market economy but insists on the obligation of the State to make adequate provision for the welfare of all citizens.

---

[15] The first twelve encyclicals are printed with helpful introductions and an excellent index in J. Michael Miller, ed., *The Encyclicals of John Paul II* (Huntington, Ind.: Our Sunday Visitor Publishing Division, 1996). For a condensed version of the same encyclicals in paraphrase form, see John Paul II, *The Encyclicals in Everyday Language*, ed. Joseph G. Donders (Maryknoll, N.Y.: Orbis, 1996). The encyclicals are available in *Origins,* and many of them are also obtainable in pamphlet form from the United States Catholic Conference and from St. Paul Books & Media, Boston, Massachusetts.

Slavorum apostoli (1985) eulogizes Cyril and Methodius, two Byzantine saints who became the first great apostles of the Slavic world. John Paul II, anxious for the Church in Europe to breathe once more with its two lungs, Eastern and Western, has proclaimed these two saints, along with Benedict of Nursia, co-patrons of Europe. This encyclical gives valuable insight into the pope's thought on inculturation.

Redemptoris mater (1987) is the fullest single presentation of the pope's Mariology. He emphasizes Mary's maternal mediation. Just as she was mother of Jesus, so is she the mother of the Mystical Body of Christ. Her mediation is prototypical for that of the Church, which is established in order to mediate the grace of Christ.

Redemptoris missio (1990) presents the pope's program for missionary activity, which is an important aspect of the new evangelization for which he has been calling since 1983. Developing the Christocentric vision articulated in *Redemptor hominis*, the pope here depicts the Church as essentially in a state of mission. In the course of his exposition he deals with a variety of themes: mission and interfaith dialogue, mission and development, and mission and inculturation. The pope attaches major importance to personal witness and proclamation.

Veritatis splendor (1993) is the first encyclical by any pope that deals in a general way with the principles of moral theology. It opposes modern errors such as consequentialism and proportionalism and cautions against an undue emphasis on the "fundamental option" as if it, rather than specific acts, were the sole index of morality. Against all these deviations the pope upholds the idea of moral absolutes.

Evangelium vitae (1995) belongs likewise, at least primarily, to the field of moral theology. It is the pope's strongest document in defense of human life and in opposition to abortion and euthanasia. It touches more briefly on the questions of just war and capital punishment.

Ut unum sint (1995) is the pope's great charter of ecumenism. It might be called a summa of Catholic ecumenical teaching in the form it has taken since Vatican II. Insisting that there is no valid unity except in the truth, the pope opposes doctrinal compromise as a method for overcoming differences.

The thirteenth encyclical, *Fides et ratio* (1998) takes up the defense of metaphysics for which the present pope had pleaded at Vatican II. Describing itself as a sequel to *Veritatis splendor*, this document warns against agnosticism and nihilism in their various forms, including historicism, positivism, and postmodernism. It calls upon philosophy to take up with courage its classical sapiential task and not let itself be marginalized as a mere study of logic or language. Reason and faith in partnership can respond to the eternal quest for meaning, which receives its ultimate answer in the Incarnate Word.

APOSTOLIC EXHORTATIONS

In comparison with the encyclicals the post-synodal apostolic exhortations are less properly the work of the pope himself.[16] They are his way of integrating, with the help of an editorial committee, the results of the synod assemblies that preceded them. Six of those thus far published are based on general assemblies of the Synod of Bishops. The seventh, *Ecclesia in Africa* (1995), summarizes the results of the special assembly of African bishops that took place in 1994. The eighth, *Une nouvelle espérance pour le Liban* (1997), followed upon the special assembly for Lebanon (1995). Most of these exhortations were published about a year after the conclusion of the respective synods. The apostolic exhortation on the special synod for America (1997) was published on January 22, 1999; those for Asia (1998) and Oceania (1998) have not been published as of this writing. A special synod for Europe is scheduled to meet in 1999.

Catechesi tradendae (1979) recapitulates the general assembly of the synod on catechetics (1977), in which the pope had participated as Cardinal-Archbishop of Kraków. *Familiaris consortio* (1981) gathers up the consensus of the synod meeting on the family in 1980. *Reconciliatio et paenitentia* (1984) presents the fruits of the synod of 1983 on reconciliation and penance. *Christifideles laici* (1988) has as its theme the role of the laity in the Church, which had been the theme of the assembly of 1987. *Pastores dabo vobis*, concerned with priestly formation, was published in 1992 on the basis of the synod dealing with that theme in 1990. *Vita consecrata* (1995) summarizes the results of the synod on the religious life in 1994. The exhortations on marriage and the family, on reconciliation and penance, on priestly formation, and on the religious life contain many passages that seem to reflect the pope's own personal thinking rather than the consensus of the synod fathers.

OTHER WRITINGS AS POPE

John Paul II considers himself charged with directing the catechesis of the Church. Responding to a request from the extraordinary synod of 1985, he charged the Congregation for the Doctrine of the Faith with supervising the production of the *Catechism of the Catholic Church*, which was completed in 1992.

---

[16] The texts of the six exhortations published after ordinary assemblies of the synod of bishops from 1979 through 1996 may be found, with helpful introductions and indices, in *The Post-Synodal Exhortations of John Paul II*, ed. J. Michael Miller (Huntington, Ind.: Our Sunday Visitor Publishing Division, 1998). Texts of the individual exhortations are also published in *Origins* and in pamphlet form by St. Paul Books & Media, Boston, Massachusetts.

Supplementing this effort, the pope has given several series of general audience "catecheses," which are then collected in books. These volumes concentrate on presenting normative Catholic doctrine without the deeper speculation that sometimes appears in the encyclicals and apostolic letters.

The Theology of the Body is a collection of catechetical talks to general audiences (1979–1984) dealing chiefly with marriage and sexuality.[17] This volume gathers into one talks that were originally published in four separate volumes.[18] The pope's exegesis of the creation account in Genesis in his talks of 1979–1980 has broad anthropological significance.

A three volume series of the pope's general audience talks between 1985 and 1991 dealing with God, Christ, and the Holy Spirit was published in English in 1997.[19] A fourth volume of the series, published in 1998, contains the 137 talks on the Church delivered in general audiences between July 10, 1991, and August 30, 1995.[20] A further sequel containing the pope's seventy catecheses on the Blessed Virgin Mary, delivered from September 6, 1995, to November 12, 1997, is scheduled for publication in the near future.

John Paul II has also issued a series of annual Holy Thursday letters directed primarily to priests. Among these *Dominicae cenae* (1980), a letter to bishops dealing with the priest and the Eucharist, merits particular attention because of its relative length and its highly doctrinal character.[21]

Much of the pope's more personal thinking appears in his apostolic letters. One of these, *Salvifici doloris* (1984) is an extended meditation on the problem of suffering in the light of the cross. The existential power of this meditation flows no doubt from the pope's own experience of bereavement, illness, and pain at many points in his life, perhaps especially during his recovery from the assassination attempt of 1981.

Mulieris dignitatem (1988), another apostolic letter, is the clearest and fullest exposition of the pope's theology of woman. It is closely connected with his Mariology.

---

[17] John Paul II, *The Theology of the Body* (Boston: St. Paul Books & Media, 1997).

[18] *The Original Unity between Man and Woman* (talks of 1979–1980); *Blessed Are the Pure of Heart* (talks of 1980–1981); *The Theology of Marriage and Celibacy* (talks of 1981–1984); and *Reflections on Humanae Vitae* (talks of 1984). All were published in Boston by St. Paul Books & Media.

[19] The three volumes are respectively entitled: *God: Father and Creator*; *Jesus: Son and Savior*; and *The Spirit: Giver of Life and Love*. All are published in Boston by St. Paul Books & Media, 1996.

[20] John Paul II, *The Church: Mystery, Sacrament, Community* (Boston: Pauline Books & Media, 1998).

[21] John Paul II, "Mystery and Worship of the Holy Eucharist," *Origins* 9 (March 27, 1980): 653–66. Reprinted in Edward J. Kilmartin, *Church, Eucharist and Priesthood: A Theological Commentary on "The Mystery and Worship of the Most Holy Eucharist"* (New York: Paulist, 1981), 69–100.

Of particular importance for the development of doctrine is the apostolic letter *Ordinatio sacerdotalis* (1994), in which the pope calls for definitive assent on the part of all the faithful to the doctrine that the Church has no authority to ordain women to the ministerial priesthood.

Tertio millennio adveniente (1994) is an apostolic letter dealing with preparations for the beginning of the third millennium in the year 2000. It sets forth some key elements of the pope's theology of time and history. Having always shown a great interest in jubilee celebrations, he wants to see that the great jubilee of 2000 is celebrated in a way that strengthens the faith and commitment of Catholics, promotes Christian unity, and avoids giving offense to non-Christians.

Orientale lumen (1995), issued shortly before the encyclical *Ut unum sint*, is an apostolic letter on the relations between the Catholic Church and the separated Eastern churches. It strongly urges renewed efforts to restore full communion with these churches.

The apostolic letter on the observance of Sunday, *Dies Domini* (1998) should be mentioned for its inclusion of the pope's ideas on work and leisure and further indications of his theology of sacred time.

Another important document, less doctrinal in character, is the "Letter to Women" issued in July 1995, while preparations were being made for the World Conference on Women held in Beijing. It approves of the presence of women in all areas of life and work and calls for an end to all discrimination against them.

The preceding survey of papal documents is far from complete. We shall have occasion to refer, in addition, to many of the pope's speeches given in the course of pastoral visitations all over the world. His apostolic constitution on Catholic universities, *Ex corde Ecclesiae* (1990), contains some important statements on the pertinence of revelation and theology to higher education.

Apart from the official teachings of the pontificate, the two previously mentioned personal books that John Paul II has published as pope should be kept in view. The first, *Crossing the Threshold of Hope* (1994), gives his candid responses to a set of probing questions put to him by an Italian journalist, Vittorio Messori. The other personal document is the pope's 1996 book *Gift and Mystery*, commemorating the fiftieth anniversary of his priestly ordination. The second half of this brief work summarizes John Paul's ideas on priestly ministry today.

CONCLUSION

The length and variety of the writings of John Paul II, both before and after his accession to the papacy, present a true *embarras de richesses*. An attempt will be made, in the chapters that follow, to distill from this abundance his essential teaching on Christian faith and doctrine. This attempt is undertaken with the confidence that the pope's achievement holds unique importance for Catholic theology between the Second Vatican Council and the end of the twentieth century. More than any other theologian, he has accomplished a brilliant and comprehensive restatement of Catholic doctrine in which the teaching of the council is expounded in relation to the contemporary world situation. His position as pope, far from detracting from his credibility as a theologian, gives an added assurance that his reflections are in full conformity to the revelation by which Christians seek to guide their thought and their behavior.

The chapters that follow are topically arranged. They begin, as most theological textbooks do, with the doctrine of God, Father, Son, and Holy Spirit, and include under the same rubric the doctrine of creation (chapter 2). Then follow Christology and Mariology—two themes closely related in the thinking of John Paul II (chapter 3). The next three chapters are ecclesiological in scope. They take up successively the Church itself and its mission to evangelize (chapter 4), its hierarchical structure (chapter 5), and the special callings to the priesthood and the religious life (chapter 6). The next five chapters deal with broader questions, impinging on secular life. Chapter 7 takes up sin, suffering, and penance; chapter 8, the laity and the family; chapter 9, culture; chapter 10, social and economic questions; and chapter 11, political society and freedom. Chapter 12 deals with the relations between the Catholic Church and other churches and religions. Chapter 13 brings the substantive portion of the book to a close with the pope's theology of history and its consummation. Chapter 14 is a recapitulation with some reflections on the theological achievement of John Paul II.

Appendix to Chapter 1

Wojtyła's Council Interventions

(References are to *Acta Synodalia*)

1. I/2, 314–15:   speech of November 7, 1962, on the liturgy
2. I/3, 294:   speech of November 21, 1962, on the sources of revelation
3. I/3, 609:   inscribed to speak, on the means of social communication
4. I/4, 598–99:   inscribed to speak, on the Church and the Virgin Mary
5. II/3, 154–57   speech of October 21, 1963, on the Church and the lay apostolate
6. II/2, 856–57:   written, attributed to Polish bishops, but largely his work, on the Church and the Virgin Mary
7. II/4, 340–42:   written, on the Church and holiness

8. III/1, 613–17: written, in the name of the Polish bishops, on collegiality and sacred orders
9. III/2, 178–79: written, on the Virgin Mary
10. III/2, 530–32: speech of September 25, 1964, on religious freedom
11. III/2, 838–39: written, on religious freedom
12. III/3, 766–68: written, on religious freedom
13. III/4, 69–70:   speech of October 8, 1964, on the lay apostolate
14. III/4, 788–89: written, on the lay apostolate
15. III/5, 298–300: speech of October 21, 1964, in the name of the Polish bishops, on the Church in the Modern World (CMW): method and outline
16. III/5, 680–83: written, in the name of the Polish bishops, on CMW (human nature, culture)
17. III/7, 380–82: written, in the name of the Polish bishops, proposed amendments to document on CMW
18. IV/2, 11–13:   speech of September 22, 1965, in the name of the Polish bishops, on religious freedom
19. IV/2, 292–93:   written, on religious freedom
20. IV/2, 660–63:   speech of September 28, 1965, on CMW (creation and redemption; atheism)
21. IV/3, 242–43:   written, on CMW (marriage and family)
22. IV/3, 349–50:   written, on CMW (culture, work)
23. IV/5, 519:   inscribed to speak, on priests

Some clarifications:

1. It will be noted that Wojtyła actually delivered eight speeches on the council floor. The rubric "inscribed to speak" is here used for the three interventions that were approved for delivery as speeches but were not actually spoken either because the opportunity was lacking or because the author decided not to ask for the floor.

2. The total number of interventions can be variously calculated. For example, in the present list I include as #6 a written intervention that is ascribed primarily to Wojtyła although he was not its sole author. On the other hand, I omit the letter to Paul VI on the importance of having a fourth session of the council in order to perfect the document on the Church in the Modern World, although Wojtyła was one of the many signers, who represented twenty-three episcopal conferences or groups of bishops from five continents. (The text may be found in AS III/5, 508–9.)

3. For further material on Wojtyła's interventions at the council the reader may consult Angelo Scola, "Gli Interventi di Karol Wojtyła al Concilio Ecumenico

Vaticano II: Esposizione ed Interpretazione Teologica," in *Karol Wojtyła: Filosofo, Teologo, Poeta,* ed. Rocco Buttiglione et al. (Vatican City: Libreria Editrice Vaticana, 1984), 289–306. Scola finds only twenty-two interventions, making no mention of my #19. John M. Grondelski, in his "Sources for the Study of Karol Wojtyła's Thought" (an Appendix to Kenneth Schmitz, *At the Center of the Human Drama* [Washington, D.C.: Catholic University of America Press, 1993], 147–63), lists only eighteen of Wojtyła's statements as a participant in the council. He omits my ##2, 6, 8, 18, and 23.

CHAPTER 2

The Triune God, Creation, Holy Spirit

KNOWLEDGE OF GOD FROM CREATION

God as Mystery

FOR JOHN PAUL II it is axiomatic that God is essentially mystery (CTH 38). Our thought about God is deficient because we are creatures, infinitely below the Creator. We need to approach the God of majesty with reverence, recognizing the inevitable shortcomings of all human conceptions of the divine (SCdn 9). Since God is utterly transcendent, we should not be surprised that he is, as St. Anselm said, "greater than all that can be conceived" (FR 14). He could not make himself an object of our inner-worldly experience, for in so doing he would, so to speak, compromise his own divinity, preventing us from perceiving that he is immeasurably exalted beyond all that human thought can master. Revelation, far from destroying the mystery, manifests it more vividly (FR 13). Even in the incarnation, which, as we shall see, is the supreme revelation of God, God's divinity is not directly seen. Referring to John of the Cross, the pope remarks that the obscurity of faith is the light that leads infallibly to God (God 125).

To imagine that God should, as it were, put himself within our grasp is a fundamental error of rationalism and idealism, which make human thought the measure of reality, rather than the reverse. As a realist, Wojtyła insists that thought must submit to what is antecedently real (CTH 38–39). The truth about God precedes human thought and is not produced by it.

Knowability from Creation

In the fathers and in the Eastern tradition of Christianity, John Paul II observes, little interest is taken in proofs for the existence of God. For them, we know God primarily from revelation. To borrow a phrase from Pascal, we may say that for

18

the fathers the true God is the God of Abraham, Isaac, and Jacob, the God of Jesus Christ, rather than the God of the philosophers.

While acknowledging the primacy of revelation, the pope insists that the approach to God through reason, limited though it be, is useful up to a point (CTH 29). He reaffirms the teaching of Vatican I that human reason, with its natural capacities, can ascertain the existence of God, the beginning and end of all things (FR 53; cf. DS 3004). Vatican II in its Constitution on Divine Revelation repeats that human speculation is capable of saying something valid about God (DV 3 and 6; CTH 28).

Our natural knowledge of God is not purely a priori. It is a posteriori since it takes its point of departure from the created world. We may say, indeed, that creation is a kind of first revelation of God. In the words of Vatican II, "God, who creates and conserves all things by his Word, gives constant testimony to himself in created realities" (DV 3, SR 46). Only on this basis can the natural light of reason achieve a certain measure of knowledge about God (DV 6; SR 46)—a knowledge that John Paul II calls "indirect and imperfect" (DM 2).

Taking up a phrase from St. Bonaventure, John Paul II speaks of an *Itinerarium mentis in Deum*—a journey of the mind to God. Human reason is driven by an innate tendency toward an absolute that can give meaning to the whole of existence (FR 24). This quest is legitimated by Scripture. The book of Wisdom blames the pagans because "from the good things that are visible they have failed to know Him who is; nor, while studying his works, have they recognized the craftsman ... for from the grandeur and beauty of created things comes a corresponding perception of their creator" (Wis. 13:1–5; SCdn 10; FR 19). Paul, in the first chapter of Romans, makes a similar assertion. "Ever since the creation of the world, [God's] invisible perfections—his everlasting power and his divinity—have been clearly perceived from the things he has made" (Rom. 1:20; SCdn 10; FR 22). Wojtyła calls this an "indirect" knowledge of God, because an exercise of human reason is required to proceed from the created realities to the reality of God the creator (SR 53; God 40).

Spontaneous Knowledge

In the ancient world the minds of most people moved spontaneously from the visible world to God, and the same remains true for many people today. The pope writes of a conversation he had with an eminent scientist who said that as a scientist he was an atheist, whereas, when confronted by the beauties of nature, he felt powerfully that God exists (SCdn 12). The pope also speaks of a Russian soldier who knocked on the door of the Kraków seminary in 1945 to discuss whether he might have a vocation to the priesthood. This soldier said he had been constantly educated to accept atheism, but that in his heart he always knew that God exists (SR 15). To know the existence of God, Wojtyła concludes, is not a matter of intelligence alone; the heart and the will are involved. In this connection he refers to the "reasons of the heart" so eloquently described by Pascal (CTH 31).

From Contingent to Necessary Being

Wojtyła shows great respect for the classical tradition, exemplified by Thomas Aquinas, which takes up from Greek philosophy the quest for the First Being, the Absolute Good (CTH 28–29). St. Thomas, he holds, continues to be the great master of philosophical and theological universalism. His five ways of proving the existence of God are still worthy of study (CTH 31). In his general audience catecheses on the Creed, the pope insists that scientific research is fully compatible with a sincere and joyful recognition of God's reality (God 101, 107). He calls attention to the need for a supreme cause to explain the movement in the universe and to account for the forward thrust of evolution (God 102–3). He refers to the marvelous beauty of the universe as a witness to the transcendent beauty of the creator (God 104).

While recommending these ways of approaching God's existence, Wojtyła does not, in the writings known to me, present his own personal version of how he would prove God's existence metaphysically. But he gives a few hints in passing statements. To arrive at the existence of God, he says, is to cross the gap from contingent being to the Necessary Being. Catherine of Siena is quoted as reporting that God, describing himself as "He who is," told her that she was "she who is not" (CTH 38). Contingent being, which has the intrinsic capacity not to be, points by its very nature to the Absolute as the ultimate ground of its existence. The Absolute, writes John Paul II, is the Necessary Being, existing by virtue of its own essence—*ipsum Esse subsistens* (SCdn 12). The absolute fullness of being, he reasons, implies every perfection. As a consequence it is evident that God infinitely surpasses the whole of creation (God 121). Among God's perfections, John Paul II reckons eternity and immutability (God 128-30).

To grasp why anything besides the one Necessary Being exists, we need to think of God as personal. Because the Absolute Being is self-sufficient, its existence alone does not explain why anything else should come to be. Possessing the fullness of perfection in himself, God does not stand to gain in any way from the world he creates (God 137). The only possible motive for creation is love, which implies that the Absolute has personal existence. God creates freely, because he wants to share his goodness with others. This truth, accessible in principle to reason, is confirmed by revelation, which tells us that God created the whole world by his Word, and "saw that it was good" and indeed "very good" (Gen. 1:12, 31; SCdn 20). Creation comes to its summit in the fashioning of human beings, whom God made "in his own image," endowing them with freedom, transcendence, and a spiritual character (SCdn 22).

Empiricism and Positivism

Since the time of David Hume and Immanuel Kant, the metaphysical approach to God has been undercut by empiricism and positivism, systems that are inherently skeptical of any knowledge that cannot be verified by sensation and experiment (CTH 33). Contemporary movements such as historical and cultural relativism, scientism, pragmatism, and postmodernism are offshoots of the so-called death of metaphysics (FR 86–91).

Although Kant was in some ways positivistic in his speculative philosophy, Wojtyła credits him with advancing beyond positivism in the attention that he gave to human moral experience. On the basis of the sense of moral obligation or duty, Kant derived practical certitude regarding the existence of God (CTH 34).

In contemporary philosophy the pope finds further signs that positivism is being overcome, at least in many circles. Ludwig Wittgenstein, in his *Philosophical Investigations*, went far beyond the positivism of his early *Tractatus logico-philosophicus*, insisting that meaningful discourse is by no means limited to propositions that can be empirically verified.

Contemporary philosophy of religion, as found in authors such as Mircea Eliade and Paul Ricoeur, builds on what the pope calls anthropological experience (CTH 36). Following Henri de Lubac, John Paul II says that the tragedy of atheistic humanism consists in stripping man of his transcendent character, thus destroying the ultimate significance of the human person (SCdn 16). The "death-of-God" movement, in its theoretical and practical consequences, demonstrates that the rejection of God makes human life meaningless and thus leads to the death of humanity. In the words of Vatican II, "Without the Creator the creature would disappear" (GS 36; D&V 38). Human dignity and human rights cannot be vindicated except on the ground of God as their absolute source.

Personalism

A close examination of Wojtyła's philosophy would lie beyond the scope of this volume, but his theology cannot be rightly understood without reference to his personalism. In his philosophical writings he strives to reconcile the ontological insights of classical metaphysics with the more subjectivist outlook of modern phenomenology. Although it is correct to define the human being, with Aristotle, as a rational animal, this definition, in Wojtyła's judgment, leaves out what is most properly human—namely, the lived experience of self-possession and self-governance. This experience, which defies metaphysical formulation, can be grasped to some extent by means of phenomenological analysis.

Modern philosophy, with its concentration on the human subject, characteristically falls short of classical metaphysics in overlooking the need to seek transcendent truth (FR 5). Max Scheler, for example, practiced phenomenology without sufficient attention to ontology. Thinkers of the Louvain and Lublin schools of Thomism have more successfully bridged the gap.

The transcendental anthropology of authors such as de Lubac is open to the philosophy of dialogue that Wojtyła finds in the Jewish philosophers Martin Buber and Emmanuel Lévinas (CTH 35). These personalist thinkers, like the Lublin Thomists, insist that man's basic experience transcends his individual existence and places him in dialogue with the other. In the dialogic framework it is possible to recover the insights reflected in the Bible, which present God as existentially related to his people. Human existence seeks its fulfillment in communion with the eternal "Thou" (CTH 36). The transcendence of the human spirit impels us to reach out for communion with an Other who is totally worthy of admiration, love, and service. Our self-fulfillment is therefore bound up with responsiveness to one who is absolute in being, goodness, truth, and beauty (SCdn 16). Only the God of infinite majesty can satisfy the deepest longings of the human heart (SCdn 17). Because this is the case, true anthropocentrism coincides, in the last analysis, with theocentrism. A philosophy centered on man must also be centered on God (DM 1).

As an illustration of how we can encounter the divine through interpersonal relationships, John Paul II often uses the example of the martyrs as "the most authentic witnesses to the truth about existence" (FR 32). Of them he writes:

> From the moment they speak to us of what we perceive deep down as the truth we have sought for so long, the martyrs provide evidence of a love that has no need of lengthy arguments to convince. The martyrs stir in us a profound trust because they give voice to what we already feel, and they declare what we would like to have the strength to express. (FR 32)

Master/Slave Paradigm

A major obstacle to belief in God, according to the present pope, is the philosophy that considers freedom to consist in absolute autonomy (that is to say, in the entitlement to do whatever one wants). In this framework, any subordination to the divine inevitably appears as servile, as enslavement. G. W. F. Hegel popularized the master/slave relationship as a paradigm of man's relationship to a transcendent God (CTH 227).

Following in the traces of Hegel, Ludwig Feuerbach and Karl Marx taught that religion alienates us by depriving us of our humanity. We enslave ourselves by groveling before the idea of God, which we construct as a projection from our experience. Wojtyła quotes Feuerbach as writing:

> In place of love of God we ought to acknowledge love of man as the only true religion; in place of belief in God we ought to expand man's belief in himself, in his own strength, the belief that humanity's destiny is dependent not on a being higher than humanity but on humanity itself, that man's only demon is man himself—primitive man, superstitious, egotistic, evil—but that similarly man's only god is man himself. (*The Essence of Religion,* quoted in SCdn 35)

Modern secularism, especially in the acute form of God-is-dead philosophies, follows along the path opened up by Hegel, Feuerbach, and Marx. These philosophical movements came to a kind of climax in the God-is-dead theologies of the early 1960s. Wojtyła interprets this curious fad as evidence of the lack of balance in modern thinking, which has seen enormous progress in what he calls the horizontal dimension, accompanied by a virtual atrophy of the vertical (SCdn 13).

Wojtyła shows that the master/slave paradigm does not stand up in the light of reason, because, as we have seen, it is evident, even philosophically, that God, as absolute goodness, creates for the sake of sharing his goodness with others. His goodness is, as the scholastic axiom had it, self-communicative (*bonum diffusivum sui,* D&V 37; God 134–35). Revelation discloses the true roots of the misconception. According to the opening chapters of Genesis the serpent tempts Adam and Eve to look upon God as the enemy, as if God were jealous of his own creature, man. By acquiring knowledge of good and evil, Satan suggests, man would become like God, thus undermining God's sovereignty and provoking God's jealousy (SCdn 30). Depicting God as man's enemy, Satan challenges man to become the adversary of God (D&V 38).

KNOWLEDGE OF GOD BY REVELATION

The Father/Son Paradigm

To overcome the master/slave paradigm, therefore, the pope turns to revelation, seen in the light of personalist philosophy. Although the desire for God may arise out of our nature, the fulfillment of that desire depends on the free initiative of God. Scripture tells us that God in fact turns toward humankind in revelation. In his retreat to the Roman curia, Cardinal Wojtyła accepts a personalist interpretation of the revelation of the divine Name in Exodus 3:14. In revealing his name, God manifests his personal character and his will to be with the people he has chosen as his own (SCdn 14–15).[1]

Divine revelation calls for the response of faith, which fulfills the dynamism of reason by providing clear and certain answers to questions of ultimate truth with which reason can only struggle. "Men and women can accomplish no more important act in their lives than the act of faith; it is here that freedom reaches the certainty of truth and chooses to live in that truth" (FR 13). Revelation sheds new light on the twofold mystery of God and human life (FR 14).

Jewish and Christian revelation overcomes the master/slave paradigm by proposing the biblical view of God as a loving Father. God's commands, as we know them from revelation, are so many helps for achieving the freedom that comes from fulfilling the highest potentialities of human nature and thereby receiving a share in the divine life. The tree of the knowledge of good and evil in Genesis is a symbol of being and value; it is linked symbolically with the tree of life (cf. Gen. 2:9; SCdn 23). The divine prohibition to eat of the fruit of that tree is a reminder that the creature cannot freely decide what is good and evil; this decision depends on God the Creator. Disobedience consists in going beyond the limits implicit in the creaturely state, the frontier that the human person may not cross (SCdn 23; D&V 36).

In the light of the biblical paradigm of the father/son relationship we can overcome the servile fear that the slave feels in the presence of the master and substitute a filial fear, the kind of loving reverence that makes us anxious not to do anything offensive to the Father. Perfect love casts out fear, as we read in the New Testament (1 John 4:18). It liberates us for loving service and enables us to obey the Gospel precept, "Be not afraid!" (CTH 226–27).

God as Merciful Father

Paul in the Letter to the Ephesians describes God as a Father "who is rich in mercy" (Eph. 2:4), but this revelation is already adumbrated in the Old Testament. In the book of Exodus, Israel is described as God's firstborn son (Exod. 4:22) and in Jeremiah God speaks of himself as "a father to Israel" (Jer. 31:9). In various passages from Hosea, Isaiah, Jeremiah, and Ezekiel, Israel is called God's beloved spouse. Throughout the Old Testament one finds a constant emphasis on

---

[1] Wojtyła here refers to the work of the Polish philosopher Jozef Tischner (*The World of Human Hope* [Kraków, 1975]) and to Joseph Ratzinger (*Introduction to Christianity* [New York: Seabury/Crossroad, 1971], 85–93).

mercy as the preeminent attribute of God. In a theophany to Moses, God proclaims, "The Lord, the Lord, a God merciful and gracious, slow to anger, and abounding in steadfast love and faithfulness" (Exod. 34:6; cf. DM 4).

Revelation of the Son

In the Old Testament we already find a clear and explicit revelation of God as Father. Certain texts in the Old Testament mysteriously point forward to the revelation of the other two divine persons, but the revelation is still somewhat obscure. In the New Testament the fundamental mission of Jesus is to give a further revelation of the Father, whose love and mercy he makes present to humankind, first in the event of the incarnation and most dramatically in that of the cross (DM 3, 7).

The mercy of God consists not merely in obliterating the memory of the past but rather in restoring the order that has been disturbed by sin. This restoration is accomplished in the incarnate Son, who accomplishes redemption on the objective plane of historical event. "In the Incarnation of the Son of God we see forged the enduring and definitive synthesis which the human mind of itself could never have imagined: the Eternal enters time, the Whole lies hidden in the part, God takes on a human face" (FR 12). Sent into the world by his eternal Father, Jesus was conscious of his own divinity and his salvific mission (Jesus 169–72, 339). He frequently alludes to his preexistence with the Father (Jesus 211–15).

The mission of Jesus came to its climax in the sacrifice of the cross, in which he pays the price of human disobedience. The resurrection clarified and completed the revelation of love by manifesting the depth of the Father's love for Christ and in him for the whole human race (DM 8). In his risen life Christ becomes manifest as the center of all history and as ontological head of the universe (Jesus 340). The eternal design of God is "to unite all things in Christ, things in heaven and things on earth . . . as a plan for the fullness of time" (Eph. 1:10; Jesus 545). These christological themes will be further explored in the next chapter.

THE HOLY SPIRIT

Revelation of the Spirit

After the Ascension the fruits of Christ's redeeming action still needed to be manifested and interiorized in the hearts of believers. This required a further mission, that of the Holy Spirit. Jesus in his final discourse at the Last Supper speaks of sending the "other advocate (Paraclete)" (D&V 3; 11). The Holy Spirit is not simply a replacement for Christ; Christ continues to be present and active in an invisible way through the Holy Spirit, the witness who receives and transmits what the Son communicates to him.

The revelation of the Holy Spirit is the crowning stage in the self-communication of God in Scripture. In the Old Testament, notably in Isaiah, there are abundant references to the Holy Spirit as gift, but it is not yet evident that the Spirit is a person. In the Farewell Discourse of Jesus as narrated in the Fourth Gospel, the Paraclete—the Holy Spirit whom the Father is to send in Jesus' name—is clearly portrayed as a distinct divine person (John 14:26; Spirit 271). Paul frequently speaks of the Holy Spirit in personalistic terms, for instance when he attributes the same charisms to the Spirit, the Son, and the Father (1 Cor. 12:4–6; Spirit 275) and when he admonishes the Ephesians to be careful not to grieve the Holy Spirit (Eph. 4:30; Spirit 176). In the baptismal formula at the end of Matthew's Gospel, the Holy Spirit is given the same divine and personal status as the Father and the Son (Matt. 28:19; cf. D&V 9; Spirit 261).

In identifying what is distinctive to the Holy Spirit, John Paul II focuses on his character as gift (Spirit 310–15). Within the godhead, he says, the Spirit is the personal expression of the mutual love and the mutual self-giving of the Father and the Son. According to Thomas Aquinas, the Holy Spirit is the uncreated gift of love (ST 1.37–38). When sent into the world, the Spirit is not simply the source of created gifts but is himself what John Paul II calls "Person-Gift" (D&V 10; Spirit 312). As the gift-element in the godhead, the Spirit is personally bestowed upon us and is the living source of all God's gifts, whether in creation or redemption (D&V 22–23; Spirit 312–13).

The inner relationships among the divine persons in the Trinity, according to John Paul II, constitute the deepest and most difficult mystery of our faith. Following Thomas Aquinas, he declares that each of the divine persons is a subsistent relation, and that all three, through their reciprocal interrelationship, constitute "the same Being, the same Life, the same God" (God, 185). The Son is therefore consubstantial with the Father who eternally generates him. And the Father, in union with the Son, is the principle of "spiration" of the Holy Spirit, who is the love in which the Father and the Son reciprocally remain united (God 162).

The pope is keenly aware that the mode of procession of the Holy Spirit has been sharply debated between the Eastern and Western churches since the tenth century. In a letter of June 4, 1980, to Patriarch Dimitrios, he speaks of the controversy about the role of the Son in the procession of the Holy Spirit as "one of the points that can and must be resolved in the dialogue between the two churches."[2] For his part, John Paul II adheres to the Latin form of the Nicene-Constantinopolitan creed, according to which the Spirit proceeds "from the Father and the Son." This formula, ratified by the councils of IV Lateran, II Lyons, and Florence, is, according to the pope, "a theological doctrine commonly accepted in the Church's teaching and therefore sure and binding" (God 176). In a general audience of November 7, 1990, he pointed out that the Council of Florence taught that this formula was compatible with the preferred Eastern formula, according to which the Holy Spirit proceeds from the Father through the Son. This conciliar text, he said, "is still a useful basis for dialogue and agreement between the Eastern and Western brethren" (Spirit 303).

In his encyclical on the Holy Spirit and in his general audience catecheses, John Paul II is concerned less with the eternal procession of the Holy Spirit than with the mission of the Spirit in time. Since the Orthodox hold, as do Roman Catholics and Protestants, that the Spirit is sent by both the Father and the Son, this theme does not constitute a point of controversy among the churches.

Activity of the Holy Spirit before Easter

The external activity of the Spirit begins with the creation of the world, which is the work of the three divine persons acting together (Spirit 211). This is already indicated in the first chapter of Genesis, which speaks of the Spirit of God moving over the waters (Gen. 1:2; Spirit 61). Insofar as creation is a gift proceeding from God's love, it is appropriated to the Holy Spirit, who is uncreated Love. But sin has intervened, contradicting the presence of the Holy Spirit in creation (D&V 13). Hence a new gift and a new beginning were needed.

The Holy Spirit was secretly at work in the Old Testament, inspiring the prophets and holy persons of Israel. The same Spirit overshadowed the Blessed Virgin, thus becoming, as the pope puts it, the protagonist of the incarnation, which John Paul II describes as "the greatest work accomplished by the Holy Spirit in the history of creation and salvation" (D&V 50). In the theophany that took place at the baptism of Jesus, the Holy Spirit descended visibly in the form of a dove. After leading Jesus into the desert, the Spirit continually guided Jesus in his public ministry. In his preaching, Jesus expressed his consciousness of being the Messiah anointed by the Holy Spirit (Luke 4:16–21; cf. D&V 18). He claimed to be working miracles and casting out demons by the power of the Spirit

---

[2] Giacomo Cardinal Biffi, "The Action of the Holy Spirit in the Church and in the World," in *John Paul II: A Panorama of His Teachings* (Brooklyn, N.Y.: New City Press, 1989), 38–47, at 39.

(Matt. 12:28; cf. Spirit 267). On the cross, Jesus offered himself without blemish through the eternal Spirit (Heb. 9:13–14; D&V 40).

For the full communication of God's self-gift in the person of the Holy Spirit, it was necessary for Christ's redemptive action to be completed. In his encyclical on the Holy Spirit and in his catechesis on the creed, John Paul II repeatedly quotes from Jesus' final discourse: "If I do not go away, the Counselor will not come to you" (John 16:7).[3] Only after his sacrifice was finished could the exalted Jesus send the Holy Spirit from the Father. In an appearance in the upper room, the risen Jesus breathes on the apostles, conferring the Spirit for the forgiveness of sins (John 20:19–22).

The Definitive Sending of the Spirit

The definitive sending of the Holy Spirit takes place at the foundation of the Church, which was born, according to John Paul II, at Pentecost. Before the glorification of Jesus, the Spirit was not permanently and publicly given. Since Pentecost the Spirit dwells continuously in the Church as his temple, acting in a covenanted way through its sacraments and ministries. The Spirit is the transcendent and principal agent of the Church's work as it discharges its divine commission to teach, to forgive sin, and sanctify the world (D&V 42). As the Spirit of truth, he keeps the Church in the truth of the apostolic heritage (D&V 4). The Spirit is likewise the invisible dispenser of the grace of the sacraments (D&V 63). When conferred upon the baptized through confirmation, the Spirit strengthens them in their life of faith. Through episcopal ordination, the same Spirit empowers bishops to carry on their office of apostolic leadership (D&V 25).

Effects of the Spirit

For individual persons, the Holy Spirit is the interior guide of conscience, prompting them to accept objective moral norms (D&V 43). The Spirit opens our eyes so that we can be conscious of the "mystery of iniquity" (D&V 39), conscious of our own sinfulness and need of conversion (D&V 30-31). John Paul gives a highly personal commentary on the text that says: "When [the Spirit] comes he will convince the world concerning sin and righteousness and judgment" (John 16:8; cf. D&V 27–32). The "sin" manifested by the Holy Spirit is essentially the lack of faith that led to Jesus' condemnation and death. "Righteousness" in this context refers to the definitive righteousness to be conferred in the final kingdom; and

[3] John 16:7 is quoted in D&V 8, 13–14, 24, 27, and 61; also in Spirit, 16, 17, 19, 32, 273, and 368.

"judgment" here means demonstration of the guilt incurred by the world in rejecting God and Christ (Spirit 30).

From passages such as these it may be seen that the pope, even while expound-
ing the Church's heritage of faith, does so with his own distinctive accents. This
is especially evident when he speaks of the Spirit's role in overcoming the slavery of sin and leading us into the freedom of adopted children—the freedom that
the truth alone can give (John 8:32). As the Spirit of truth, the Paraclete bears witness to Christ and leads the Church into all truth (Spirit 20–25). The Spirit as
God's personal self-gift imparts a deeply personal quality to our relationship with
God. We find in the Holy Spirit the deepest expression of God's inner life as Love
and of the definitive triumph of grace over sin (Spirit 31, 312).

The Holy Spirit and Prayer

St. Paul, followed by all the saints and mystics of Christian tradition, teaches us
that authentic prayer is inspired and directed by the Holy Spirit (Spirit 389–94).
The pope frequently declares his personal conviction that there is no real prayer
without the Holy Spirit: "It is a beautiful and salutary thought that wherever
people are praying in the world, there the Holy Spirit is, the living breath of
prayer" (D&V 65). This is true, he says, because it is the Spirit who "breathes"
prayer into the human heart. He adds that according to Paul, "we do not know how
to pray as we ought, but the Spirit himself intercedes for us with sighs too deep
for words" (Rom. 8:26).

These ideas recur in a more personal style in *Crossing the Threshold of Hope*.
Early in the book, when asked how the pope prays, he replies that he prays as the
Holy Spirit permits him (CTH 19). He finds that the Spirit comes to help him in
his weakness. Prayer, he says, is always God's initiative within us, for in prayer
the true protagonist is God (CTH 17).

Later in the same book John Paul II recalls how, when he was a boy, his father
gave him a prayerbook that contained a prayer to the Holy Spirit, telling young
Karol to say it every day. That prayer, which he still recites daily, taught him to
appreciate Jesus' words to the Samaritan woman about how the hour had come for
people to worship God in the Spirit and in truth. This directive of his father, the
pope declares, set him on course toward living as a true worshiper in the community of the Holy Spirit—a community even larger than the Church in its visible
structure (CTH 141–42). As we shall later see, the Holy Spirit figures prominently
in what the pope has to say about ecumenism and interreligious dialogue. The
prayer meetings with leaders of different religions at Assisi reflect the pope's confidence that all who sincerely pray enjoy a certain community in the Holy Spirit.

CONCLUSION

Building on the contributions of modern personalist phenomenology, John Paul II has recast traditional natural theology. His system is simultaneously theocentric and anthropocentric. The deep hunger of the human spirit for life, truth, and love is the mirror image of what the Creator wills to give. Human reason is in principle capable of knowing the existence of the loving creator, but this natural knowledge is impeded by sin, so that we project false images of God as the enemy of our freedom.

Revelation, accepted in faith, provides the divine answer to human sinfulness. The missions of the Son and the Spirit jointly manifest the supreme mystery of God as love, and thereby also manifest the meaning and goal of human life. The Son, by taking on human flesh and by his atoning death on the cross, manifests the depth of the Father's love and illuminates the riddles of suffering and death.

The Holy Spirit, as the personal expression of God's uncreated love, is sent into our hearts so that we may appropriate the meaning manifested in the Son. As a principle of truth, freedom, and communion, the Spirit is omnipresent in the theology and personal piety of John Paul II. Cardinal Giacomo Biffi begins his essay on the pneumatology of the pope with a pregnant sentence that may serve as a conclusion for this chapter and as a prelude to some themes that lie ahead:

> The name of the Holy Spirit recurs very frequently on the lips of John Paul II, who sees in him the secret source of all ecclesial vitality, the guarantor of a possible transformation of the world, the principle of a renewed human psychology, the hope of a more complete intercommunion among the Churches.[4]

[4] Biffi, "Action of the Holy Spirit," 38.

CHAPTER 3

Christology and Mariology

⟨∞⟩

To deal with the Christology and Mariology of John Paul II in a single chapter may seem like a rather large order, since he maintains that "the Redeemer of man, Jesus Christ, is the center of the universe and of history" (RH 1) and, furthermore, that "the decisive answer to every one of man's questions, his religious and moral questions in particular, is given by Jesus Christ, or rather is Jesus Christ himself" (VS 2). It may nevertheless be possible to accomplish what is essential for our purposes. I have already given a preliminary sketch of the pope's Christology in my presentation of his doctrine of the Trinity. I there pointed out that Jesus Christ both reveals the merciful love of God and accomplishes redemption by making atonement for human sin. In the present chapter these rather concise statements may be amplified and put in a broader context.

The Christology of John Paul II is closely bound up with his personalism and his philosophy of action, as expounded in his book *The Acting Person*. For him, persons constitute themselves existentially by what they do. Approaching Christology from this background, Wojtyła develops it in dynamic and relational terms. His interest focuses not primarily on the ontological constitution of Christ as God-man but rather on the work of Christ within the cosmos and human history. He refuses to separate the constitution of Christ from the work of Christ, the incarnation from the redemption, or Christology from soteriology.

John Paul II sees himself as charged with the mandate to direct the gaze of the Church and of the world to Christ the Lord, the Redeemer of humanity. The fundamental task of the Church, he says, is to point the awareness of all humanity toward the mystery of God and toward the redemption made available in Jesus Christ (RH 10). Again in the concluding section of *Redemptor hominis* he writes: "The aim of any service in the Church, whether that service is apostolic, pastoral, priestly or episcopal, is to keep this dynamic link between the mystery of the Redemption and every man" (RH 22). The revelation of God in Christ is not the private property of Christian believers; it is a message entrusted to the Church as

31

good news for all humanity—that humanity to which the pope at his inaugural mass of October 22, 1978, addressed the exhortation, "Do not be afraid. Open wide the doors for Christ!"[1]

CHRISTOLOGY

Predestination

Far from being an interloper in the world, Christ belongs to the essential plan of creation. If we wish to distinguish "moments" in the eternal plan of God, we shall have to say with St. Paul that Christ is the "first-born of all creation" (Col. 1:15) and that all who are called to salvation were chosen in Christ from before the foundation of the world (Eph. 1:4; God 263). For John Paul II, as for St. Paul, Christ is "before all things, and in him all things hold together" (Col. 1:17). The world, created in Christ the eternal Son, bears in itself from the beginning the call and pledge of predestination in Christ (God 264). Through the incarnation, God granted definitively the participation in divine life that he intended human beings to have from the beginning (RH 1).

Christ as God-man

Pope John Paul II is of course convinced of the utter uniqueness of Jesus Christ as a divine person having two integral natures, divine and human. This is simply the doctrine defined by the early councils, which no Catholic can call into question. In its doctrine of the incarnation, he writes, Christianity has greatly enriched the philosophy of the person, which had been very undeveloped in classical antiquity, since the distinction between person and nature was still unknown. By the teaching that God is three persons in one nature, and that Christ is one person with two natures, revelation set philosophy on the path to discovering that important distinction. In his catechetical lectures on the creed John Paul II recognizes the historic contribution of the Council of Chalcedon for the clarification of technical concepts such as "person" and "hypostasis" (Jesus 329–31).[2]

While acknowledging that the terminology of Christian doctrine may be adapted to the modern mentality, the pope cautions against being enmeshed in new categories in which the substance of revealed truth could be manipulated

---

[1] John Paul II, "The Inauguration Homily," *Origins* 8 (November 2, 1978): 305–8, at 307.

[2] For further discussion of the concept of person and its importance, see John Saward, *Christ Is the Answer: The Christ-centered Teaching of Pope John Paul II* (Edinburgh: T. & T. Clark, 1995), 81–82.

(Jesus 338). For this reason he is reluctant to speak of Christ as a "human person," as do some contemporary theologians. This manner of speaking, based as it is on a phenomenological concept of personality, tends to obscure the ontological mystery of the incarnation so successfully protected by the formulas of the ancient Church, which referred to Christ as a divine person subsisting in two natures (ibid.).

Although his theology is Christocentric, John Paul II points out that Christ himself is not Christocentric. On the contrary, Christ's entire life is oriented toward the Father. In his divinity he proceeds from the Father and is essentially Son. His personal existence is that of a subsistent relation: sonship. His incarnate life replicates that relationality. Jesus is totally faithful to the mission he receives from the Father. His food is to do the will of the Father who has sent him (John 4:34; cf. Jesus 178).

While remaining completely faithful to the doctrine of Scripture and of the councils, John Paul II explains this doctrine in relation to the human situation. His Christology might be said to follow a "method of correlation," in the sense that he points out the correspondence between human questions and the divine answer proffered in Christ. The questions that arise in the human heart are echoes of a call from God, who is the origin and goal of human existence (VS 7). While the contents of revelation cannot be altered to suit the changing human situations, we may be sure that there is no human question that does not take on light through the mystery of Christ. The answers are not merely abstract. Jesus' actions, and especially his passion and death on the cross, "are the living revelation of his love for the Father and for others" (VS 20).

Following Vatican II, the pope distinguishes between three aspects of the mission of Christ. He is prophet, priest, and king (SC 119-35). As prophet he reveals what we need to know for the sake of our salvation. As priest he mediates between God and creation, effecting reconciliation. And as king he inaugurates and governs the reign of God, establishing the people of God as an organic and organized society.

Prophetic Office

As we saw in chapter 2, a Christocentric theology is both theocentric and anthropocentric, because Christ has two natures. He is able to redeem us because he is both God and man. He becomes incarnate and dies on the cross for us and for our salvation, as we say in the creed. His mission is from the Father and to humankind.

Revelation of the Father. Jesus is sent, in the first place, to reveal the Father (Jesus 360, 364). John Paul II quotes the passage from the Gospel of John in which Philip turns to Christ and says, "Lord, show us the Father, and we shall be satisfied." Jesus replies, "Have I been with you so long, and yet you do not know me . . . ? He who has seen me has seen the Father" (John 14:8–9; DM 1). In the encyclical *Veritatis splendor* the pope makes the further point that "the light of God's face shines in all its beauty on Jesus Christ, 'the image of the invisible God' (Col. 1:15), the 'reflection of God's glory' (Heb. 1:3), 'full of grace and truth' (John 1:14)" (VS 2). Although the Son is really distinct from the Father, those who see Jesus may, in a certain sense, be said to see the Father, for the Son possesses the fullness of the divine nature, communicated to him by the Father.

More especially, Christ reveals the Father's love, which under the conditions of the present order means the Father's mercy. According to John Paul II, "Mercy is an indispensable dimension of love; it is, as it were, love's second name and, at the same time, the specific manner in which love is revealed and effected vis-à-vis the reality of evil that is in the world" (DM 7).

In the career of Jesus Christ, it is the cross that above all discloses the depth of God's love. With the light shed upon our situation by the Holy Spirit we are able to grasp more adequately the depth of human sin, to which the love of the Father responds. Only in the light of the cross is it possible to understand the malice of sin, the *mysterium iniquitatis* (D&V 32), and the inexhaustible mercy of the Father (DM 8).

Revelation of humanity to itself. Christ therefore reveals not only the mercy of God but the situation and destiny of humankind. In this connection the pope frequently quotes from Vatican II's Pastoral Constitution, *Gaudium et spes,*

> It is only in the mystery of the Word incarnate that light is shed on the mystery of man. For Adam, the first man, was a figure of the future man, namely, of Christ the Lord. It is Christ, the last Adam, who fully discloses man to himself and unfolds his noble calling by revealing the mystery of the Father and the Father's love. (GS 22; cf. RH 8; DM 1; VS 2)

The original revelation in Genesis, of course, tells us that human beings were created in the image and likeness of God and were given dominion over the rest of creation. The rational nature with which humans were endowed is a participation in the eternal reason of God, which exists personally as the divine Logos, who became incarnate in Christ. Thus we may speak of a christological dimension of creation itself. All creation takes place through God's word, but human beings, by sharing in the divine reason, have a special affinity with the eternal Logos, being endowed with the capacity to contemplate and understand the order of creation.

In his incarnation and redemptive death, Jesus gives us a further proof of our value in the eyes of God. Human dignity appears in a new and clearer light when viewed in the perspectives of the cross, inasmuch as God deemed it fitting to deliver up his beloved Son to win us back from our sinful condition (cf. Rom. 5:8).

The cross likewise permits us to find meaning in human suffering and death, which might otherwise appear as riddles or absurdities (cf. GS 22). Revelation teaches us that suffering is not an absolute evil, since it can be embraced by God.

> Thanks to Christ, the meaning of suffering changes radically. It no longer suffices to see in it a punishment for sin. One must discern in it the redemptive, salvific power of love. The evil of suffering, in the mystery of Christ's redemption, is overcome and in every case transformed. It becomes a force of liberation from evil, for the victory of the good. All human sufferings, united to that of Christ, complete "what is lacking in Christ's afflictions for the sake of his body" (cf. Col. 1:24). The body is the Church as the universal community of salvation. (Jesus 454)

While not offering a theoretical solution to the problem of evil, revelation enables us to cope with the negative experiences of life and integrate them into God's plan for the redemption of the world (SD 26). Although nothing was qualitatively and intensively lacking in the sufferings of the Christ as head, still he allows us to participate in his sufferings by applying them to our own place and time (SD 24). We shall return to this theme when we take up suffering and penance in chapter 7.

The resurrection of Jesus is also important for our self-understanding. We naturally recoil before the inevitability of death, but Christ enables us to know by faith that death has been swallowed up in victory. The risen Christ discloses to us that we are called to reign with him in eternal life not simply as detached souls but as complete human persons.

As the God-man, Jesus is the norm for morality. Because he is the perfect man, like us in all things except sin, his example and his teaching reveal what human life at its best ought to be. He provides a living norm by which everything human can be measured. In *Veritatis splendor* John Paul II explains that "Jesus' way of acting and his words, his deeds and his precepts constitute the moral rule of the Christian life" (VS 20). In the same encyclical the pope gives a concrete, personalistic exposition of the principles of Christian morality based primarily on Jesus Christ as revealer. The beatitudes, he explains, are not specific rules of behavior but are rather invitations to discipleship and communion with Christ. They may best be understood as a sort of self-portrait of Christ (VS 16).

Priestly Office

The second office of Christ is the priestly. In his apostolic exhortation on priestly formation John Paul II takes up the doctrine of Hebrews that Jesus is in his very being the perfect mediator between the Father and humanity. Hebrews 10:5–7 makes it clear that priesthood belongs essentially to the existence of the God-man. It quotes from Psalm 40 (LXX): "A body thou hast prepared for me. . . . Then I said, 'Lo, I have come to do thy will, O God, as it is written of me in the roll of the book.'" According to the pope, Jesus carries out his priestly mission throughout his earthly life, but especially in the central event of his passion, death, and resurrection (PDV 13; cf. Jesus 117). This priestly mediation begins with the incarnation itself, which adds a new dimension to human existence inasmuch as one of our race, one of our blood brothers, is God. John Paul II takes every opportunity to quote Vatican II to the effect that Christ by his incarnation united himself in some sort with every human being and in so doing elevated human nature to an incomparable dignity (GS 22 cited in RH 8; 13; cf. 14; 18).

Jesus carries out his priestly activity especially in those actions that are directed to his Father—his prayer, his worship, and his total obedience to the Father's will. This aspect of his work comes to its peak in his sacrifice on the cross. The cross is not just a parable intended to teach us a lesson; more fundamentally it is an event that makes reparation for human sin and restores the order of divine justice. John Paul II maintains that Jesus suffered the greatest pain endured or endurable by a human being (SD 18). He bore our sins and carried our sorrows. In terms reminiscent of John Henry Newman's famous sermon on the mental sufferings of Our Lord, the pope speaks of the agonizing weight and the abominable filth of sin as it was poured forth upon the refined and sensitive soul of our blessed Redeemer (Jesus 440–41). By enduring physical and mental agony in such great intensity Jesus showed forth the depth of God's love for his sinful creatures, atoned for their sin, and transformed the very nature of human suffering, so that in union with his own it could become salvific (Jesus 442, 447, 454). This last point has already been mentioned in connection with the rather difficult passage from Paul about filling up what is lacking in the sufferings of Christ.

In *Salvifici doloris* and in his catecheses on the creed, John Paul interprets in some detail the cry of Jesus from the cross: "My God, my God, why hast thou forsaken me?" (Matt. 27:46; Mark 15:34). As he explains it, this cry does not express resentment or anger, still less doubt and despair, but rather "a pained bewilderment at that suffering which had no merely human explanation, but which was a mystery to which the Father alone possessed the key" (Jesus 471). Throughout his sufferings Jesus was intellectually conscious that the Father still encompassed him with his love, for he himself had said, prior to his passion, "I am not alone, for the Father is with me" (John 16:32; Jesus 472). In quoting the beginning of Psalm 22, the Lord undoubtedly did not forget that the same psalm concludes with a triumphant hymn of liberation and an announcement of the universality of salvation (Jesus 473).

Royal Office

The regal aspect is the third element in John Paul II's dynamic Christology. As we know from Holy Scripture, Jesus was announced as the son and successor of David, whose throne was to endure forever. When interrogated by Pilate, he did not deny that he was a king but indicated that his kingship was totally unlike any temporal office. Jesus entered into the glory of his kingdom through humiliation and suffering. By becoming obedient even unto death on the cross, he restored the divinely willed order, which had been disrupted by human sin. By the grace that he has won for us, Christ enables us to overcome sin in ourselves and to lead others to the glory of heaven. "Every Christian who conquers sin by imitating Christ achieves the royal self-dominion that is proper to human beings; by so doing he shares in the *munus regale* of Christ and helps to bring about Christ's kingdom" (SR 263). In this way we can become members of the body of the redeemed, the Mystical Body of Christ. Through the members of his Mystical Body Jesus achieves his own kingship; he becomes the supernatural center of a new human solidarity, a community of faith and love.

The kingdom of God, though it is already present in mystery in the Church, is not identical with the Church. The mission of the Church is to establish God's kingdom in history (Jesus 255). The kingdom is constituted by the victory of God over the power of evil and over Satan, the principal and mysterious author of evil (Jesus 369). The kingdom was born and develops in time as a seed inserted into history (Jesus 349) but will reach its consummation only when Christ returns in glory (Jesus 540).

Cosmic Redemption

It would be too narrow to look at the work of Christ simply in terms of its impact on humanity. As John Paul II points out in his encyclical on the Holy Spirit, "the incarnation of God the Son signifies the taking up into unity with God not only of human nature, but in this human nature, in a sense, of everything that is flesh: the whole of humanity, the entire visible and material world" (D&V 50). The pope goes on to say: "The Incarnation, then, has also a cosmic significance, a cosmic dimension. The 'first-born of all creation' (Col. 1:15), becoming incarnate in the individual humanity of Christ, unites himself in some way with the entire reality of man, which is also 'flesh'—and in this reality with all 'flesh,' with the whole of creation" (ibid.).

Cosmic redemption plays a part in the eschatology of John Paul II. He quotes from Colossians 1:19–20 that it was the Father's good pleasure to reconcile to himself all that exists on earth and in heaven. Although God allows evil to manifest

itself in history, still he is secretly leading all things toward the final consummation in Christ (SC 175). According to Paul in 1 Corinthians 15:27–28, all things are
to be made subject to Christ, who will in the end subject himself and all creatures
to the Father, so that God may be all in all (SC 177). In Christ as Lord of history
all creation finds its transcendent fulfillment (Jesus 545). We shall return to this
theme toward the end of this study, when we take up John Paul II's eschatology.

Conclusion

The Christology of John Paul II, like his anthropology, is dynamic and relational.
He avoids a static essentialism that would isolate the constitution from the work
of Christ. He emphasizes the unity between the Creator Logos and the Incarnate
Word, Jesus Christ. In treating the ontological constitution of Jesus Christ, the
pope adheres to the full biblical and dogmatic heritage, which he restates in a pastorally effective way. His interest, however, gravitates toward the work of Christ
as redeemer of the world in all its dimensions, including the cosmic. He speaks
with particular animation about Christ as the one who displays the mercy of the
Father, who unlocks the riddles of suffering and death, and discloses the meaning
and goal of human life. Coming into the world as the way, the truth, and the life,
Christ is the truth that sets us free.

MARIOLOGY

Devotional Context

John Paul II, like Pius XII and Paul VI, is outstanding for his devotion to Mary.
This attitude was inculcated in him from his early youth, when he became accus-
tomed to visiting the great Marian shrines of Poland. When ordained to the episcopate, he placed on his coat of arms the words, "Totus tuus," "totally yours." In
his account of his vocation, *Gift and Mystery*, he explains that this motto is an
abbreviation of the formula of consecration found in the writings of St. Louis-
Marie Grignion de Montfort, "I am totally yours and all that I possess is yours. I
accept you in all that is mine. Give me your heart, O Mary" (GM 30).[3] When
elected pope, he had inscribed on his papal coat of arms a large M beneath the
cross.

[3] This theme runs as a kind of refrain through the celebrated work of Louis-Marie Grignon de
Montfort, *A Treatise on the True Devotion to the Blessed Virgin* (London: Burns & Oates, 1904). The
spelling of the author's last name in the French original, followed by the pope in RMat 48 and in my
text, is Grignion de Montfort.

To give thanks for his almost miraculous escape from the attempted assassination on May 13, 1981, the pope made a pilgrimage to Fatima a year later, the sixty-fifth anniversary of the first apparition there (May 13, 1917). In *Crossing the Threshold of Hope,* he speaks glowingly of Mary. From September 6, 1995, to November 12, 1997, he devoted a series of seventy Wednesday audience catecheses to the subject of Mary. Most of his important letters and encyclicals contain, usually at the end, passages invoking the intercession of Mary. For purposes of a briefer discussion we are fortunate in having a single encyclical, *Redemptoris mater*, in which he presents the essentials of his Marian doctrine. Departing somewhat from the pope's own order, I shall here take up a few points that seem especially worthy of emphasis.

Divine Motherhood

The title of the encyclical, "Mother of the Redeemer," is significant. In the first place, it links Mary with Jesus, the divine Redeemer. John Paul II wants to make it clear that there can be no competition between devotion to Christ and to Mary. Mary cannot be rightly understood except in the light of Christ, toward whom her entire life was directed and from whom she received all that made her great and glorious. As he says more than once in his encyclical, "Only in the mystery of Christ is her mystery made clear" (RMat 4; cf. 19). In *Crossing the Threshold of Hope,* he cautions against any separation between the devotion we should have toward Jesus and toward the Blessed Virgin. As a young factory worker during World War II he learned from the works of St. Louis Grignion de Montfort that true devotion to the Mother of God is actually Christocentric, since it is rooted in the mysteries of the incarnation and redemption (CTH 213, cf. RMat 48).

The title of the encyclical also points to what John Paul II regards as the fundamental source of Mary's dignity: her role as Mother of the Son. The Council of Ephesus in 431 defined the fundamental Marian dogma, that she is *theotokos*, "God-bearer." This dogma is a bond of union between Eastern and Western Christians. Later in his encyclical the pope adverts to the praise of Mary in the Eastern liturgies, e.g., that of John Chrysostom, where Mary is called higher than the cherubim and more glorious than the seraphim (RMat 31–32). Mary is "full of grace," says the pope, "because it is precisely in her that the Incarnation of the Word, the hypostatic union of the Son of God with human nature, is accomplished and fulfilled. . . . Because of this gift of sublime grace she far surpasses all other creatures, both in heaven and on earth" (RMat 9).

Prior to Vatican II many theologians searched for a single fundamental principle to give unity and coherence to Mariology. Karl Rahner, for instance, constructed his Mariology around the theme of Mary as the human person most perfectly redeemed. The synthesis of John Paul II is centered rather on Mary's divine motherhood.

Mary as the New Eve

Beginning with Justin and Irenaeus, many of the church fathers depicted Mary as the New Eve (RMat 19). At various points in his encyclical, the pope underlines the parallels and the contrasts between Mary and Eve. The first Eve was so called, according to Genesis, because she was the "mother of all the living" (Gen. 3:20). In a deeper sense, this is true of Mary, who is the Mother of Christ and of all who are redeemed in Christ. The first Eve, although created free from sin, fell into the sin of disobedience when misled by the words of the Tempter. Mary, in her response to the message of the angel, exemplifies total obedience. Genesis 3:15 speaks of the lasting enmity between the serpent and the woman. In the spiritual exegesis that comes into the tradition with the early fathers, Mary is identified as the woman under whose heel the serpent will be crushed. She is also identified with the woman of the twelfth chapter of the book of Revelation, who is fiercely opposed by the dragon (RMat 11). The "woman clothed with the sun," with twelve stars about her head, is none other than Mary in her role as queen of heaven and queen of the apostles. John Paul II accepts these spiritual interpretations in his Marian encyclical (RMat 11 and 47).

In answering the angel, Mary said, "Let it be done to me according to your word" (Luke 1:37). Her "fiat," as the reversal of Eve's disobedience, exemplifies the full submission that pertains to faith (RMat 13). In the course of his encyclical the pope many times speaks of Mary as the model for the Church in its pilgrimage of faith (RMat 5–6; 25). At the Annunciation and often during the public life, she had to believe, contrary to appearances, that God's promises would be fulfilled. At the visitation Elizabeth saluted Mary with the words, "Blessed is she who believed that what was spoken to her by the Lord would be fulfilled." Mary's faith was to be severely tested on many occasions, beginning with the Flight into Egypt and then the Loss and Finding in the Temple. On this latter occasion Luke mentions that, although Mary did not understand what was spoken to her, she "pondered it in her heart" (RMat 20). The supreme test of Mary's faith was undoubtedly the crucifixion. At the cross, says the pope, she willingly consented to the immolation of her Son. And he adds: "This is perhaps the deepest 'kenosis' of faith in human history" (RMat 18).

John Paul II speaks frequently of Mary's intimate association with her Son in the whole of his redemptive action. This association, he holds, in no way infringes on the necessity and sufficiency of Christ's own action, in which Mary participated in a way unique and proper to herself. All of us can cooperate with Christ, but Mary, he says, does so during the event of Calvary itself and in her capacity as mother. In union with Christ, therefore, she collaborated in obtaining salvation for all the redeemed.[4]

Mary's Spiritual Motherhood

In the biblical scenes of Nazareth and Bethlehem we are taught about the physical motherhood of Mary, who conceives and gives birth without detriment to her virginity. The virginal conception is important because it signifies that the incarnation is totally a gift and requires no prior action on the part of human beings. Mary is purely and simply receptive.

Mary's motherhood is not merely physical, though it is of course physical too. Motherhood in its full reality includes spiritual bonds. John Paul II therefore speaks of an "other dimension" of Mary's motherhood that was revealed by Jesus during his public life. This dimension is apparent in the pope's interpretation of the incident in which an unnamed woman says to Jesus: "Blessed is the womb that bore you, and the breasts that you sucked!" (Luke 11:27). To this Jesus replies, "Blessed rather are those who hear the word of God and keep it." Is not Mary, asks the pope, the first of those who "hear the word of God and keep it"? Already at the Annunciation she believed the message of the angel and described herself as the handmaid of the Lord (Luke 1:38). She received her sublime vocation before the other apostles and can therefore be called, in a sense, the first disciple of her son (RMat 20).

Mary's maternal care is brought out by several passages in the Fourth Gospel. At the wedding feast at Cana, she appears as the "Mother of Jesus" (John 2:1–2). Mary's spiritual motherhood is indicated also by the words of Jesus from the cross. Jesus says to his mother, "Woman, behold your son!" and to the beloved disciple, "Behold your mother!" (John 19:26–27; cf. RMat 23–24). In this case there is no question of physical motherhood, but only of a new spiritual relationship. All members of the Church are urged to take Mary into their lives as the beloved disciple took her into his home (John 19:27; cf. RMat 45).

Mary's Mediation

John Paul II develops the doctrine of Mary's mediation in the light of her divine motherhood, which distinguishes her intercessory role from that of other saints. Her motherhood, he says, is the first and most fundamental instance of the mediation she was to exercise at Cana and throughout her career. In his reflection on the wedding feast the pope makes the point that Mary "places herself between her

---

[4]General Audience of April 9, 1996; text in *L'Osservatore Romano* (English language edition), April 16, 1996, p. 7.

Son and mankind in the reality of their wants, needs, and sufferings." Her mediation takes the form of intercession. Her only action consists in her implicit request that Jesus should act. In telling the servants, "Do whatever he tells you," she directs them to obey her Son. "The Mother of Christ therefore presents herself as the spokeswoman of her Son's will," seeking only that his will be accomplished (RMat 21).

Conscious of the danger that Mary's mediation could be seen as detracting from that of Christ, the pope quotes Vatican II's important statement, "Mary's maternal function toward mankind in no way obscures or diminishes the unique mediation of Christ, but rather shows its efficacy" (GS 60). Her mediation is simply a participation in the mediatorship of Christ, who is described in Scripture as the one Mediator between God and men (1 Tim. 2:5; cf. RMat 22).

Mary and the Church

In the first chapter of Acts we see the apostles in the upper room, praying together with Mary the mother of Jesus and other disciples (Acts 1:14). They are praying for the descent of the Holy Spirit, which will give life to the Church on Pentecost. By her prayer with the apostles, Mary contributes to the birth of the Church. Each year the Church celebrates a novena to the Holy Spirit in the days between Ascension Thursday and Pentecost, praying with Mary for a renewed outpouring of the Holy Spirit (Spirit 37–44).

At the end of the third session of Vatican II, Paul VI made a speech in which he conferred upon Mary the title "Mother of the Church." That speech caused some consternation, especially among the Protestant observers, because the council deliberately avoided that very title. In his Marian encyclical John Paul II recalls that incident and adds that in the credo of the People of God issued in 1968, Paul VI restated this doctrine in an even more forceful way (RMat 47). John Paul II strongly agrees. As we have seen in chapter 1, he spoke up at the council to say that just as Mary was the Mother of Jesus in his physical body, so she was to become the Mother of the Church as the Mystical Body. This is the foundation for what John Paul II calls the "special presence of the Mother of God in the mystery of Christ and his Church" (RMat 48).

Prominent theologians have written about Mary as model or type of the Church. John Paul II fully accepts this designation. The Church, he holds, imitates Mary in believing the word of God, in obeying Christ the Lord, in mediating the grace of Christ, and in interceding for the needs of the human race. All disciples of Christ should have a Marian dimension in their lives. Mary is preeminently a model for women. In her, women can find an exemplar of "the loftiest sentiments of which the human heart is capable: the self-offering totality of love; the strength that is capable of bearing the greatest sorrows; limitless fidelity and tireless devotion to work; the ability to combine penetrating intuition with words of support and encouragement" (RMat 46).

Conclusion

In his Mariology John Paul II continues to draw on his youthful piety and the work of St. Grignion de Montfort. He stands with Henri de Lubac and Hans Urs von Balthasar in maintaining that Marian devotion is not outdated and that the Second Vatican Council did nothing to authorize Marian minimalism. The present pope, like his recent predecessors in the see of Peter, makes no apologies for his robust devotion to the Mother of Christ.

Mary, in his view, is not simply a venerable figure from the past who made it possible for the Redeemer to come into the world and who nurtured his physical and spiritual development. She continues her spiritual mediation from heaven, cooperating unceasingly in the work of salvation accomplished by Christ (RMat 49). Because she continues to play an important part in the unfolding of salvation history, she is to be devoutly invoked by those who are still on their journey of faith. In her active receptivity she is a model and type of the Church and of its faithful members, especially women. Before the coming of Christ she was the "morning star" (*stella matutina*) preceding the rise of the Sun of Justice (RMat 3). After her assumption into glory she is invoked as "star of the sea" (*stella Maris*) for those who are still struggling amid the adversities and uncertainties of this earthly existence (RMat 6). Glorified as she is by the side of her Son in heaven, she inspires the hope that she may become, for those who rely on her, the "gate of heaven" (*porta coeli*) (RMat 51).

CHAPTER 4

The Church and Evangelization

THE CHURCH

K AROL WOJTYŁA'S SENSE of the Church was brought to maturity by his participation in the Second Vatican Council. Ecclesiology stands at the heart of his
Sources of Renewal, composed with a view to implementing the council in his
archdiocese of Kraków. His thought on the Church can be gathered, additionally,
from his catechetical lectures on ecclesiology delivered between July 1991 and
August 1995. Particular aspects of the Church are also treated in various occasional articles and speeches to which reference will be made in the present chapter. With special attention to Holy Scripture and Vatican II, Wojtyła relates his
ecclesiological vision to the Christocentrism and the dynamic personalism to
which we have already referred.

The Church as Object and Subject

The dignity of the human person consists above all in being called to communion
with God through Jesus Christ, the universal Redeemer. According to the divine
plan this goal is to be achieved not by lonely individuals finding God in isolation
but by integration into a community that takes its origins from Christ (SR 116–17)
and is continually vitalized by the Holy Spirit (SR 120).

Throughout the centuries the Church has loyally preserved the deposit of faith.
Within that deposit the reality of the Church is one item, mentioned in the creed
after the realities of God, creation, and redemption (SR 38). But from another
point of view the Church may be seen as the corporate subject of faith. As a
believing subject, the Church is viewed as prior to all the content that is believed.
It is the community that consciously and consistently accepts and affirms the
word of God. The Church, therefore, is both the believer and the believed. "We

ourselves are the Church, and at the same time we believe in it; it is the object of our faith, and it is ourselves" (SR 38).

Just as persons constitute themselves by free and conscious decision, so the Church is called to realize itself through free and deliberate appropriation of the faith. It is this enrichment of the faith which John Paul II sees as having been inaugurated by Paul VI in his first encyclical, *Ecclesiam suam* (1964), and by Vatican II in its two constitutions on the Church (LG and GS). The council's first question, he says, was: "*Ecclesia, quid dicis de teipsa?*" ("Church, what do you say of yourself?")[1]—a question that called upon the Church and all its members to identify themselves consciously. The answer is formulated principally in *Lumen gentium*, which is the key to the whole accomplishment of Vatican II. This constitution, however, should be read in connection with the other council documents, especially the Pastoral Constitution on the Church in the Modern World, *Gaudium et spes* (SR 35). In order to realize the promise of the council, says John Paul II, the faithful must enrich their faith and their Christian life by more intense appropriation of the divine truth of revelation (SR 15).

Mystical Body and People of God

In the perspectives of his personalist philosophy, John Paul II brings out the communitarian and conscious aspects of the Church's existence. The Church, for him, is not an objective institution that cramps its members but rather an organic body that throbs with divine life. Conscious that the work of redemption continues to be accomplished within her, the Church understands herself in a mystical sense as Christ's Body, living by the grace that flows from Christ the head (SR 86).

Already at Vatican II Wojtyła intervened to insist that the "Mystical Body of Christ is more than an image, for it is a determining aspect of the Church's very nature under its christological aspect and likewise under the aspect of the mysteries of the Incarnation and Redemption."[2] But the image of the Mystical Body, according to the pope, needs to be completed by that of the People of God, which is the main topic of *Lumen gentium*, chapter 2. The two images are mutually complementary, illuminating each other (SR 90; Church 97). If the first image were taken in isolation, we might be tempted to look on the Church as a biological organism and to forget the multiplicity of human subjects. But if the second were taken alone, we might conceive of the Church too much as a merely human com-

[1] A thematic question for the pope in his *Sources of Renewal: The Implementation of the Second Vatican Council* (San Francisco: Harper & Row, 1979), 35–36, 203, and 420.

[2] *Acta synodalia* II/3, 857. This intervention was coauthored by Karol Wojtyła and John Jaroszewicz.

munity, to be analyzed sociologically. We might forget that it is a real participation in the divine through Jesus Christ. The Church, we may say, has vertical and horizontal dimensions, neither of which can be separated from the other.

Church as Sacrament and Institution

As a living body, the Church has an inner life and an outer visible form. According to Vatican II it is "a kind of sacrament, or sign and instrument, of intimate union with God and of the unity of all mankind" (LG 1; cf. RH 3 and 18; Church 99). A sacrament is a divinely instituted, visible, and efficacious sign of an invisible grace. It in some way contains the grace that it signifies and confers. "The Church is the sign and instrument of the presence and action of the life-giving Spirit" (D&V 64).

As a visible sign, the Church is an organized society; it has an institutional aspect. "The Church, a priestly, sacramental and prophetic community, was instituted by Jesus Christ as a structured, hierarchical and ministerial society, to provide pastoral governance for the continual formation and growth of the community" (Church 201). The choice of the Twelve by Jesus was an institutional act giving the Church a permanent hierarchical structure (Jesus 373; Church 206–9). But the external signs and structures of unity exist for the sake of interior spiritual unity, which is effected by the Holy Spirit.

The Spirit sanctifies the members with interior grace and energizes them with charismatic gifts. The institutional framework of the Church assists the charismatic element by preserving the space in which the charisms can effectively function; it also protects the faithful from being deluded by false claims to charismatic inspiration (CL 24). Because all ministries come from the one Spirit, there can be no opposition between institution and charism (Church 198).

Vatican II speaks of the Church as a unitive sacrament (LG 1). The Church draws its members together in a mysterious and intimate communion. Their union in faith and love is a sign to the world because it palpably corresponds to a deep yearning on the part of the human race, who are in quest of a peace and harmony that otherwise elude them. By conscious self-insertion into the great mystery of redemption, the Church finds the light and strength she needs for her universal mission (RH 18).

Church as Communion and Family

John Paul II's favorite category for ecclesiology would seem to be that of communion. "The reality of the Church as communion," he writes, "is, then, the integrating aspect, indeed the central content of the 'mystery,' or rather, the divine plan for the salvation of humanity" (CL 19). A communion, he explains, is more than a mere community. It cannot be understood in merely sociological or psychological terms. Its bonds are spiritual, since they arise from the Holy Spirit, who is poured forth on all the members. The Church may therefore be described as a community in which the members are brought into a supernatural relationship by their "reciprocal membership" in the Body of Christ (SR 120).

The Holy Spirit, touching the members in what is quintessentially personal to them, gives the Church a unique interpersonal unity (SR 135). The supreme model for the Church, Wojtyła explains, is the divine Trinity as a *communio personarum* (SR 121). Although the Church in a mystical sense is the Body of Christ, the term "body," suggesting organic unity, needs to be complemented by images of human society, which better indicate that the members preserve their distinct personalities. Vatican II therefore speaks of the Church as the People of God, God's household, and God's family. This last image is particularly dear to John Paul II.

Already in the Old Testament the covenant between God and Israel established a quasi-familial relationship. This relationship is intensified under the "new and everlasting covenant" proclaimed at the Eucharist.[3] The image of God's household, according to the pope, is fundamental:

> [This image] is in some way contained in all the others. It figures in the Pauline analogy of the body of Christ (cf. 1 Cor. 12:13, 27; Rom. 12:5), to which Pope Pius XII referred in his historic encyclical *Mystici corporis*. It is also found in the notion of the people of God, to which the Council made reference. The Year of the Family is for all of us a call to make the Church ever more "the household of God, in which his family lives." (LG 6)[4]

In speaking of the Church as a people, family, or household, the pope intends to accent the personal relationships by which it is constituted. What is distinctive to family relationships is the personal love and care extended to each member individually. Persons are not simply assigned to categories and treated as members of a class. The Church is a special kind of family because the members are bound together by a supernatural love that is poured into the hearts of the members by God. They love one another with a love that originates in the most holy Trinity (Church 122).

In his apostolic exhortation on Christian marriage, *Familiaris consortio*, John Paul II explores the analogies between the family and the Church. The Christian family, he says, is a "Church in miniature (*Ecclesia domestica*)." It represents the Church and participates in her saving mission. Just as the Church is animated and

---

[3] Karol Wojtyła, *Sign of Contradiction* (New York: Seabury/Crossroad, 1979), 25.

[4] John Paul II, Holy Thursday Letter "Priesthood and Pastoral Care of the Family" §3, *Origins* 23 (March 31, 1994): 719–23, at 722.

held together by the Holy Spirit, so the Spirit gathers the members of the Christian family into a mysterious fellowship with one another and with Christ in the unity of the Church (FC 21). As a fruit and sign of the supernatural fecundity of the Church, the Christian family is "a symbol, witness, and participant of the Church's motherhood" (FC 49).

Diverse Relationships to the Church

There are many different degrees of communion and ways of being associated with the Church (SR 125). In his discussion of the "dialogue of salvation" in *Ecclesiam suam*, Paul VI already indicated that people are related to the Church in various ways and degrees, which he and the council distinguished. In gathering up the council's teaching, John Paul II brings out features that resonate with his own personalist philosophy. Vatican II, he says, expressed the truth concerning the necessity of the Church for salvation not in merely objective terms but with due consideration for the consciousness and choice whereby the individual person responds to the love and grace of God (SR 125–26).

Full incorporation, as Vatican II asserted, requires the acceptance of the entire visible structure of the Church and all the means of salvation given to her (LG 14). But this does not suffice unless the objective elements are personally appropriated. Full incorporation, therefore, requires inward adherence through faith and love. Without this one would belong to the Church in body but not in heart (SR 127).

Vatican II spelled out the various relationships that can be had by those who are not members of the Roman Catholic communion (LG 15–16). It speaks of catechumens who may be in the Church by an explicit intention to belong, without yet being baptized. Then it speaks of non–Roman Catholic Christians, who are related to the Church by the ecclesial elements present in their own communion. Next the council treats of the great monotheistic religions, Judaism and Islam, which share with Christianity certain true elements of divine revelation. After this, *Lumen gentium* speaks of other religions, which express a sincere search for the God who is revealed in Christ. And finally, it deals with those who strive to live a good life without yet having arrived at an explicit knowledge of God.

In all these cases the decisive factor, according to John Paul II, is the inner relationship of God to the soul. God leads different persons to himself in ways that are uniquely appropriate to them in their individual and concrete history. Some who belong to the Church exteriorly may not belong to it interiorly, but others, who display no outward sign that they are related to the Church, may be associated with it by interior and invisible bonds. In their virtuous actions they may be responding to the grace of God even without recognizing God or Christ as the source and goal of what is good and honorable in their lives. With an implied reference to the famous theory of Karl Rahner he asks, "Are these the 'anonymous Christians' of whom contemporary theologians write?" (SR 131).

For the pope, therefore, the interior relationship imparted by the Holy Spirit is all-important. External means of grace (such as the creeds and sacraments) are signs and helps, but their purpose is to foster the interior, not to replace it. Where access to the external means of grace is physically or morally impossible, a person can be saved without sacramental baptism and full incorporation in the Church. Conversely, baptized members of the Church can, through personal sin, fall from grace and place themselves on the road to perdition.

Unity in Diversity

In the first draft of the Constitution on the Church the discussion of the hierarchy preceded that of the People of God as a whole. The order was then changed, and Bishop Wojtyła, as we have seen, spoke in favor of the change. The People of God, he said, is presupposed by the hierarchical office, which is an instrument for the sake of serving the common good of the whole body of the faithful.[5] Paul in 1 Corinthians 12 gave the classic exposition of the different callings, gifts, and charisms and of the harmony that must obtain among them (SR 137–40). In later chapters we shall follow *Lumen gentium* in treating the distinctive services of the bishops, priests, deacons, religious, and laity.

Not only are there many individuals in the Church, but there are many local and regional churches. The relationships among the components can best be understood, says the pope, on the analogy of individuals in a family. As individuals find themselves through self-giving, the parts of the Church flower in the community of the whole, placing their own proper gifts at the disposal of the other parts and of the whole Church. Particular churches, whether local or regional, should not strive for total autonomy, which would impoverish them by cutting them off from communion with the rest, but rather for dynamic union in which they contribute to, and receive from, the others. *Communio* in this sense, according to John Paul II, is the foundation of catholicity or universality (SR 136).

The Threefold Office

In chapter 3 notice was taken of the threefold office of Christ as prophet, priest, and king. Following Vatican II, John Paul II applies this threefold schema to the Church. In her life, as in that of Christ, the three offices (*munera*) interpenetrate,

[5] Intervention of October 21, 1963; text in *Acta synodalia* II/3, 154–57.

qualifying one another. The Church's prophetic work is priestly and royal; her priestly role is prophetic and kingly; her royal activity is prophetic and priestly. By imprinting on the Church the features of his own threefold mission, Christ guides the supernatural development of the whole People of God (SR 270).

(a) The priestly office consists in the self-offering of the Church to God in Christ. It takes place preeminently in the liturgy, from which (as Vatican II taught in SC 10) flows all the power of the Church. In the liturgy the priest-celebrant and the people have distinct roles, but the people are called to active participation. The liturgy should not be viewed as an end in itself; it is a means of acquiring the true Christian spirit, thus making one's whole life a "sacrifice of praise" (SR 240).

The priestly office of the Church has a certain primacy because the essential purpose of the Church is to bring people into communion with God. In two interventions at Vatican II, Bishop Wojtyła emphasized that the Church's ultimate goal is sanctification. The tasks of teaching and ruling are therefore subordinate to the priestly function of communicating holiness, as is apparent from biblical texts such as John 17:18–19 and Ephesians 5:25–27.

In *Sources of Renewal* Wojtyła devotes some ten pages (189–200) to the holiness of the Church. Expressed by the term "communion of saints," holiness is the fundamental basis on which the People of God is formed. Holiness is always personal; it is a response to the divine gift of grace; and it finds in Christ its source and model. The holiness of the Church on earth is imperfect; it is a vocation and aspiration rather than an achieved reality. Yet we find it realized in remarkable purity by the saints and especially by Mary. In the likeness of Mary, the Church is constituted as a mediatrix of divine grace. Or rather, Christ through the Church continues his own work of mediation.[6]

In chapters 6 and 7 we shall have more to say about the sacerdotal office of the Church in connection with the Eucharist and penance.

(b) Turning to the prophetic office, Cardinal Wojtyła in *Sources of Renewal* describes a prophet as one who speaks in the name of the Lord, bears the truth of God's word within himself, imparts it to others, and guards it as a sacred heritage (SR 244). In this sense the whole Church is prophetic. It lives by the revelation of God in Christ, which it preserves and transmits as effectively as it can. According to *Redemptor hominis* the Church is "the social subject of responsibility for divine truth" (a phrase that may perhaps be taken as the pope's definition of the prophetic office). This responsibility for divine truth is shared in various ways by all—by the pope, the bishops, the priests, the catechists, the theologians, and laity. John

---

[6] See written intervention of December 1962 in *Acta synodalia* I/4, 598, and that of October-November 1963 in *Acta synodalia* II/4, 340–42.

Paul II speaks in this connection of the special assistance by which the Holy Spirit gives infallibility to those charged with the transmission of revealed truth, and in the same connection he speaks of the whole people of God as being endowed with a supernatural sense of the faith (RH 19).

Already at the council Bishop Wojtyła had called for greater emphasis in the council documents on the laity and their personal consciousness of apostolic responsibility. Their possession of the faith should not be portrayed as merely passive. All Christians are coresponsible for the supernatural good of the Church.[7] In *Redemptor hominis* the pope maintains that all members of the laity have the assistance of the Holy Spirit to guide them in receiving and appropriating the authentic teaching of the Church (RH 19).

The prophetic office, for John Paul II, includes all the Church's ministry in the service of truth. It therefore includes theology and catechesis (RH 19). In 1979, shortly after publishing his first encyclical, the pope issued his apostolic exhortation *Catechesi tradendae*. His concern for catechesis was also expressed in his enthusiastic support for the *Catechism of the Catholic Church*, completed in 1992. In his judgment the Catechism was indispensable to give a new direction to the teaching of the Church in the light of Vatican II (CTH 164).

(c) In chapter 3 we have seen that Christ fulfilled his kingly office through suffering and humiliation, which were the paths to his glorification. In his various writings on the Church, the pope emphasizes its assignment to tread the path already marked out by Christ, "whom to serve is to reign." Human beings attain royal freedom when they are liberated by the grace of Christ from the slavery of sin and death. That liberation, of course, does not become complete until after the present life, but we can receive a foretaste of it by our personal imitation of Christ and by our solidarity with the Church, which is already the first installment of the final kingdom (SR 263–66).

In *Redemptor hominis* John Paul II expands on the servant-character of the Church's kingship (RH 21). Like Christ, he says, the Church came not to be served but to serve, and it finds its royal dignity precisely in being a servant. In serving Christ we overcome sin in ourselves and in others, and thereby acquire a share in the freedom for which Christ has set us free (cf. Gal. 5:1). The Church's kingly office does not assure it of an easy mission. On the contrary, John Paul II expects the Church to remain throughout history a "sign of contradiction." Martyrdom is for him the paradigm of the Christian life. "By their eloquent and attractive example of a life completely transfigured by the splendor of moral truth, the martyrs and, in general, all the Church's saints, light up every period of history by reawakening its moral sense" (VS 93).

---

[7] Intervention of October 21, 1963; *Acta synodalia* II/3, 154–57, at 156.

Necessity of the Church

Since Christ, the Incarnate Word of God, is the sole Redeemer, and since the Church is his Mystical Body, salvation necessarily involves a relationship both to Christ and to the Church. In calling the Church an instrument for the salvation of all (LG 9), Vatican II indicated that all who are redeemed are indebted to the instrumental mediation of the Church (RMis 9). This mediation may take various forms, such as intercessory prayer, vicarious suffering, and evangelization (RMis 78).

The Church is catholic or universal because of God's eternal decision to offer salvation to all humanity through Jesus Christ. According to *Lumen gentium* 1, the Church may be viewed as "a sacrament (or sign and instrument) of intimate union with God and of the unity of all mankind." For this reason, says the pope, the Church's consciousness requires universal openness (RH 4).

The Church is the ordinary means of salvation, for she alone possesses the fullness of the means of salvation (RMis 55). For all who have an opportunity to know and accept the Church, salvation is made available by explicit faith and full incorporation. But salvation is also possible for those who are related to the Church in other ways. For them "salvation in Christ is accessible by virtue of a grace which, while having a mysterious relationship to the Church, does not make them formally a part of the Church but enlightens them in a way which is accommodated to their spiritual and material situation" (RMis 10).

Anyone who refuses to enter the Church after having come to know that it was established as necessary for salvation would cut oneself off from salvation. But the council abstained from specifying who in the concrete has so cut himself or herself off. It leaves the verdict to God alone (SR 126, 133). "The consciousness of the Church is in the last analysis a consciousness of mystery" (SR 133).

Conclusion

In his writings on the Church, occasional rather than systematic, John Paul II shows an awareness of the various ecclesial "models" operative in contemporary theology. Partly because of his philosophical background, he exhibits a marked preference for the *communio* model, but he expounds it in a way that takes cognizance of the merits of other approaches, such as those depicting the Church as institution, sacrament, herald, and servant. As a personalist, Wojtyła clearly subordinates the institutional and the external to the communal and the spiritual. He sometimes uses the category of sacramentality to integrate the visible and invisible, the external and the internal. The visible Church is an effective instrument because it contains and signifies God's invisible grace.

Convinced of the inseparability of being from acting, John Paul II sees the entire Church in a state of mission. Placed as it is in history, the Church is never static. Just as the human person achieves maturity by free and conscious commitment to the service of others, so the Church, according to the pope, comes to full self-realization in loving service to God and to the human family. Its self-realization within history is always incomplete, but by its striving for holiness it already anticipates something of the glory of the everlasting kingdom.

EVANGELIZATION

Bishop Wojtyła's interest in evangelization was already apparent in his two interventions on the lay apostolate at Vatican II.[8] Inspired by his philosophy of the "acting person," he insisted that Christians as individuals are called to bear witness to Christ and the gospel even if they do not belong to Catholic Action or any such organization. Faith by its very nature demands to be personally appropriated and shared with others. This is, I think, the basic anthropological insight that underlies his writings on the missionary mandate.

Already in *Sources of Renewal* Cardinal Wojtyła emphasizes the dynamic character of faith. In an important section he points out that the missionary thrust of the Church is simply the prolongation of the divine missions of the Son and the Holy Spirit, from which the Church took its origin and by which it is maintained in existence (SR 206).

As already noted, Wojtyła as a cardinal played an important part at the Synod on Evangelization in 1974. Some of his ideas presumably found their way into the apostolic exhortation *Evangelii nuntiandi* issued by Paul VI in 1975. Throughout his apostolic journeys since becoming pope, John Paul II ceaselessly sounds the theme of missionary urgency. Beginning with his address to the bishops' council of Latin American churches at Port-au-Prince, Haiti, on March 9, 1983, the pope has frequently called for commitment to a new evangelization—"new in ardor, methods, and expression."[9]

The Necessity of Evangelization

In his great encyclical on missionary activity, *Redemptoris missio* (1990), the pope insists, as did Paul VI, that missionary evangelization is "the primary service which the Church can render to every individual and to all humanity in the modern world" (RMis 2). Such missionary activity, he holds, "renews the Church,

---

[8] *Acta synodalia* III/4, 69–70 (speech of October 8, 1964) and 788–89 (written intervention of late 1963).

[9] John Paul II, "The Task of the Latin American Bishop," *Origins* 12 (March 24, 1983): 659–62, at 661.

revitalizes faith and Christian identity, and offers fresh enthusiasm and new incentive. *Faith is strengthened when it is given to others!*" (ibid.). In this encyclical he links the urgency of mission with the approach of the third millennium. "As she prepares to celebrate the Jubilee of the year 2000, the whole Church is even more committed to a new missionary advent. We must increase our apostolic zeal to pass on to others the light and joy of the faith, and to this high ideal the whole People of God must be educated" (RMis 86). Here and elsewhere he predicts a "new springtime of the Church and of the gospel" (ibid.; cf. CTH 105, 114).

The pope is concerned about the decline of missionary zeal in recent decades—a decline he attributes in part to a religious relativism in which the unique mediatorship of Christ is questioned or denied, so that all religious are placed on a par. In the face of this challenge he recalls that the Church is under a strict mandate from Christ to proclaim the gospel to all peoples. He reaffirms the faith of the New Testament that the name of Jesus Christ is the only name "given among men by which we must be saved" (Acts 4:12; cf. RMis 5).

In answer to other objections the pope asserts that the gospel in no way detracts from human freedom or from the respect that is owed to every culture and to non-Christian religions (RMis 3). The Church, he declares, proposes her message but imposes nothing (RMis 38). As Vatican II affirmed, she esteems whatever is true and good in every religion (RMis 3; cf. NA 2). Later in this chapter we shall see how the pope links evangelization with interreligious dialogue.

The Church and the Kingdom

Some contemporary ecclesiologists, subordinating the Church to the kingdom, tend to instrumentalize the Church, speaking as though it were only one of a number of agencies working to bring about the kingdom of God, which is then defined in terms of abstract secular values such as peace, justice, freedom, and brotherhood (RMis 17).

John Paul II insists on a more biblical and theological concept of the kingdom. It is an essentially religious entity, and according to the New Testament—which is of course normative for Christians—the kingdom does not exist without Christ the King, in whom it has, so to speak, its very core (RMis 18). No one can be properly incorporated in the kingdom without recognizing the lordship of Christ. The Church, as Christ's Mystical Body, is the seed and the beginning of the kingdom, as we read in *Lumen gentium* 5. Living in the joy of its paschal faith, the Church bears witness to the kingdom (Jesus 135). At the end of time Jesus Christ, who is head of the Church and of all creation, will bring about the fulfillment of both. The glory of God, which is the goal of all creation, includes both the salvation of humanity and the renewal of the cosmos (SR 186–88).

The Holy Spirit and the Mission of the Church

The Holy Spirit, described in the book of Wisdom as filling the universe (Wis. 1:7), is the principle of the Church's universality or catholicity (Spirit 336). At Pentecost the Spirit moved the apostles to bear witness to pilgrims of many races, languages, and nationalities, thus signifying the essentially catholic and missionary character of the Church (Church 73–74). *Redemptoris missio*, following up some themes already broached in *Dominum et vivificantem*, characterizes the Holy Spirit as the principal agent of mission (RMis 21 and 30). On various occasions the pope has dwelt on the role of the Holy Spirit in effecting a personal relationship with the living Christ. "Missionary dynamism," he asserts, "is not born of the will of those who decide to become propagators of their faith. It is born of the Spirit, who moves the Church to expand, and it progresses through faith in God's love."[10] The new evangelization, in particular, "is not a matter of merely passing on doctrine but rather of a personal and profound meeting with the Savior."[11]

The Holy Spirit moves certain individuals to dedicate their lives to the cause of carrying the gospel to new audiences. Just as the Spirit transformed the apostles into courageous witnesses and enlightened heralds of his word, so does he strengthen great missionaries of every age (RMis 87). More importantly for ecclesiology, the Spirit imprints a missionary character upon the Church as a whole. Vatican II reminds all Christians of their responsibility to participate in the missionary apostolate by virtue of their baptismal dignity and calling (RMis 71).

The Scope of Missionary Activity

In recent decades there has been a dispute in the Church between a more traditional school, which tends to restrict the term "missionary activity" to the evangelization of regions where the faith is not yet planted, and a more innovative school, which contends that in present circumstances missionary activity must be carried on everywhere, even in traditionally Christian parts of the world. In the judgment of this second group the term "foreign missions" should be abandoned as a reflection of the colonialist mentality, which must be superseded. Missiologists of the first group reply that to speak of the whole world as mission country would divert attention, funds, and personnel from the parts of the world where the Church still depends on support from countries where the Church is firmly established and flourishing.

[10] Address of February 12, 1988, to Italian bishops on Liturgical Course, *L'Osservatore Romano* (Eng.), March 14, 1988, p. 5.

[11] "Commissioning of Families of the Neo-Catechumenal Way," January 3, 1991, *L'Osservatore Romano* (Eng.), January 14, 1991, p. 12.

The pope in *Redemptoris missio* takes what may be called a mediating position. He uses the Latin term *missio ad gentes* as the equivalent of what used to be called "foreign missions," thus satisfying a concern of the more traditional group. But he also says, with the innovative school, that many traditionally Christian parts of the world are no longer Christian except perhaps in name, and are in need of what he calls "re-evangelization." In the end he makes a threefold distinction (RMis 33):

(a) Pastoral activity is needed in areas where the population is on the whole Christian and practicing.

(b) Re-evangelization or new evangelization is needed where the faith has been dominant but is no longer vital.

(c) *Missio ad gentes,* or missionary activity in the strict sense, is needed where the gospel has not yet been proclaimed or where the Church has not been planted. Its proximate aim is conversion and the implantation of the Church.

In a very intriguing section of *Redemptoris missio* John Paul II points out the difficulty of clearly differentiating between the various sectors, since there are vast regions or populations within supposedly Christian countries who have never been evangelized. He speaks of the very poor, of migrants and refugees, and of new cultural sectors, including the new world of electronic communications, which constitutes, he says, a present-day "Areopagus" (RMis 37–38). In using the term "Areopagus" the pope is alluding to Paul's preaching of the gospel at the cultural center of the ancient world, the Areopagus of Athens. Those who undertake the evangelization of the new worlds of science, culture, and the media may be seen as following the example of Paul (CTH 112). These observations of John Paul II are reminiscent of the words of Teilhard de Chardin when he exclaimed, with regard to the new worlds of science, "Ah, there lie the Indies that draw me more strongly than those of St. Francis Xavier."[12]

Although the contemporary sectors of science and technology undoubtedly present difficult challenges for missionary evangelization, they may also be seen as opening up new opportunities. Materialism itself, in the pope's estimation, often provokes a desperate search for meaning, which cannot be adequately satisfied except by Christian revelation, for it is in Christ that God reveals the true meaning of human existence and of the world. "The Church has an immense spiritual patrimony to offer mankind, a heritage in Christ, who called himself 'the way, and the truth, and the life'" (RMis 38).

---

[12] Pierre Teilhard de Chardin, *Letters from a Traveler* (New York: Harper, 1962), 127.

The Forms of Missionary Activity

Missionary activity can be conducted in a variety of modes, including the witness of Christian life and that of social action on behalf of the poor and the oppressed. Commendable though these apostolates be, they cannot simply replace verbal proclamation. John Paul II, like Paul VI, speaks of the necessity of verbal proclamation, which he calls "a permanent priority of mission" (RMis 44). But proclamation must always be accompanied by the witness of a Christian life, apart from which the proclamation itself would not be attractive or credible. Before we can pass on the gospel to others, it must have penetrated our own lives. "It is important to recall that evangelization involves *conversion*, that is, interior change."[13]

The conversion of individuals, expressed in a sincere and dynamic faith, is an important goal of mission. But the ecclesial aspect must not be neglected. According to the will of Christ, conversion is necessarily joined to baptism and incorporation into the Church. Proclamation of the gospel, therefore, cannot be separated from the further objective of founding Christian communities and developing mature local churches, which will themselves become missionary (RMis 46–49).

In an important section of his encyclical on the missionary mandate, John Paul II turns to the relationship between proclamation and interreligious dialogue. Some have contended that the new attitude toward non-Christian religions should no longer be proclamation, aimed at conversion, but rather dialogue, aimed at an exchange of insights and values. The pope is in favor of both proclamation and dialogue. He says, in fact, that dialogue is a necessary element in proclamation. We cannot proclaim the message properly without entering into dialogue with those to whom we proclaim. But dialogue is not an alternative to proclamation (RMis 41-49). This relationship is spelled out in greater detail in a document entitled "Dialogue and Proclamation," issued by the Congregation for Evangelization in 1991, shortly after the publication of *Redemptoris missio*.[14]

Still another controverted question, the relationship between evangelization and development or liberation, also engages the attention of John Paul II (RMis 58-60). Like Paul VI, he wants to avoid a secularization or politicization of missionary activity. As already stated, he holds that the primary element in missionary activity is evangelization, the proclamation of the truth about Christ, which is proximately aimed at personal conversion. But such evangelization indirectly contributes to political and economic development or liberation, because those who have sincerely embraced the gospel are more generous, loving, and considerate of the needs of the poor and oppressed.

---

[13] "Address to the Bishops of Malawi on Their *Ad Limina* Visit," *L'Osservatore Romano* (Eng.), September 5, 1988, p. 4.

[14] Vatican Paper, "Dialogue and Proclamation," *Origins* 21 (July 4, 1991): 121–35.

Where the gospel is explicitly proclaimed and believed, people have the motivation and guidance that are needed for the full development of their humanity and for building a society of peace and love. Society cannot be saved without the missionary activity of the Church. The Church aspires to communicate the fullness of its faith, but even when it falls short of this goal it can spread certain gospel values such as "the rejection of violence and war; respect for the human person and for human rights; the desire for freedom, justice and brotherhood; the surmounting of different forms of racism and nationalism; the affirmation of the dignity and role of women" (RMis 86; cf. 20).

Various themes connected with evangelization, such as social action, inculturation, ecumenism, and interreligious dialogue, will be further explored in chapters yet to come.[15]

Conclusion

John Paul II's theology of evangelization, like his teaching on many other points, is a creative appropriation of the utterances of Vatican II and Paul VI. His is not an inward-looking Church concerned only with its own structures and activities. The Church for him is in a constant state of mission, charged with bringing the good news and healing love of Christ to all nations. The message, centered on Christ the Lord, must be heralded in ways that respect the freedom and integrity of all to whom it is addressed. Evangelization does not end with the first proclamation of the gospel but involves the total transformation of individuals and cultures in Christ. It is the task not of a few specialists but, in one way or another, of all Christians. The principal agent of evangelization is the Holy Spirit.

[15] See chapters 9, 10, and 12 below.

CHAPTER 5

Office and Teaching
in the Church

OFFICE: POPE AND BISHOPS

A CCORDING TO ESTABLISHED Catholic doctrine the Church was from the beginning a structured community under the direction of Peter and the other apostles, who were charged by the Lord himself with the tasks of evangelizing all nations, baptizing, celebrating the Eucharist, and forgiving sins (Jesus 373–77; Church 201–5). The pope and the bishops, as successors of Peter and the Twelve, are responsible for carrying out these and other essential functions (Church 206–9).

The Papal Office

Acutely conscious of his position as successor of Peter, John Paul II finds the responsibilities of the Petrine office a sobering thought. In the opening chapter of *Crossing the Threshold of Hope* he meditates on Peter's frailty as a man, but he adds that, thanks to the prayer of Jesus and the outpouring of the Holy Spirit at Pentecost, Peter no longer had to rely on his merely human strength. Though of himself he was only shifting sand, he had become the rock. In a deeper sense, however, Christ was the rock who built his Church on Peter (CTH 8–9).

The pope does not care much for adulatory titles such as "Your Holiness," "Holy Father," and "Supreme Pontiff." He accepts the title "Vicar of Christ" only with the reservation that it indicates a service rather than a dignity. He alludes to the text from the sermon of Augustine quoted by Vatican II: "When what I am for you frightens me, what I am with you consoles me. For you I am a bishop, with you I am a Christian. The former is a title of duty, the latter is one of grace. The former is a danger, the latter is a title to salvation" (LG 32; cf. CTH 14). According to Vatican II (LG 27), the pope recalls, every bishop is a vicar of Christ with regard to the church entrusted to his care. The idea is not that the pope or the bishop takes the place of Christ but rather that Christ is true to his promise, "I will be with you all days, even to the end of the age" (Matt. 28:20).

The pope is the vicar of Christ with respect to the Church of Rome, and through that church, of the other churches that are in communion with Rome. The special place of Rome has to be understood in terms of the universal communion of churches and the collegiality of all the bishops of the churches in the communion (CTH 13).

In his encyclical on ecumenism John Paul II emphasizes the task of the pope as visible sign and guarantor of unity. The popes, he acknowledges, continue to show the weakness that was present in Peter himself. For this reason they must repeatedly ask for forgiveness and show mercy. How could they fail to do so, he asks, since Peter was the first to experience the mercy of Christ after his threefold denial? As successor of Peter, the pope knows that he must be a sign of mercy (UUS 88, 91–93).

Within the college of bishops the special mission of the bishop of Rome, according to John Paul II, is to keep watch "like a sentinel" so that the true voice of Christ may be heard in all the churches. He is the first servant of unity. He must recall the requirements of the common good of the Church and admonish any element in the Church tempted to overlook the common good in the pursuit of personal interests. By bearing witness to the truth, the pope serves unity (UUS 94). The truth to which the pope bears witness is not simply a set of abstract doctrines, but is more fundamentally Jesus Christ, the living Truth, who will always remain the vital force of the Petrine ministry (Church 285).

Collegiality and Its Expressions

The doctrine of collegiality came to the fore in Vatican II, which pointed out that in the Catholic Church the entire body of bishops, together with the pope as their head, constitute a stable group that succeeds to the college of the apostles with and under Peter. As a group they are coresponsible for the supreme direction of the universal Church. They exercise their collegiality in the strict sense when the pope calls the entire body of bishops to collegial action, as happens, for instance, at an ecumenical council.

The Synod of Bishops was set up by Paul VI toward the end of Vatican II (September 15, 1965). It serves as a sign and an instrument of the collegial relationship of all the bishops, even though its members are only a relatively small number of bishops chosen from the different conferences, primarily by election. Because of his heavy involvement in the Synod of Bishops John Paul II, before and since becoming pope, has spoken extensively about collegiality. The second synod meeting, in 1969, was devoted to the theme of collegiality, which was being intensely discussed in the light of the crisis following the encyclical *Humanae vitae* (1968). At that meeting Cardinal Leo Suenens of Mechlin, Belgium, came in with an elaborate scheme of coresponsibility that would have required the pope to conduct a public consultation with the whole episcopate before issuing doctrinal pronouncements.[1] But other bishops, including Wojtyła, wished to maintain the pope's power to consult in less formal ways according to his own discretion.

Cardinal Wojtyła made an important speech on October 15, 1969, insisting that collegiality could not be conceived unless the bishops were gathered "with and under Peter" as their head—a phrase that he took over from Vatican II (AG 38). Collegiality, he explained, must be understood not in a merely political or sociological sense, but in relation to the communion with God that binds together the whole People of God in a mysterious supernatural unity. The collegial action of bishops, he said, is a visible expression of the *communio* of their churches. The bishops come together representing the heritage of different peoples, cultures, and local churches in order to achieve unity under the presidency of the successor of Peter.[2]

The college of bishops, therefore, is not a parliament that might serve as a check or balance to restrain the excesses of papal authority. The pope plays an essential role of primacy within the college. Speaking as pope, John Paul II, in a carefully crafted speech to the General Secretariat of the Synod of Bishops on April 30, 1983, declared:

> In the mystery of the Church all the elements have their own place and function. And so the function of the bishop of Rome inserts itself deeply into the body of bishops as the heart and hinge of episcopal communion. His primacy, which is at the service of the good of the whole Church, places him in a much more intense relationship of union and collaboration. The synod itself exhibits the intimate connection between collegiality and primacy. The task of the successor of Peter is also a service to the collegiality of the bishops, and conversely the effective and affective collegiality of the bishops is an important help for the primatial Petrine service.[3]

The terms "effective" and "affective," derived from Vatican II's Dogmatic Constitution on the Church (LG 23), may require some explanation. Effective col-

---

[1] See José de Broucker, *The Suenens Dossier: The Case for Collegiality* (Notre Dame: Ind.: Fides, 1970). Cardinal Suenens launched his proposals in a highly publicized interview published by *Informations catholiques internationales* on May 15, 1969. This interview is reprinted by de Broucker on pp. 7–45. Two of Cardinal Suenens's interventions at the Synod are reproduced in the appendix, pp. 253–58.

[2] See Giovanni Caprile, *Il sinodo dei vescovi: prima assemblea straordinaria (11-28 ottobre 1969)* (Rome: Civiltà Cattolica, 1970), 121-22; also George H. Williams, *The Mind of John Paul II* (New York: Seabury, 1981), 228–29.

[3] The Latin text (here followed) is in *Acta apostolicae sedis* 75 (1983): 648–51, at 651. For a slightly different Italian version, see Jozef Tomko, ed., *Il sinodo dei vescovi: natura, metodo, prospettive* (Vatican City: Libreria Editrice Vaticana, 1985), 9–12.

legiality is present when the entire college is engaged in strictly collegial action, for example, at an ecumenical council. Lesser forms of collaboration that manifest the collegial union of the bishops, such as episcopal conferences or the synod of bishops, are said to express the collegial spirit, or affective collegiality.

The conferences—Wojtyła goes on to say—reinforce the collegial character of the synod of bishops because each meeting of the synod is preceded by a period of preparation in which national and regional conferences are involved. They formulate responses to the working paper that is circulated in advance, and they elect the large majority of the members of the synod. Because of this involvement of the episcopal conferences, the synod expresses the communion of the particular churches and strengthens the organic unity of the universal Church. "In this way the Synod stands at the service of ecclesial communion, which is nothing other than the unity of the Church itself in its dynamic dimension."[4]

In his first encyclical, *Redemptor hominis*, the pope paid warm tribute to the college of bishops for its action "with and under the guidance of the successor of Peter" (RH 5). He referred to the Synod of Bishops as a "permanent organ of collegiality" and asserted that the synod had contributed significantly to the renewal and revitalization of the Church, notably at the 1974 assembly on evangelization that led to the apostolic exhortation of Paul VI, *Evangelii nuntiandi.*

In *Redemptor hominis* the pope made it clear that he favors collegiality and coresponsibility at all levels of the Church's life. He spoke of the episcopal conferences as "collegial structures." Diocesan pastoral councils, parish councils, and councils of priests manifest the same spirit of collegiality and collaboration (RH 5). Collegiality, however, cannot be rightly understood except with reference to papal primacy. The pope has the right and the obligation to rely on the special assistance of the Holy Spirit when he exercises his primatial office in order to "confirm his brothers" in their doctrinal and pastoral ministry (Church 252).

Much as he encourages episcopal conferences and meetings among bishops on regional levels, John Paul II is on guard against two possible abuses. On the one hand, the conferences might erect a kind of "national church" that would be injurious to the universal communion of Catholics throughout the world. On the other hand, they might absorb functions that properly belong to individual bishops, who have the task of being teachers and pastors of their respective dioceses. Responding to this twofold concern, the pope issued a *motu proprio* on May 21, 1998, in which he explained that episcopal conferences are primarily intended for exchanges of views and consultation among the bishops of a territory and for coordinating their pastoral activity. If all the bishops in the territory concur, their joint decision can assume the force of law in each particular diocese. In other cases the doctrinal and legislative acts of conferences do not have binding force

[4] Ibid.

unless adopted by a two-thirds majority and confirmed by an official *recognitio* from the Holy See.

The Office of Bishop

Wojtyła's views regarding the role of bishops are powerfully expressed in a paper he composed for the European Bishops' Symposium in Rome on October 14–18, 1975.[5] His exposition of the episcopal office has a characteristically Christocentric emphasis. The bishop's task, he says, is to make Christ present, as the bishop is able to do because he stands in the apostolic succession that links him with the apostles and gives him a share in the guidance of the Holy Spirit promised to the bishops in the apostles. In this article and elsewhere the author quotes from *Lumen gentium* the sentence: "These shepherds, chosen to nourish God's flock, are the ministers of Christ and the dispensers of the mysteries of God (cf. 1 Cor. 4:1), for they have been entrusted with bearing witness to the gospel of God's grace (cf. Rom. 15:16; Acts 20:24) and with the service of the Spirit and of the righteousness of [the dispensation of] glory" (cf. 2 Cor. 3:8–9)."[6]

In *Sources of Renewal* Cardinal Wojtyła wrote at some length about the three-fold office of bishops—their *munus sanctificandi*, *munus regendi*, and *munus docendi*. As ministers of sanctification their office is to pray, to offer sacrifice, and to administer the sacraments in the name of Christ and in that of the whole Church. As rulers, bishops govern the flock of Christ by exhortation, example, and the use of sacred power. In all three offices bishops must act as servants of Christ and servants of God's people. They must not dominate the flock but build it up, recognizing and encouraging the various charisms that God has been pleased to bestow upon his people (SR 219–71).

Among the functions of the bishop, the pope dwells especially on the third, the *munus docendi* or *munus propheticum*, which is ordered to the fostering of faith. This is the principal theme of Cardinal Wojtyła's paper for the European Bishops' Symposium of 1975. As one might expect, he accents the subjective or existential dimension of faith as a response of the whole person to the word of God. In order to serve the faith, he says, bishops must be personally conscious of the mystery at the core of their faith. The apostolic mandate of the bishops guarantees that Christ will be mysteriously present with them through the light and power of the Holy Spirit. "In fact Bishops represent Christ with the People entrusted to them and make Him present amongst this People."[7] This they do in a preeminent way, Wojtyła maintains, through proclamation and magisterial teaching.

---

[5] Karol Wojtyła, "Bishops as Servants of the Faith," *Irish Theological Quarterly* 43 (1976): 260–73.

[6] Ibid., 262; cf. LG 21.

[7] Ibid., 266; cf. 263.

Proclamation. The bishop is called to preach and to teach, but his teaching is subordinate to his preaching. By preaching Wojtyła here means the proclamation of the gospel, the kerygma, which points people to the way of salvation. In proclaiming the gospel the bishop subjects himself to the message and even disappears behind it to make room for the Spirit of God. Bishops proclaim the faith in all their official actions, most of all when they administer the sacraments, which have a word of proclamation built into them.[8]

Proclamation, as understood by John Paul II, has two dimensions, *ad intra* and *ad extra*. The first dimension is directed to church members; the second to those who are not formally incorporated. "Bishops must become men of creative coordination because they are the 'meeting point' of Christ and the Church"—the point at which the Church intersects with contemporary society and culture.[9] They can play a key role in the dialogue with the world of our day, for which Vatican II appealed. While avoiding a narrowly apologetical attitude, bishops must leave nothing undone to demonstrate that "only the gospel can give human life its full meaning and assure it of salvation."[10]

In these observations on proclamation *ad extra* Cardinal Wojtyła anticipates what would become a major thrust of his pontificate. Bishops, he would later declare, "are the pillars on which rest the work and the responsibility of evangelization, which has as its purpose the building up of the Body of Christ."[11] In his pastoral visits to different countries, he frequently exhorts the bishops of the local conference to preach the gospel and be, first and foremost, heralds of the faith.[12]

Teaching. In addition to preaching the faith, the bishops must teach. Their doctrinal function safeguards the truth and objective certainty that belong to God's word and to the Church's faith. The deposit of faith must be faithfully guarded, even while it is proclaimed in ways attuned to the needs of the times. Bishops, by reason of their office, have a special responsibility for preventing the faith from being adulterated or diluted.[13] Their authoritative teaching may best be considered in relation to other sources of teaching in the Church.

---

[8] Ibid., 266–69.

[9] Ibid., 270–71.

[10] Ibid., 272.

[11] Address to Italian Bishops' Conference, May 18, 1989; text in *L'Osservatore Romano* (Eng.), June 5, 1989, pp. 7 and 16, at 16.

[12] Notable examples are his speech "Bishops as Heralds of Faith," given on his visit to Canada in 1984 (*Origins* 14 [October 4, 1984]: 251–54, at 251), and his speech "Beyond Violence and Hate: Church and Society," given on his visit to Chile in 1987 (*Origins* 16 [April 16, 1987]: 780–84, at 781).

[13] "Bishops as Servants," 269–70.

TEACHING AUTHORITY AND SCHOLARSHIP

The Hierarchical Magisterium

In his writings on the nature and functioning of the magisterium, John Paul II adheres closely to the teaching of Vatican I's two dogmatic constitutions, *Dei Filius* and *Pastor aeternus*, and of Vatican II's two dogmatic constitutions, *Lumen gentium* and *Dei Verbum*—all of which are extensively referenced in his Wednesday audience talks and his encyclicals (Church 281–91; RH 19; VS 27). Among the principal duties of bishops, the pope believes, is that of personal vigilance over the transmission of sound doctrine in the diocese (VS 116). Each diocesan bishop represents the universal magisterium in a particular diocese. In order to teach with authority bishops must always preserve full communion with the pope:

> Obviously, the Council [in LG 25] specifies that an essential condition for the value and obligatory quality of the bishops' teaching is that they are in communion with the Roman Pontiff and speak as such. Certainly each bishop has his own personality and presents the Lord's teaching by using the talents at his disposal. But precisely because it is a question of preaching the Lord's teaching entrusted to the Church, he must always remain in communion of mind and heart with the visible head of the Church. (Church 229)

The pope speaks of the assistance of the Holy Spirit promised to those who receive the mandate of transmitting and teaching the truth of revelation. When the bishops (together with the pope as their head) universally agree on a doctrine of faith and morals, they are able to speak with the charism of infallibility (Church 230–31).

The pope, as bishop of Rome, is in an eminent degree responsible for the purity of doctrine. He can teach infallibly either as representative head of the college of bishops, expressing the general consensus, or *ex cathedra* as successor of Peter and supreme teacher of the visible Church. John Paul II is conscious of his power to speak *ex cathedra*. In his encyclical on ecumenism he distinguishes between two ways in which the pope can exercise his supreme doctrinal authority:

> When circumstances require it, he speaks in the name of all the pastors in communion with him. He can also—under very specific conditions clearly laid down by the First Vatican Council—declare *ex cathedra* that a certain doctrine belongs to the deposit of faith. By thus bearing witness to the truth, he serves unity. (UUS 94)

Thus far John Paul II has not issued any *ex cathedra* pronouncements. But on several occasions he is thought to have spoken infallibly, using his authority as successor of Peter to "confirm the brethren" in teachings that have become the common doctrine of the Church. Instances of this confirmatory exercise of infallibility may be found in his teaching on the Church's lack of authority to ordain women to the priesthood (*Ordinatio sacerdotalis*, 1994) and, some would hold, in three italicized propositions in *Evangelium vitae* (1995) dealing respectively with the taking of innocent human life, with abortion, and with euthanasia.[14]

The pope is fully aware that in some of his pronouncements he must accept the burden of unpopularity. After quoting from the Second Letter to Timothy, "Proclaim the word; be persistent whether it is convenient or inconvenient . . . [even] when people will not tolerate sound doctrine" (2 Tim. 4:2–3), he comments:

> What Paul recommended to Timothy also applies to Bishops today, and especially to the Roman Pontiff, who has the mission of protecting the Christian people from errors in faith and morals, and the duty of guarding the deposit of faith (cf. 2 Tim. 4:7). Woe to him if he should be frightened by criticism and misunderstanding. His charge is to give witness to Christ, to his word, his law, his love. However, in addition to being aware of his responsibility for doctrine and morals, the Roman Pontiff must, like Jesus, be committed to being "meek and humble of heart" (Matt. 11:29). Pray that he may be so and will become ever more so. (Church 286)

Sense of the Faithful

The pope frequently quotes from Vatican II the statement that the Holy Spirit endows the whole People of God with a special sense of the faith (LG 12; RH 19). Specialists in the various disciplines, such as scientists, physicians, jurists, and teachers, as members of the People of God, "all have their own part to play in Christ's prophetic mission and service of divine truth"; they all have a share in the Church's responsibility for the truth of revelation (RH 19).

In his apostolic exhortation on the Christian family, *Familiaris consortio* (1981), the pope mentions that married couples who live faithful Christian lives can make a unique contribution to the right understanding of the word of God. But he adds that the supernatural sense of the faith does not consist solely or necessarily in consensus. The truth does not always correspond to the majority opinion in the Church, nor can it be determined by public opinion polls. The pastors, as bearers of the apostolic ministry, "must promote the sense of the faith in all the faithful, examine and authoritatively judge the genuineness of its expressions, and educate the faithful in an ever more mature evangelical discernment" (FC 5).

John Paul II recognizes that members of the laity may on occasion be inspired, as was Catherine of Siena, to admonish members of the magisterium, including popes. But the authenticity of such prophetic impulses cannot be taken for granted. Relying on the New Testament, the pope sets forth four criteria for the evaluation of charismatic gifts. First of all, the content must agree with the

---

[14] See Avery Dulles, "John Paul II and the Teaching Authority of the Church: Like a Sentinel," Twentieth Annual Nash Lecture (Campion College, Regina, Saskatchewan, 1997), 19 pp.

Church's faith in Christ (cf. 1 Cor. 12:3; 1 John 4:2). Second, the initiative must be accompanied by joy, peace, and the other fruits of the Holy Spirit (cf. Gal. 5:22). Third, it must exhibit conformity with the Church's authority and docility to the pastors (cf. 1 Cor. 14:37). And finally, it must make a constructive contribution to the building up of the community (cf. 1 Cor. 14: 4–5, 12, 18–19, 26–32) (Church 196–97).

Philosophy and Theology

John Paul II, building on his lifelong interest in both philosophy and theology, frequently emphasizes the mutual reinforcement of the two disciplines. He likes to speak of philosophy in the etymological sense of the word as a "love of wisdom." In all cultures, he maintains, people ask similar questions: Who am I? Whence do I come and whither am I bound? Why does anything exist? Why is there evil? (FR 1).

Philosophy arises out of the native tendency of reason to seek understanding. Because of the rational structure of the human mind, philosophers have been able to produce systematic bodies of knowledge. Certain insights, such as the principle of contradiction, the freedom and rationality of the human subject, the obligation to do good and avoid evil, are the common property of the human race (FR 4).

Because of human finitude and the effects of original sin, human reason runs up against its limits. Many people fail to attain truths that are in principle available to all, such as the existence of God, the spirituality of the human soul, and the primary precepts of the moral law. But human reason is rescued from its weakness by divine revelation. Under the Old Law, God revealed his existence and his basic attributes. In the New Testament he bestowed the plenitude of his revelation. The enigmas of evil and death take on light when seen, with the help of the Holy Spirit, in relation to the mystery of Christ (FR 22–23; 12).

The word of God as it comes to us in Christ has inherent intelligibility. We are called not only to hear that word (*auditus fidei*) but in some measure to understand it (*intellectus fidei*). Faith comes to flower in understanding and wisdom (RH 19). Theology, as a systematic reflection on the word of God in the light of faith, makes use of the achievements of philosophy (FR 64–66). "If the *intellectus fidei* wishes to integrate all the wealth of the theological tradition, it must turn to the philosophy of being" (FR 97).

At some moments in the past, philosophy has made exorbitant claims, as though pure reason could attain universal wisdom without any dependence on faith. But these pretensions have proved hollow. Since the eighteenth century philosophy has retreated into excessive modesty. Systems such as empiricism and pragmatism renounce the quest for objective and universal truth. Some forms of postmodernism proclaim the total absence of meaning, thus turning philosophy against its true and original vocation (FR 47, 86–91).

The decomposition of philosophy, according to John Paul II, has baneful repercussions on faith and theology. Contemporary believers are reluctant to make any claim to know universal and abiding truth. Theology, forsaking its lofty aspirations, limits itself to biblical studies and religious phenomenology. It sometimes takes refuge in the merely narrative mode of "telling the Christian story" (FR 94).

In his encyclical on *Faith and Reason* John Paul II issues a ringing call to philosophers and theologians alike. He challenges philosophers not to allow their discipline to be marginalized but to recover the full range of reason. Theologians, for their part, are called to affirm that the truths of faith, like all genuine truths, are universally and permanently valid. The bonds between philosophy and theology must be forged anew.

In an important address to professors of theology at Salamanca on November 1, 1982, John Paul II spoke of the necessary connection between theology and philosophy.[15] Today, he said, this demands that theology be anthropological. It must probe the essential structures of human existence and establish the capacity of the human person to receive and respond to the word of God. Vatican II recommended this process of theological reflection, particularly in its pastoral constitution *Gaudium et spes*. This type of philosophical anthropology is, of course, what Wojtyła has been practicing throughout his career.

In his first encyclical, *Redemptor hominis*, the pope laid down several cautionary rules for theologians. One of them is to recognize that the word of God is not theirs but God's. Thus theology cannot be a simple meditation on the theologian's own personal ideas. Theology must be centered on Christ, whose word was that of the Father who sent him. The word of God, moreover, has been delivered to the Church, the body of Christ. Since one cannot adhere to Christ without adhering to his body, theology is necessarily an ecclesial discipline. Because the faith of the Church is authoritatively taught by the popes and bishops, it follows that theology must be faithful to the hierarchical magisterium. Theologians must also place themselves at the service of the apostolic commitments of the whole People of God (RH 19).

Relation of Theology to the Magisterium

Standing as it does at the service of the Church and its magisterium, theology must regard itself as dynamically integrated into the Church's mission to disseminate the truth. In other words, theology is a participation in the prophetic mission of the Church. As collaborators with the papal-episcopal magisterium theologians

[15] John Paul II, "Theology in an Age of Renewal" §3, *Origins* 12 (November 18, 1982): 366–69, at 368.

may appropriately receive a canonical mission or mandate from ecclesiastical authority.[16]

In his Salamanca address John Paul II elaborated on the intrinsic relationship between theology and the ecclesial magisterium. The two are closely connected because both are bound to the word of God, to the documents of tradition, and to the pastoral and missionary task of the whole Church. But magisterium and theology are not the same; they have different functions. That of the magisterium is to proclaim the doctrine of faith and morals; that of theologians is to seek an understanding that is critical, methodical, and systematic. The pope explains each of these terms. Theology is "critical" in the sense that it must be conducted with consciousness of its presuppositions and of its exigency to be universally valid. It is "methodical" because it must be in conformity with the norms imposed by its object and its end. It is "systematic" insofar as it is oriented toward coherent understanding of the revealed truths in their relation to the center of faith, Christ, and in their salvific significance. Because the magisterium and theology are so closely interrelated and yet different, the pope feels justified in speaking of them as mutually complementary.[17]

Relation of Theology to Science

Throughout his pontificate the pope has shown a constant concern to reestablish the positive links between religion and science that existed in the Middle Ages. He holds that the two disciplines, far from being antithetical, are mutually complementary. Speaking at Kraków on the six hundredth anniversary of the Jagiellonian University, in June 1997, he remarked that scientists are well aware that "the search for truth, even when it concerns a finite reality of the world or of man, is never-ending, but always points beyond to something higher than the immediate object of study, to the questions that give access to Mystery" (cf. FR 106). While expressing admiration at the breathtaking achievements of science, the pope urges scientists to be conscious of the sapiential horizon within which their achievements coalesce with philosophical and ethical values that are distinctively human (ibid.). John Paul II is sensitive to the need for the Church and its members to be respectful of the autonomy of science in its own sphere.

In the Pastoral Constitution *Gaudium et spes*, Vatican II included a discreet footnote reference to Galileo, implying that his condemnation might have been a mistake (GS 36). Building on this initiative, John Paul II, in a 1979 address to the

---

[16] On the canonical mission required for professors in ecclesiastical faculties, see the apostolic constitution *Sapientia christiana* (1979), General Norms, art. 27; on the mandate for other university professors of theology, see the apostolic constitution *Ex corde Ecclesiae* (1990), General Norms, art. 4.

[17] "Theology in an Age of Renewal" §5, p. 368.

Pontifical Academy of Sciences, called for an honest examination of the Galileo case conducted with full recognition that the truth of faith and the truth of science must both be respected.[18] That same year he set up a commission which concluded in 1984 that Galileo's judges had overstepped the boundaries between faith and science and had committed an "objective error" in condemning the heliocentric theory.[19]

In a number of addresses the pope has attempted to clarify the relationships between theology and science. In Cologne in 1980, he spoke of the contemporary dialogue between science and faith, holding forth the example of Albert the Great as one who acknowledged the freedom of scientific research without detriment to the integrity of revealed truth.[20] In 1983, on the occasion of the 350th anniversary of Galileo's *Dialogues Concerning Two New Sciences*, the pope remarked that the Church's experience during and after the Galileo affair "has led her to a more mature attitude and a more accurate grasp of the authority proper to her." He added: "It is only through humble and assiduous study that she learns to dissociate the essentials of faith from the scientific systems of a given age, especially when a culturally influenced reading of the Bible seemed to be linked to an obligatory cosmogony."[21] Again in 1988 he published his reflections on a study week he had sponsored the previous year at Castelgondolfo marking the three hundredth anniversary of Isaac Newton's *Principia mathematica*. In this important paper he insisted that faith cannot do the work of science, nor can the Bible function as a textbook of astronomy or biology.[22]

In 1996 the pope addressed the question of evolution with the evident desire to put an end to the mutual suspicions and apparent conflicts between scientists and theologians. "New knowledge," he said, "leads to the recognition of the theory of evolution as more than a hypothesis." But evolution would not be acceptable if understood in materialist and reductionist terms. Although science may establish that the human body took its origin from preexistent living matter, believers must hold in faith that the spiritual soul is immediately created by God.[23]

---

[18] John Paul II, "Faith, Science and the Search for Truth," *Origins* 9 (November 29, 1979): 389-92.

[19] See the marginal note in *Origins* 19 (October 26, 1989): 339-40 and, for a fuller account, *Galileo Galilei: Toward a Resolution of 350 Years of Debate, 1633-1983*, ed. Paul Poupard (Pittsburgh: Duquesne University Press, 1987).

[20] John Paul II, "Science and the Church," *Origins* 19 (December 4, 1980): 395–98.

[21] John Paul II, "A Papal Address on the Church and Science," *Origins* 13 (June 2, 1983): 49–52; quotations from 51.

[22] John Paul II, "A Dynamic Relationship between Theology and Science," *Origins* 18 (November 17, 1988): 375–78. A volume of essays on this letter has been published under the title *John Paul II on Science and Religion* (Vatican City: Libreria Editrice Vaticana, 1990).

[23] John Paul II, "Message to Pontifical Academy of Sciences on Evolution," revised translation, *Origins* 26 (December 5, 1996): 414-16; quotation from §4, p. 415.

The Galileo case and the disputes about evolution exhibit the excesses to which zeal for orthodoxy can lead when it does not include proper respect for the competence of experts in specialized disciplines. This tendency to excess, manifested in many religions and churches, has led in the past, and leads even today, to persecutions and religious wars. In his apostolic letter on the approach of the third millennium, John Paul II makes the point that authentic witness to the truth cannot justify suppressing or ignoring the opinions of others (TMA 35).

Criticism and Dissent

In *Redemptor hominis* the pope observes that at Vatican II there was frequent discussion of the need to overcome what some bishops called "triumphalism." He agrees that "it is right that, in accordance with the example of her Master, who is 'humble in heart,' the Church also should have humility at her foundation, that she should have a critical sense with regard to all that goes to make up her human character and activity, and that she should always be very demanding on herself" (RH 4). But in the years following the council, he remarks, critical attitudes attacking the Church, her institutions and structures, and churchmen and their activities, have been carried to excess. "Criticism too should have its just limits; otherwise it ceases to be constructive and does not reveal truth, love, and thankfulness for the grace in which we become sharers principally and fully in and through the Church." Too often criticism does not express an attitude of service but rather an ambition to promote one's own opinions (ibid.).

In particular the pope deplores the contemporary trend in some quarters to set aside the firm and repeated teaching of the magisterium on questions of faith and morals and to substitute for it the opinions of private theologians. This is true dissent and should be treated as such. Toward the end of *Veritatis splendor* he exhorts the bishops of the world to be vigilant to see that the word of God is faithfully taught. "It is part of our pastoral ministry," he declares, "to see to it that this moral teaching [expounded in this encyclical] is faithfully handed down and to have recourse to appropriate measures to ensure that the faithful are guarded from every doctrine and theory contrary to it. . . . Theological opinions constitute neither the rule nor the norm of our teaching" (VS 116).

A similar note was sounded by John Paul II in an address at Los Angeles on September 16, 1987. Responding to a speech in which Archbishop John R. Quinn had called for greater encouragement of moral theologians, the pope declared that it will never be easy to accept the gospel teaching in its entirety. But the Church is committed to presenting the gospel in its fullness, even at the price of becoming a "sign of contradiction" and embracing the cross. One striking paragraph deserves to be quoted in its entirety:

It is sometimes reported that a large number of Catholics today do not adhere to the
teaching of the Church on a number of questions, notably sexual and conjugal
morality, divorce and remarriage. Some are reported as not accepting the Church's
clear position on abortion. It has also been noted that there is a tendency on the part
of some Catholics to be selective in their adherence to the Church's moral teachings.
It is sometimes claimed that dissent from the magisterium is totally compatible with
being a "good Catholic" and poses no obstacle to the reception of the sacraments.
This is a grave error that challenges the teaching office of the bishops of the United
States and elsewhere. I wish to encourage you in the love of Christ to address this
situation courageously in your pastoral ministry, relying on the power of God's truth
to attract assent and on the grace of the Holy Spirit, which is given both to those who
proclaim the message and to those to whom it is addressed.[24]

A little later in the same address the pope made a remarkably forthright statement on dissent:

Within the ecclesial community, theological discussion takes place within the
framework of faith. Dissent from Church doctrine remains what it is, dissent; as
such it may not be proposed or received on an equal footing with the Church's
authentic teaching.

    Moreover, as bishops we must be especially responsive to our role as authentic
teachers of the faith when opinions at variance with the Church's teaching are proposed as a basis for pastoral practice.[25]

As can be seen from these quotations, the pope does not delude himself about
the extent to which even the Catholic people accept the entire doctrine of the
Church. But while recognizing the existence of dissent, he is no pessimist. The
current difficulties regarding doctrine and discipline, he holds, "are not serious
enough to present a real threat of new divisions." Thanks to the collegial solidarity of the Catholic bishops, the Catholic Church, transcending national boundaries, remains a strong witness to the *splendor veritatis*, the radiance of the truth
of Christ (CTH 169).

CONCLUSION

Concerned for the Church's inner unity and solidarity, and for its adherence to the
full deposit of faith, John Paul II seeks to weave together the respective responsibilities of the pope, the bishops, and Christian intellectuals. His theology of the
papacy and the episcopate shows an acute consciousness of their personal rela-

---

[24] John Paul II, "The Pope's Address," Part II, §5; *Origins* 17 (October 1, 1987): 254-67, at 261.
[25] Ibid., §6, p. 261.

tionships with Christ in their particular callings. He calls upon all in authority to have the courage to preach and teach, even in the face of opposition.

As a humanist, John Paul II exhorts believers to be bold in seeking to understand what they believe and to relate it to the universal human questions about the meaning of human existence. He deplores fideism, which fails to put faith to work in the quest for wisdom. But he also recognizes the dangers of overweening pride. Faithful members of the Church will not rashly contradict the teaching of the Church as it comes through tradition and the sacred magisterium. Conscious of the occasional failures of the hierarchical leaders, he recommends humble acknowledgement of past mistakes. Yet the occasional abuses of authority that have occurred should not, in his judgment, be used as excuses for avoiding or rejecting the due exercise of authority as needed to maintain the integrity of the Catholic faith. It is urgent, this pope believes, for the Church to be a sign of unity and truth, challenging the agnosticism and relativism that are so pervasive in our day.

CHAPTER 6

Priesthood and Consecrated Life

THE PRIESTHOOD

JOHN PAUL II IS PREEMINENTLY a priest. He has written a deeply appreciative account of his own priestly vocation on the golden jubilee of his ordination.[1] His entire adult life offers a striking example of priestly ministry lived out to the full. Since becoming pope, he has written annual Holy Thursday letters to priests expressing his affection and concern. These letters, notwithstanding their predominantly hortatory and devotional tone, contain important doctrinal elements.

The pope presents his teaching on priesthood most comprehensively is the apostolic exhortation *Pastores dabo vobis*, issued in 1992 on the basis of the 1990 Synodal Assembly on Priestly Formation, and in the eighteen catecheses on priesthood presented at general audience talks in 1993. Other apostolic exhortations, such as *Catechesi tradendae* (1979), *Reconciliatio et paenitentia* (1984), and *Vita consecrata* (1996), contain significant passages dealing with priesthood. Additional materials are provided by presentations to priests given on the pope's apostolic journeys, such as the talk given in Philadelphia on October 4, 1979. In all this documentation there is inevitably a certain amount of repetition.

It seems appropriate to include in this chapter John Paul II's teaching on the consecrated life, since in his view the religious state bears a close affinity with priesthood. More than once the young Wojtyła seriously considered becoming a Carmelite.[2] His thoughts on the consecrated life can best be gleaned from the fifteen talks on the subject in his general audiences from October 29, 1994, to March 29, 1995, and from his apostolic exhortation *Vita consecrata*, published in 1996.

---

[1] John Paul II, *Gift and Mystery: On the Fiftieth Anniversary of My Priestly Ordination* (New York: Doubleday, 1996).

[2] George Huntston Williams, *The Mind of John Paul II* (New York: Seabury, 1981), 81; Jonathan Kwitny, *Man of the Century* (New York: Henry Holt, 1997), 78, 93-94.

The Ministerial and the Common Priesthood

Vatican II, reacting against the clericalism of the preceding centuries, which seemed to isolate priests from the rest of the Church, gave a more ecclesial and pastoral interpretation, situating priesthood among the many charisms bestowed by the Holy Spirit for the service of the community. The council revived the concept of the universal priesthood of the faithful, but it continued to insist, with the whole Catholic tradition, that the priesthood of the ordained is distinct in kind, and not simply in degree, from the priesthood common to the baptized (LG 10).

Since the council some "progressive" Catholic theologians have tried to advance further, as they see it, in the direction taken by Vatican II. They depict the ministerial priesthood in merely functional terms, as a particular way of exercising the baptismal priesthood. They deny that the ministerial priesthood is distinct in kind, and in particular they reject the doctrine of the so-called priestly character as a medieval fabrication. Hans Küng, going still further in the direction of Protestant theology, questioned the very idea that ministers of word and sacrament should be called priests.[3]

John Paul II stands by the teaching of Vatican II on all these points. "The ministerial priesthood conferred by the sacrament of holy orders," he writes, "and the common or 'royal' priesthood of the faithful, which differ essentially and not only in degree, are ordered to one another—for each in its own way derives from the one priesthood of Christ" (PDV 18; cf. SR 221-31). The sacramental character of ordained priesthood involves a special configuration of those who are ordained to Christ the Priest, enabling them to exercise ministerial powers in the name of Christ as head and shepherd of the Church (PDV 16-17; Church 303).[4] By virtue of this consecration the priest participates ontologically in the priesthood of Christ and becomes "a man of the sacred" (Church 304).

In a commentary on the pope's Holy Thursday letter of 1990, Father Edward Kilmartin, S.J., remarked on the pope's neglect of the pneumatological dimension of priesthood and Eucharist.[5] Even in this letter, however, the pope holds that eucharistic worship is directed to the Father through Jesus Christ in the Spirit, so that priesthood cannot be understood without the gift of the Spirit (DC 3). Elsewhere he asserts that the Holy Spirit confers the mysterious power for the com-

---

[3] Hans Küng, *Why Priests? A Proposal for a New Church Ministry* (Garden City, N.Y.: Doubleday, 1972), 41–42.

[4] Under Paul VI, the Congregation for the Doctrine of the Faith had strongly insisted on the permanent priestly "character" in *Mysterium Ecclesiae* §6; *Origins* 3 (July 19, 1973): 97–100, 110–12, at 112. Under John Paul II this doctrine was reaffirmed by a letter to bishops from the Congregation for the Doctrine of the Faith, "The Minister of the Eucharist," *Origins* 13 (September 15, 1983): 229–33.

[5] Edward J. Kilmartin, *Church, Eucharist and Priesthood* (New York: Paulist, 1981), 7.

pletion of the eucharistic consecration, as the Church acknowledges at the *epicle-sis* in her eucharistic prayers (Spirit 354). A similar intervention of the Holy Spirit occurs in priestly ordination. "Just as in the Mass the Holy Spirit brings about the transubstantiation of the bread and wine into the Body and Blood of Christ, so also in the Sacrament of Holy Orders he effects the priestly or episcopal conse-cration."[6]

The Origins of the Priesthood

The historical origins of the ministerial priesthood have become a topic of intense discussion in recent years. Some hold that it was a creation of the apostolic Church or even of the sacerdotalism that overlaid the gospel in the third century. Such views, long in vogue in the churches of the Reformation, have recently been popularized in Catholic theology.

John Paul II, following Vatican II, holds that in calling the Twelve Jesus made a decisive choice whereby they became "a special, distinct socio-ecclesial reality" (Church 202). From the Gospels the pope finds evidence that Jesus gave the apos-tles a share in his own authoritative mission of evangelizing, forgiving sins, and shepherding the community (Church 203–4). On the basis of the command of Jesus, "Do this in memory of me" (Luke 22:19; 1 Cor. 11:24), he concludes that the priesthood was effectively established at the Last Supper and indeed at the very moment of the institution of the Eucharist (DC 2; cf. Trent, DS 1752). The gift of the Holy Spirit at Pentecost enabled the apostles to fulfill their mission (Church 204).

The apostles, according to John Paul II, understood that they were commis-sioned to provide for successors to continue the Church's ministry to the end of time. The hierarchical structuring of the Church's ministry can therefore be traced to Christ's institution of the apostolic office (Church 205).

In the New Testament itself one cannot easily distinguish between the status of bishops and presbyters, but the distinction becomes clear in the subapostolic period (Church 302). As Vatican II authoritatively taught (LG 21 and 28), bishops enjoy the fullness of the priestly office, and presbyters are their co-workers (Church 299–302). When I use the term "priest" in the present paper I shall be speaking primarily of presbyters.

Who Can Ordain?

Following the Council of Trent (DS 1777), Vatican II spoke of the bishops as "dis-pensers of sacred orders" (LG 26). In the rite of priestly ordination, as revised

---

[6] John Paul II, GM 44.

after the council, the bishop is informed of the Church's request that he ordain the candidate, and the people express their consent by applause or some such appropriate sign.

These efforts to involve the laity might seem to suggest that ordination is the work of the entire community, with the bishop "presiding" as an official witness. Some in fact contend that all the baptized have the radical capacity to ordain and that in an emergency, where a regularly ordained priest is lacking, the congregation can designate one of its own members to exercise the office of priest, at least temporarily, so as to celebrate a true Eucharist.

In opposition to these trends, John Paul II insists that the sacramental priesthood does not take its origin from the community, "as though it were the community that 'called' or 'delegated'" some of its members to take on priestly functions.[7] The Church must always retain its apostolic structure, which enables the bishops, as successors of the apostles, to impart the sacrament of holy orders.[8]

Who Can Be Ordained?

Insisting as he does that the call to priesthood is a free gift of God, John Paul II goes on to affirm that no one has a right to it. In calling men only as apostles, he says, "Christ acted in a completely free and sovereign manner" (MD 26). Although he involved women in many aspects of his mission, he did not give them the sacramental charge that is joined to the institution of the Eucharist. After teaching many times that women cannot receive priestly orders (as had Paul VI and other popes before him), John Paul II in May 1994 declared that all the faithful are to hold definitively that the Church has absolutely no authority to confer priestly ordination on women.[9] The Congregation for the Doctrine of the Faith on October 28, 1995, in a document approved by the pope, declared that this doctrine, based on a long-standing consensus of the hierarchical magisterium, was infallibly taught and pertained to the deposit of faith.[10]

While maintaining that Christ acted freely in reserving ordination to men, the pope sometimes gives a theological explanation of the reason for Christ's decision. Following a well-established theological tradition, he holds that the priest

---

[7] John Paul II, "A Letter to Priests" (1979) §4, *Origins* 8 (April 19, 1979): 696-704, at 698.

[8] Under John Paul II, the Congregation for the Doctrine of the Faith in 1983 declared that the opinion that the community can designate its own president and confer on him the faculties needed to preside at the Eucharist "undermines the entire apostolic structure of the Church and distorts the sacramental economy of salvation itself." See "The Minister of the Eucharist," III/1, p. 231.

[9] John Paul II, Apostolic Letter on Ordination and Women, *Ordinatio sacerdotalis* §4; *Origins* 24 (June 9, 1994): 49-52, at 51.

[10] Congregation for the Doctrine of the Faith, "Response to the *Dubium*," *Origins* 25 (November 30, 1995): 401-3, at 401.

must represent Christ precisely in his capacity as Bridegroom of the Church. This
is notably the case at the Eucharist, when the priest acts in the person of Christ the
Head (*in persona Christi capitis*). At the consecration, the priest speaks the very
words uttered by Jesus with reference to the sacrifice by which he offered his life
for the Church, his beloved Bride (cf. Eph. 5:25–26). The pope spells out this
argument most extensively in *Mulieris dignitatem*, where he speaks of the
Eucharist as "the sacrament of the Bridegroom and of the Bride" (MD 26).

In answer to the objection that Christ or the Church discriminates against
women, the pope points out that the ministerial priesthood is not a position of
social privilege or dominative power. It consists in humble service toward Christ
and the entire People of God.[11] The ministry of the priest exists for the sake of
building up the whole Church in holiness and promoting the common priesthood
of the faithful (PDV 16). In his teaching on the family, the lay apostolate, and the
religious life, John Paul II maintains that women play an indispensable role in
Church and world. In the person of Mary, who is without spot or wrinkle, the
Church has already reached its perfection. The "Petrine" or hierarchical aspect of
the Church exists in order to strengthen the Church in its "Marian" aspect—the
ideal of sanctity exemplified in the Mother of Jesus (MD 27).

Functions of the Priesthood

As we have noted in earlier chapters, John Paul II frequently refers to the teaching of Vatican II on the three offices of Christ: the prophetic, the priestly, and the
regal. The whole Church participates in the threefold office, but in a special way
this is true of the ministerial priesthood, which receives what the pope calls a
"threefold ministry of word, sacrament, and pastoral charity" (PDV 26). Although
it would be wrong to separate these three functions by allotting some of them to
some priests and others to other priests, there can be a certain division of labor
since individual priests and groups of priests may receive different charisms. Paul,
for example, was sent primarily to proclaim the gospel rather than to administer
the sacraments (1 Cor. 1:14, 17; Church 312–13).

(a) The proclamation of the word, according to Vatican II, is the first and most
fundamental task (LG 28; Church 305). Not limited to the pulpit, this ministry may
consist in activities as diverse as teaching, writing, publishing, radio, and television
(Church 309). The Catechism of the Catholic Church is entrusted above all to

[11] John Paul II, "Women in the Life of the Priest" §7, *Origins* 24 (April 20, 1995): 749–55, at 754.
In *Gift and Mystery* (pp. 44–46) the pope explains that the ultimate meaning of all priestly spirituality is expressed by the rubric in the rite of ordination requiring the ordinand to lie prostrate on the floor
in the form of a cross. Priests, he says, must become a "floor" for their brothers and sisters.

priests as pastors of God's people.[12] The Church expects them "to neglect nothing with a view to a well-organized and well-oriented catechetical effort" (CT 64).

Priestly ministry, according to John Paul II, is missionary to its very core.[13] It means being sent out for others, in order to bring the good news to all strata of humanity. As evangelist, the priest must proclaim that salvation is to be found in Jesus Christ, the Son of God. "It is his name, his teaching, his life, his promises, his kingdom, and his mystery that we proclaim to the world."[14] The priest is not the author or proprietor of the word, but a minister and witness. To be an effective witness he must be a faithful disciple, docile to the living tradition of the Church (PDV 26). "Continuing theological study is necessary if the priest is to faithfully carry out the ministry of the word, proclaiming it clearly and without ambiguity, distinguishing it from mere human opinions" (PDV 72).

(b) The second major task of the priest, which presupposes the ministry of the word, is that of sacraments and sanctification. Quoting the final message of the synod of 1990, John Paul II declares that the principal task of ordained priests is to be "ministers of the Eucharist and ministers of God's mercy in the sacrament of penance" (PDV 4). These two sacraments call for special consideration in these pages.

Following Vatican II, which depicted the eucharistic sacrifice as "the center and root of the whole priestly life" (PO 14; cf. PDV 23), the pope declares: "The priest cannot be understood without the Eucharist."[15] Elsewhere he writes: "The presbyter is above all the man of the Eucharist" (Church 320). The priesthood and the Eucharist presuppose each other. On the one hand, the Eucharist could not exist without the priest, and on the other, priesthood would be reduced to a lifeless shadow without the Eucharist.[16]

The Eucharist, as seen by John Paul II, has three dimensions: sacrifice, communion, and real presence (RH 20). Against the recent tendency to insist almost exclusively on its character as a meal, the pope moves in a contrary direction. In his Holy Thursday letter of 1980, *Dominicae cenae*, he declares: "The Eucharist is above all else a sacrifice," one that restores humanity to its right relationship with God. He warns against the false opinion that the Mass is "only a banquet in which one shares by receiving the body of Christ in order to manifest, above all else, fraternal communion" (DC 11). While the congregation join in the offering

---

[12] John Paul II, "1993 Holy Thursday Themes: Catechism, Celibacy" §2, *Origins* 22 (April 8, 1993): 746–48, at 747.

[13] John Paul II, "Dimensions of the Priesthood" §3, *Origins* 9 (October 18, 1979): 281–84, at 283.

[14] Ibid.

[15] John Paul II, "Priests and the Eucharist," *The Pope Speaks* 29 (1984): 197–99, at 198.

[16] Ibid.

by virtue of their royal priesthood, the priest alone effects the holy sacrifice, as he can do by virtue of the powers conferred through sacred ordination (DC 9).[17] The full participation of the congregation cannot mean that everyone does everything. At the consecration the priest-celebrant acts in union with Christ, the author and principal subject of the sacrifice. Distinguishing between his own part in the sacrifice and that of the congregation, the priest asks the people to pray "that my sacrifice and yours may be acceptable to God, the almighty Father" (DC 8–9).

While everything possible should be done to gather the faithful for the Eucharist, situations may arise in which there is no congregation. It would be a mistake, says the pope, to omit celebration on that account. "Even if the priest is alone, the Eucharistic offering which he performs in the name of Christ has the effectiveness that comes from Christ and always obtains new graces for the Church" (Church 338).

During and after Vatican II some theologians minimized devotion to the Blessed Sacrament outside of Mass. Opposing this tendency, Paul VI in his encyclical *Mysterium fidei* (1965) defended the solemn exposition of the sacrament and the carrying of consecrated hosts in procession (§56). John Paul II likewise recommends personal prayer before the Blessed Sacrament, hours of adoration, eucharistic benediction, eucharistic processions, and eucharistic congresses (DC 3). He assures priests that the time they spend in adoration of the Blessed Sacrament will contribute to the dynamism of their ministry (Church 339).[18]

Ever since his days as a seminarian, the present pope has had a great devotion to St. John Mary Vianney, the Curé of Ars, who would often hear confessions for more than ten hours a day. "My encounter with this saintly figure," he writes, "confirmed me in the conviction that a priest fulfills an essential part of his mission through the confessional—by voluntarily making himself a prisoner of the confessional."[19] Of all priestly ministries, says the pope, "this is undoubtedly the most exhausting and demanding . . . , but also one of the most beautiful and consoling" (RP 29). Here, as in the Eucharist, the priest acts in the person of Christ (*in persona Christi*), who in this sacrament heals, comforts, and absolves (ibid.).

(c) The third aspect of priestly ministry, in the view of the pope, is that of governance (*munus regendi*). This ministry is at once hierarchical and ministerial. It is hierarchical because it is connected with the power of forming and governing the priestly People of God, and ministerial because it is a service exercised in the

---

[17] In holding that the ordained priest alone confects the eucharistic sacrifice, John Paul II is following the teaching of Vatican II (LG 10 and PO 2) and that of many other official documents.

[18] See also John Paul II, "Priests and the Eucharist," 198.

[19] John Paul II, *Gift and Mystery*, 58.

name of Christ, who came not to be served but to serve.[20] In carrying out this ministry the priest must be guided by pastoral charity, imitating Christ in his self-giving and service (PDV 22). As a pastor the priest has the task of coordinating all the gifts and charisms that the Spirit raises up in the community (PDV 26). Gathering the family of God about its Lord, he builds up the community over which he presides.[21]

Relationality in the Priesthood

From the standpoint of his dialogic personalism, John Paul II welcomes the new emphasis of Vatican II on the relational quality of the priestly office. Priestly ministry is meaningful, he holds, only within the community of faith and in relation to the various components of the Body of Christ—the pope, bishops, fellow priests, and lay persons.

(a) In accepting ordination the priest enters into an organized community in which the bishops, as successors of the apostles, have the task of teaching and governing in the name of Christ. In the ordination rite the new priest promises filial respect and obedience to ecclesiastical superiors (PDV 28). The entire pastoral activity of the priest is an extension, as it were, of the ministry of the bishop. The grace of orders creates a special bond among priests and bishops, described by Vatican II as "hierarchical communion" (Church 373; cf. PO 7).

(b) Priestly obedience is necessarily exercised in solidarity with the presbyterate, which is called as a body to cooperate harmoniously with the bishop and, through him, with the pope (PDV 28). Christ's prayer for unity at the Last Supper is a reminder to priests that they must live out their ministry in fraternity and friendship.[22] Structures such as senates or councils of priests give concrete expression to the unity of bishop and priests in shepherding the flock of Christ.[23] John Paul II favors common life for priests, access to a common table, and fraternal gatherings for rest and relaxation (Church 381–82).

(c) Besides being related to various groups of clergy, priests have a crucially important relationship to the laity, since they are ordained for service to the entire People of God. Pastors have the duty to recognize the dignity of the lay faithful as persons raised by baptism to divine adoption (Church 384–85). The Church

---

[20] John Paul II, "A Letter to Priests" (1979) §4, p. 698; "To All Priests," *The Pope Speaks* (1985): 166-73, at 166.

[21] John Paul II, "Holy Thursday Letter to Priests" §6, *Origins* 18 (April 6, 1989): 729-34, at 733.

[22] John Paul II, "Dimensions of the Priesthood" §4, p. 283.

[23] Ibid. §1, p. 281.

develops organically according to the principle of the diversity of gifts, all of which are bestowed for the sake of the common good.[24] With ample quotations from Vatican II, the pope recalls the importance of developing and utilizing the distinctive gifts of lay Christians and making use of their prudent advice.[25] The laity have an indispensable role, since they can bring the gospel to bear on areas of life not ordinarily accessible to priests, such as the family, civil society, professional life, and culture. It is the task of priests to discern, acknowledge, and foster the charisms of the lay faithful (CL 23; Church 385).

John Paul II dwells by preference on certain groups of the laity to whom priests must relate themselves. One of these is youth. Thinking perhaps of his own experience in Poland, he remarks that the priest must make himself accessible to young people and be their companion in tourism, sports, and cultural interests. He should know how to listen and answer, giving guidance about the most fundamental questions that young people will ask. In such contexts the pope refers repeatedly to the conversation between Jesus and the rich young man in the Gospels who asked about the way to salvation and perfection.[26]

In his 1995 annual letter to priests, the pope chose as his topic "Women in the Life of the Priest." He there repeats the exhortation of Paul to Timothy: "Treat . . . . older women like mothers, younger women like sisters, in all purity" (1 Tim. 5:2). In our ministry, he says, we priests must give scope to the participation of women as well as men in the threefold mission of Christ—prophetic, priestly, and royal.[27] In this connection the pope recalls the significant role played by women in the public life of Jesus, at the cross, and in bearing witness to the resurrection.[28] We shall take up the theology of woman in chapter 8 below.

Priestly Identity

The primary office of priests, according to the pope, is to represent Christ the priest (DC 11). Configured as they are to Christ by the sacramental character received in ordination, priests are called "to prolong the presence of Christ, the one high priest, embodying his way of life and making him visible in the midst of the flock entrusted to their care" (PDV 15). Participating as he does in the priesthood of Christ, the priest is a "man of the sacred," called to disseminate and distribute sacred realities. "This is the priest's true identity" (Church 304).

John Paul II emphatically denies that the ministerial priesthood should take on

[24] John Paul II, "Holy Thursday Letter to Priests" §4, p. 732.
[25] Ibid. §7, p. 733, with references to LG 30 and 37 and GS 43.
[26] John Paul II, "To All Priests," 168–73.
[27] John Paul II, "Women in the Life of the Priest" §7, p. 754.
[28] Ibid. §6, p. 754.

a more "secular" style so as to draw closer to the laity. On the contrary, he maintains, the person of the priest must be a clear sign of his specific identity and mission. Only by way of exception should priests involve themselves in professional or cultural activities that are not directly Church-related. Worker-priests run a particular risk of reducing their spiritual ministry to a secondary role or even eliminating it (Church 359).

Even more specifically, John Paul II warns that priests should abstain from political activism (Church 362–67). They must certainly share in the concern of all Christians for truth and justice, but as priests they must perform this service in the perspective of eternal salvation. "Our brethren in the faith, and unbelievers too, expect us always to be able to show them this perspective, to become real witnesses to it, to be dispensers of grace, to be servants of the word of God. They expect us to be men of prayer."[29]

On many of his pastoral visits to foreign countries the pope has urged priests to render their own specific service and to avoid involvement in partisan politics, which is contrary to their particular calling.[30] When priests become enmeshed in political struggles or run for electoral office, an element of ambiguity is introduced into their ministry. It becomes unclear whether they are speaking and acting as witnesses to the gospel or submitting to the practicalities of politics and the demands of party discipline. By taking stands on purely secular issues priests can alienate lay persons who may have different economic or political positions. Besides, says the pope, the clergy should not infringe on the proper territory of the laity, whose responsibility it is to apply Christian principles to social situations through the mechanisms of the economy and government. The lay faithful, by reason of their "secular" vocation, have a particular obligation to work for the Christian animation of the social order (CL 36) in ways that will appear more clearly in chapters 8 through 11.

Some recent proposals for bringing priestly life up to date are, in the estimation of John Paul II, inadequate and ill-conceived. The holiness and zeal that characterized priests such as St. Vincent de Paul, the Curé of Ars, St. John Bosco, and others are as relevant today as they ever were. "In practical terms, the only priest who will always prove necessary to people is the priest who is conscious of the full meaning of his priesthood: the priest who believes profoundly, who professes his faith with courage, who prays fervently, who teaches with deep conviction,

---

[29] John Paul II, "A Letter to Priests" (1979) §7, p. 700.

[30] See in this connection his address "Be Mediators, Not Politicians," to the assembly of priests in Zaire on May 4, 1980, *Origins* 10 (May 22, 1980): 10–12, at 11; also his address on "Communion, Participation, Evangelization," to the bishops of Brazil on July 10, 1980, *Origins* 10 (July 31, 1980): 129–36, at 136.

who puts into practice in his own life the program of the beatitudes. . . ."[31] John Paul II contends that priestly service, included in the "today" of Christ the Redeemer (cf. Heb. 13:8), is never in danger of falling "behind the times."[32]

Priestly Vocation

In his exhortation on priestly formation, John Paul II devotes an entire chapter to the subject of the call that comes from Christ. He is convinced that any priestly vocation begins with a living dialogue between the Lord who calls and the individual who freely responds.

Freedom, however, implies the possibility of a negative response, such as that given by the rich young man in the Gospels, who went away sorrowful because he had great possessions (Matt. 19:22; PDV 36; cf. VS 19–21). In the affluent societies of our day, which urge young people to make an absolute out of personal satisfaction and riches, there are many obstacles to the hearing and acceptance of God's call. The Church must strive mightily to create an environment in which young people can make a full and free commitment to Christ in faith. Priests have a special responsibility to pray to the Lord of the harvest to send more laborers into the field (Matt. 9:38; PDV 38; Church 389–90).

The freedom of the priestly vocation is demonstrated in an outstanding way by the full and irrevocable self-disposition that it demands and elicits. For John Paul II, the priesthood is permanent not only because the sacramental character of ordination is indelible but also because of the quality of the call and the response. Since priesthood involves a total gift of self, it cannot be merely temporary or provisional. "The priesthood," he writes, "cannot be renounced because of the difficulties that we meet and the sacrifices asked of us. Like the apostles, we have left everything to follow Christ; therefore we must persevere beside him also through the cross."[33]

Holiness and Prayer

Priestly spirituality is the cultivation of the specific form of holiness that flows from the very identity of the priest as a sacramental representation of Christ, whom he makes visibly present in the midst of the people (PDV 15). To be a competent preacher of the word, a guide of souls, and a pastoral leader the priest must excel in pastoral charity. The priesthood of Christ, whose headship coincides with

---

[31] John Paul II, "A Letter to Priests" (1979) §7, p. 700.

[32] John Paul II, *Gift and Mystery,* 84.

[33] John Paul II, "A Letter to Priests" (1979) §4, p. 698.

his character as servant, must be the model of every priest (PDV 12; 21). Because Christ's servanthood comes to its fullest expression in his death on the cross, the priest is required to make a total gift of himself to the service of the Lord and of the Church, his Bride (PDV 22-23). As Christ's instrument, the priest must be, like him, a victim (*sacerdos et victima*) (Church 330).

Jesus invites all priests to share in the intimacy enjoyed by the first apostles.[34] As his close companions, they may hear as addressed to themselves the words, "No longer do I call you servants . . . but . . . friends, for all that I have heard from my Father I have made known to you" (John 15:15; PDV 46).

Although there are no limits to the holiness to which lay Christians can be called, the priest, specially consecrated through ordination, has a particular vocation to holiness. In the rite of ordination the Church prays that the new priest will be enriched with God's Spirit of holiness. This communion with the Spirit, as the pope told a group of priests, "calls for your personal sanctification."[35]

In his first Holy Thursday letter to priests (1979) John Paul II linked priestly identity with prayer and holiness. He wrote:

> Perhaps in these recent years—at least in certain quarters—there has been too much discussion about the priesthood, the priest's "identity," the value of his presence in the modern world, etc., and on the other hand there has been too little praying. . . . It is prayer that shows the essential style of the priest; without prayer this style becomes deformed.[36]

Since prayer is so essential to the beginning and growth of every priestly vocation, and to the observance of celibacy, it is imperative for the priest to be a man of prayer. By their prayer in the offering of the Eucharist and in the Liturgy of the Hours, priests offer the voice of the Church which intercedes on behalf of all humanity (Church 334). The faithful commonly look to priests for instruction in the art of prayer. "The priest," writes the pope, "will only be able to train others in this school of Jesus at prayer if he himself has been trained in it and continues to receive its formation" (PDV 47).

Evangelical Counsels in the Life of the Priest

Tracing the origins of the priesthood to Christ's call of the Twelve, John Paul II speaks of the "radicalism of the gospel," which holds forth the ideals of the evangelical counsels to all who are called to follow Jesus in his ministry (PDV 27). By

[34] John Paul II, "Dimensions of the Priesthood" §4, p. 283.

[35] These words, from a homily of John Paul II to priests given in October 1984, are quoted in *Pastores dabo vobis* §33.

[36] Ibid. §10, p. 703.

embracing the evangelical counsels of obedience, chastity, and poverty, priests can insert themselves more deeply into the mystery of Christ and render their ministry more fruitful.

Reference has already been made to the obedience owed by the priest to ecclesiastical superiors. In his exhortation on priestly formation John Paul II points out that this obedience is apostolic and pastoral in character (PVD 28). It is based on a readiness to be consumed by the demands of the flock, setting the needs of the Church ahead of any personal preference or convenience.

John Paul II attaches great importance to priestly celibacy. At the Synod of Bishops in 1971 Cardinal Wojtyła strongly defended the discipline as a sign of priestly commitment. Confirming the expressed will of the synod of 1990, he reiterates in *Pastores dabo vobis* that no doubt should be left in anyone's mind regarding the Church's firm will to maintain the current discipline, which he describes as a precious charism maintained in the Western Church. This practice, he holds, harmonizes with the meaning of sacred ordination, which configures the priest to Christ as spouse of the Church. Celibacy "for the sake of the kingdom" is both an eschatological sign and a significant help in enabling the priest to make himself totally available for the service of the People of God.[37] Celibacy, therefore, is to be welcomed and continually renewed with a free and loving decision to accept it as a precious gift (PDV 29). The gift does not, however, dispense the individual from personal effort to remain faithful to it and carry it out generously and joyfully (PDV 50).

In an address to the presidents of the European episcopal conferences the pope took note of challenges to priestly celibacy arising, as he said, from the general climate of secularization. He appealed to the bishops not to give in to these pressures or surround this vocation with an atmosphere of discouragement.[38]

Priestly poverty, which the pope generally treats last among the three evangelical counsels, is expressed in "detachment toward money, in renunciation of all greed for possessing earthly goods, in a simple lifestyle," and the like (Church 360). It enables the priest to stand in solidarity with the poor and makes him more available to be sent wherever he is most needed, even at the cost of personal sacrifice. In consumerist societies, priestly poverty takes on prophetic significance inasmuch as it expresses trust in God's providence rather than excessive reliance on money and material possessions (PDV 30).

[37] John Paul II, "A Letter to Priests" (1979) §8, p. 701.
[38] Reflections at conclusion of meeting with presidents of European episcopal conferences, *Origins* 22 (April 8, 1993): 747–48, at 748.

THE CONSECRATED LIFE

Through religious institutes, secular institutes, and other forms of dedication, many men and women explicitly consecrate themselves to the evangelical counsels through sacred bonds officially recognized by the Church. In this way they closely imitate Jesus' own form of life, express the full meaning of their baptism, and realize what the pope calls the radicalism of the gospel. His approach to the consecrated life in *Vita consecrata* is at once trinitarian, Christocentric, ecclesial, evangelical, and ecumenical.

Near the beginning of the exhortation the pope presents a highly personal meditation on the Transfiguration, an episode in which three specially chosen disciples are privileged to hear the words of the Father, "This is my beloved Son: listen to him" (Matt. 17:5; VC 14–16). Beholding the countenance of Jesus radiantly transformed, they are caught up in ecstasy. They are engulfed in a bright cloud which the pope, following a text from St. Thomas, interprets as a theophany of the Holy Spirit (VC 19).[39]

The ascent to Mount Tabor before the incident, and the subsequent descent from the mountain may be interpreted respectively as illuminating the meaning of the contemplative and the active life. Contemplative religious men and women image forth Christ praying on the mountain (VC 8; 32), whereas those in the active life follow him in his proclamation of the kingdom of God, his healing of the sick, and his work of converting sinners to a better life (VC 9; 32). By committing themselves to the evangelical counsels, these Christians are configured to Christ the Lord and reenact in the Church the form of life that he embraced for the sake of the kingdom of God (VC 22). By consecrated chastity, they make his pure love their own; by poverty they imitate his total dependence on the Father's providential care, and by obedience they imitate his unwavering conformity to the Father's will (VC 16). Because the way of the counsels bears eloquent testimony to the beatitudes and fosters a deeper awareness of the demands of the gospel, it has an "objective superiority" in comparison with other states of life (VS 18; 32). The profession of commitment to the counsels strengthens the Church in standing up against the ever-present temptations of hedonism, materialism, and the selfish abuse of freedom (VC 87–91).

The consecrated life belongs inalienably to the life of the Church, for it palpably expresses her inmost nature as Bride (VC 3, 29, 105). By their community life cenobitic religious seek to reflect the mystery of the Church as communion (VC 41). Consecrated virgins constitute a special image of the Church as Bride and by their form of life foretell the resurrected state and the glory of the heavenly king-

---

[39] Cf. Thomas Aquinas, *Summa theologiae*, III, q. 45, a. 4, ad 2.

dom (VC 7, 26, 34). Contemplative and apostolic religious in diverse ways enable the Church to reveal her true face to the world of our day, whether by prayer and worship or by apostolic and charitable labors (VC 45). Animated as they are by a keen sense of the Church, consecrated Christians of all these types, and of new types now emerging in the Church, are able to make their own the words of Thérèse of the Child Jesus, "In the heart of the Church, my mother, I will be love" (VC 46).

The pope takes the occasion offered by this theme to recall the glories of Eastern monasticism, which flourished in the early centuries and still flourishes in our own day, especially in the Orthodox churches. He also takes note of the reemergence of monastic congregations in the communities stemming from the Reformation (VC 2). Consecrated religious have a special obligation to demonstrate, pray for, and promote Christian unity and to develop cordial relationships with the monastic communities of other religions (VC 100).

The priestly and religious vocations, according to the pope, are mutually supportive. Consecration to the evangelical counsels can dispose a man to accept the grace of priestly ordination. Conversely, commitment to the demands of the sacred ministry prompts significant numbers of diocesan priests to join religious institutes (Church 597-600).

Some religious institutes quite properly enjoy exemption in order to govern themselves according to their own constitutions and pursue the apostolate on a universal scale. But when religious priests engage in ministry within a diocese, they should obtain a mandate from the bishop. Like diocesan priests, religious priests are to that extent co-workers of the bishop (Church 374).

CONCLUSION

John Paul II's writings on priesthood and the consecrated life pertain integrally to his ecclesiology. In accordance with Vatican II, he gladly accepts the new emphasis on the collegial and pastoral character of ministry and the enhanced role for the laity. But he integrates these features into the longer Catholic tradition. Vatican II, he insists, did not desacralize the priesthood. Nor did it diminish the links between priesthood and Eucharist or between priesthood and prayer. Nor did it cast doubt on the value of the evangelical counsels, which effectively serve the mission of the Church.

Important and indispensable though they be, the priestly office and the consecrated life are special vocations given to a relatively small number of persons for building up the Body of Christ in unity and holiness. Our account of the pope's vision of the Church, therefore, will not be complete until we have considered the laity and the manifold charisms distributed among the whole People of God.

Suffering, Sin, and Penance

∞

A S WE HAVE SEEN in the biographical sketch in chapter 1, the young Wojtyła knew suffering at first hand by experiencing bereavement, the horrors of the Nazi occupation, the ravages of war, and the brutality of Marxist Communism. As pope he has experienced painful hospitalization and illness. An instance of this was his month-long stay at the Gemelli Polyclinic in Rome after breaking his hip in May 1994. Reflecting on this mishap he said:

> I understand that I have to lead Christ's Church into this third millennium by prayer, by various programs, but I saw that this is not enough: she must be led by suffering, by the attack 13 years ago [when he was shot in St. Peter's Square] and by this new sacrifice. Why now, why in this year of the Family? Precisely because the family is threatened, the family is under attack. The Pope has to be attacked, the Pope has to suffer, so that every family may see that here is, I would say, a higher Gospel: the Gospel of suffering by which the future is prepared. . . . Again I have to meet the powerful of the world and I must speak. With what arguments? I am left with the subject of suffering. And I want to tell them: understand it, think it over! . . . I meditated on all this and thought it over during my hospital stay. . . .[1]

In this chapter we shall see how the pope's experience of suffering feeds into his theology of sin and penance.

SUFFERING

Suffering and the Problem of Evil

Suffering, John Paul II asserts, is a feature of every individual life. We all know from experience both the physical suffering of bodily pain and the moral suffer-

---

[1] Quoted in Tad Szulc, *Pope John Paul II: The Biography* (New York: Scribner, 1995), 30.

ing of humiliation and disappointment. Suffering also takes on a corporate or collective dimension in cases of natural disasters, epidemics, wars, and the like. By events of this type whole "worlds of suffering," as the pope calls them, are brought into being. The world of suffering has a solidarity of its own (SD 5, 8).

Sacred Scripture is in great part a book about suffering. It abounds in descriptions of terrible afflictions, such as those endured by the individual prophets and kings and by the whole People of God in famine, plagues, slavery, war, and captivity. The books of Job, Qoheleth, Psalms, and Jeremiah are full of lamentations and even complaints against God (SD 6; God 268).

Modern literature likewise presents a bleak picture of the human condition, as may be seen from the novels of Dostoyevsky, Kafka, and Camus (CTH 61). Not infrequently, the prevalence of suffering and evil is used as an argument against the existence of God, or against his power, wisdom, and goodness. How can a good and powerful God, it is asked, permit so much evil and pain?

One possible answer is that evil is a punishment for sin. Many of the prophets used this explanation to account for the setbacks of Israel. Thus, Azariah in the book of Daniel can say to God in prayer: "For thou art just in all that thou hast done to us, and all thy works are true and thy ways right . . . for in truth and justice thou hast brought all this upon us . . . because of our sins" (Dan. 3:27–28; SD 10). If only the people had obeyed God's law, they would prosper. This moralistic explanation is valid up to a point, but John Paul II points out its limitations. He writes:

> . . . [M]any cases of physical evil in the world happen independently of human causes. Suffice it to mention, for example, natural disasters or calamities, and also all the forms of physical disability or of bodily or psychological diseases for which people are not blameworthy. [God 269]

The Bible shows a deep preoccupation with the agonizing question, Why do the innocent suffer? In many cases the pure and innocent suffer as much as, or more than, sinners do. This objection was acutely raised, for instance, in the book of Job.

We may turn, therefore, to a second answer, that of the book of Job. The upshot of this drama seems to be that we have no right to question God. Supreme and absolute, he is not subject to any human judgment (CTH 62). This answer, like the first, contains a true insight, and indeed a profound one, but Wojtyła's probing intelligence is unwilling to let the human quest for understanding run up against a blank wall of incomprehensibility.

As a first step, he makes a distinction between physical and moral evil. Physical evil is not absolutely opposed to the will of God. "As regards . . . the fact that material beings (among them also the human body) are corruptible and undergo death, it must be said that this belongs to the very structure of the being of these creatures." How could the world accommodate the unending existence of every human being? Just as a parent or physician may inflict pain or fail to prevent it for the sake of a beneficial effect, so God may permit physical evil, including even suffering, for the sake of a greater good (God 271).

Moral evil, or sin, is a more serious problem because "it is radically opposed to God's will" (ibid.). Here Wojtyła appears as a champion of human freedom. The existence of free beings is for God, we must say, "a more important and fundamental value than the fact that these beings may abuse their freedom against the Creator, and that freedom can therefore lead to moral evil." Without willing moral evil, God tolerates it in view of a greater good. That greater good is not fully known except by revelation (God 271–72).

According to John Paul II, God does not have to justify himself to man, but he nevertheless desires to do so. He is not an impersonal absolute that remains outside the world, indifferent to human suffering, as some Enlightenment philosophers imagined. He is Emmanuel, God-with-us, and therefore he plunges into the world to share our destiny. A distinctive trait of Christian faith is its confidence that God stands in solidarity with human suffering (CTH 63).

The Cross: God's Response to Suffering

In his entire life Christ drew near to the world of human suffering. He had compassion on the hungry, the sick, and the poor, and went about freeing people from these afflictions. More importantly, he took suffering upon himself, experiencing fatigue, condemnation by religious and civil rulers, abandonment by his own disciples, scourging, and crucifixion. In some mysterious way he seems to have experienced a kind of abandonment even by his Father. Taking on the penalty for all human sin, he was treated by the religious leaders of his day—and almost, it would seem, by God—as a sinner, a blasphemer (SD 18; SCdn 150–52, 159).

Jesus did not shrink from the cross, but willingly embraced it as the instrument by which he would accomplish his mission and strike at the very roots of evil. He suffered voluntarily and innocently, and in so doing he gives us the answer to the problem of evil. In his encyclical on mercy and in his apostolic letter on suffering the pope meditates on the relationship between justice and mercy, both of which are shown forth in their perfection in the cross of Christ. The crucifixion, grossly unjust on the part of the executioners, is a work of divine justice because Christ compensates adequately and indeed superabundantly for all sin. This deed of justice springs from God's merciful love, since the Father freely surrenders his Son for our sakes and since the Son freely accepts his painful mission. Because Christ has paid the price for human sin, we who are sinners can hope for pardon and forgiveness (DM 7). As the supreme mystery of divine love, the cross is the source from which flow the living waters of redemption (SD 18).

The Old Testament had not made a clear distinction between suffering and evil (SD 6), but the cross of Jesus teaches us to make that distinction. Thanks to the death of Jesus, suffering ceases to be ultimately and finally evil (CTH 70). The cross is the instrument through which humanity is rescued from the loss of eternal life, which is the ultimate evil (SD 14).

The cross is the answer to the problem of evil, but it is not an abstract answer by which to refute all objections. We can learn the answer only in the measure that we become sharers in the sufferings of Christ, who transforms suffering from within (SD 26). Those who follow the vocation to take up their own cross discover Christ himself as the personal answer to the problem of suffering. For them it is clear that the evil we find in the world, far from contradicting God's love and power, is an indispensable element in his providential plan. God's love is manifested in weakness and humiliation—in what John Paul II calls "the omnipotence of humiliation on the Cross" (CTH 63). Christ triumphs over evil and enables us to share in his triumph, provided that we follow in the path to which he calls us (SD 26). The scandal of the cross thus becomes the key to the interpretation of the great mystery of suffering (CTH 63). The *mysterium pietatis*, which coincides with the mystery of redemption, is God's response to the *mysterium iniquitatis* (RP 19).

Christian Attitudes toward Suffering

In the perspectives of the Old Testament, as I have mentioned, suffering was often seen as a punishment for sin. The book of Job makes a further advance by recognizing suffering that is not a punishment for sin but is a test to establish an innocent man's loyalty to God (SD 12). But only with the advent of Christianity does it become clear that suffering is also a divinely appointed means of conversion and sanctification. By taking on human suffering, Christ raised it to the level of the redemption. He made it possible for each of us to become a sharer in his own redemptive suffering (SD 19).

This theme permeates the New Testament. Peter admonishes his readers: "Rejoice insofar as you share in Christ's sufferings, that you may also rejoice and be glad when his glory is revealed" (1 Pet. 4:13; SD 22). Paul writes to the Romans: "We rejoice in our sufferings, knowing that suffering produces endurance, and endurance produces character, and character produces hope, and hope does not disappoint" (Rom. 5:3–5; SD 23). In a moment of high mysticism Paul, writing to the Galatians, glories in the cross of Christ, by which, he says, the world has been crucified to him, and he to the world (Gal. 6:14; SD 20).

Jesus in the Gospels summons all Christians to take up their cross, following him in suffering. He wills to be united with those who suffer, and in a mysterious way allows their tribulations to complete his own (SD 24). This theme too finds expression in Paul, who writes to the Colossians: "In my flesh I complete what is lacking in Christ's afflictions for the sake of his body, that is, the Church" (Col. 1:24; SD 1). In his rather lengthy commentary on this verse, John Paul II denies that there is any insufficiency in the redemptive suffering of Christ. Because of its redemptive efficacy, other persons may enter lovingly into the redemptive mystery by uniting their sufferings to those of the Lord (SD 24).

The salvific value of suffering, however, provides no excuse for inflicting suffering or failing to alleviate it when we can. Jesus was moved to compassion in the presence of human misery, and he proposed the parable of the Good Samaritan to illustrate how we should relate to those who suffer. The last judgment scene in Matthew 25 makes it clear that we will be rewarded or punished for our mercy or lack of mercy toward those who suffer hunger, thirst, loneliness, nakedness, and imprisonment (SD 28–30).

As a personalist, John Paul II insists that suffering calls for a personal response of love. No institution, he says, can replace the human heart when it is a question of dealing with suffering. It would be completely false to imagine that the gospel justifies passivity. On the contrary, suffering constitutes an appeal for mercy and compassion. The proper response to suffering is therefore a double one. We are called to do good both by patient acceptance of our own suffering and by compassionate assistance toward others who suffer (SD 30).

Division and Conflict; Need for Reconciliation

A particular form of suffering that is widespread in the world today consists in conflict and division. This provides the point of departure for the pope's apostolic exhortation on Reconciliation and Penance, in which he gathered up the fruits of the 1983 meeting of the Synod of Bishops. The world of our day, he said, is torn by deep and painful divisions (RP 1). This is true not only on the individual and domestic level, in evils such as fratricide, divorce, spousal abuse, and child abuse, but also at the level of larger groups—classes, ethnic groups, nations, and whole blocs of nations. Forms of violence such as discrimination, oppression, torture, terrorism, and civil and international wars are reported by the news media on a daily basis. We are living in a world that is fractured to its very foundations (RP 2).

Christianity, which ought to bring a remedy to these divisions, is itself split into factions and denominations that all too often use violence against one another. For centuries the Christian faith has suffered from the mutual separation and hostility of different Christian communions, and in our day, as at various times in the past, the Catholic Church is weakened by mutual antipathy among its own members. Yet people of good will are moved by a sincere desire to mend the divisions and heal the wounds. In the world and in the Church there are signs of longing for peace and reconciliation (RP 3). Reconciliation cannot be achieved without a remedy that goes to the very roots of the hostility and fragmentation (RP 2).

The Ministry of Reconciliation

The divine remedy for human conflict and division is given in Jesus Christ. Paul writes to the Corinthians, "God was in Christ, reconciling the world to himself" (2 Cor. 5:18; RP 7). We are all called to gather up the fruits of this reconciliation. Thus Paul can write to the Ephesians: Christ "is our peace, who has made us both one, and has broken down the dividing wall of hostility . . . , so making peace" that he "might reconcile us both to God" (Eph. 2:14–16; SD 10). While these words refer directly to the division between Jews and Gentiles, they signify more broadly the multi-racial and multi-ethnic reconciliation that God wills to bring about through Christ.

According to Vatican II, the Church is a kind of sacrament—"a sign and instrument of communion with God and of the unity of the entire human race" (LG 1). As a reconciled and reconciling community, the Church is by its very nature a great sacrament of reconciliation (RP 11). She is called to give an example of reconciliation within herself (RP 9). She is also called to carry on what Paul describes as a ministry of reconciliation (2 Cor. 5:18) and to spread the message of reconciliation entrusted to her (2 Cor. 5:20; cf. RP 8, 9, 11). Among the principal means of reconciliation given to the Church are prayer, preaching, and pastoral action (RP 12). By fostering peace and friendship among peoples, the Church helps to build up what Paul VI called a "civilization of love" (RP 12).

Reflecting on this subject, John Paul II observes that such a civilization can never be achieved by justice alone. It must go beyond the principle "an eye for an eye, a tooth for a tooth" (Matt. 5:38; cf. Deut. 19:21). In a world of unfeeling justice, people would be locked in an incessant struggle to vindicate their rights, and there would be no real peace. Forgiveness, says the pope, is an indispensable condition for reconciliation in society (DM 14).

SIN

Sin as the Root of Conflict and Division

Division entered into the world as a consequence of sin. In the book of Genesis we learn how Cain's jealousy of his brother Abel led to the first homicide. "Man's revolt against God in the earthly paradise is followed by the deadly combat of man against man" (EV 8). We also read the story of the Tower of Babel, in which human ambition, pursued without reference to God, resulted in conflict and misunderstanding. The behavior of the two brothers in the parable of the Prodigal Son illustrates the hostility that comes about through selfishness (RP 13–14).

Sin disrupts the original unity of the paradisal state (MD 9). It has vertical and horizontal dimensions. It is directed against God, against self, and against one's fellow human beings. As an act directed against God, it ruptures our relationship to him. But since God is the source of our life, sin is also suicidal. By excluding God, it throws our inner life out of balance and sets us in opposition to ourselves. Damaged in our personal integrity, we then become sources of conflict with others. Sin therefore brings about social as well as personal disintegration (RP 15). It even has repercussions in the world of nature, which constitutes man's environment (God 219–20).

Because conflict and division are results of sin, the only effective remedy will be one that cures and prevents sin. This is precisely the ministry committed to the Church by Christ. Merely sociological and psychological remedies do not get to the root of the matter.

The Nature of Sin

Sin is by its nature a free personal act by which a person disobeys God and destroys the right relationship with God (RP 15–16). The book of Genesis describes the disobedience of Adam, which is the first sin and the principle and root of all the others (D&V 33). Satan, "the father of lies," incessantly tempts human beings to "exchange the truth about God for a lie" (VS 1; cf. John 8:44 and Rom. 1:25). The children of Adam are darkened in their minds, so that they cannot know the truth, and weakened in their will, so that they do not submit to the truth (VS 1).

The subject of sin is always an individual person. The responsibility cannot be transferred to structures, institutions, or societies. It is true, however, that unfavorable social conditions may influence people to fall into sin and may diminish their personal responsibility. For example, abortion is always a sin on the part of those who perform it, but responsibility for abortion in today's world goes beyond the initiative of individuals and attests to a serious wound festering in our society and culture. Organizations that systematically campaign to legalize and spread abortion in the world enter into a network of complicity which John Paul II does not hesitate to call a "structure of sin" (EV 59).

In recent years it has become common to speak of "social sin." This term is unacceptable if it means that social structures can commit sin or that sin can be impersonal and anonymous. But the term "social sin" may be legitimate if it is understood to mean that unjust social structures are conducive to sin, that every sin has social effects (in greater or lesser degree), and that struggles among social groups, such as classes or nations, may be sins in an analogical sense (RP 16).

After discussing these points in his exhortation on reconciliation and penance, the pope turns to the distinction between mortal and venial sin. He defends this traditional distinction on the ground that some acts, if performed with full knowledge and deliberate consent, are of such a nature as to destroy a person's relationship to God. Some other sins, however, do not turn persons away from God as their last end, but arise from a hesitation or lack of fervor that delays them in their progress toward God. Thus, John can write in his first letter that not all sin is unto death (1 John 5:16–17; RP 17). Mortal sin, if unforgiven, leads to eternal punishment, whereas venial sin merits only temporal punishment (RP 17). This teaching in the apostolic exhortation on penance is taken up by the pope again in his encyclical *The Splendor of Truth* without significant change, except for a more explicit condemnation of the view of some theologians that no single act of choice can itself be mortally sinful (VS 69).

This rejected theory about mortal sin rests on a certain understanding of what is called a "fundamental option," an enduring personal orientation toward or against God. True responsibility is said to lie at the inner, core level of one's personal orientation and not on the level of concrete, specific choices. In several documents John Paul II discusses this theory. He does not deny the existence of a fundamental option. A basic and stable choice is essential, indeed, to the life of faith and discipleship. But the pope insists that the option is always brought into play by particular, conscious decisions. It can accordingly be revoked by actions that seriously violate the responsibilities previously assumed (VS 67). The thesis that no particular act could cancel out the fundamental option could lull people into a false sense of security and weaken their sense of sin (RP 17; VS 70).

Loss of Sense of Sin

The sense of sin, according to John Paul II, is rooted in conscience, which is intimately connected with the sense of God. The world of our day is suffering from an eclipse of the sense of God (EV 21). As a result we are seeing the loss of the sense of sin. Already in 1946 Pius XII warned: "The sin of the century is the loss of the sense of sin" (RP 18).[2]

One source of the difficulty is the prevailing secularism, which treats the world as completely autonomous and promotes a humanism that seeks to build the world without God. In this mentality, moral convictions are held to have their

---

[2] John Paul II is here quoting from Pius XII's Radio Message to the U.S. National Catechetical Congress in Boston (October 26, 1946).

ground not in the law of God but in social or psychological conditioning. Subjectivism and relativism undermine all binding obligations. Confusing a bad conscience with morbid guilt-feelings, psychologists sometimes strive to rid their patients of any sense of sin or guilt (RP 18; DV 47).

PENANCE

The Virtue of Penance

Jesus began his preaching with the call to repent and believe the gospel (RP 1). The Greek term *metanoeite* (and the corresponding noun, *metanoia*) has three meanings, all of which should be kept in mind. In the first place it carries the idea of turning around, turning toward God, and in that sense being converted. Second, it implies repentance, that is to say, sorrow for the evil one has done. Third, it conveys the thought of reparation or, as we say, "doing penance," so as to reestablish the right order broken by sin (RP 4).

Men and women of our time, according to the present pope, find it difficult to be converted, to repent, and to do penance. There is a general reluctance to admit one's misconduct, to say "I am sorry," and to make restitution. Catholic catechesis can, however, support the Church's traditional penitential discipline. Practices such as prayers of atonement, fasting, and almsgiving are still valuable in bringing about the reconciliation of persons with one another and with God (RP 18).

All seven sacraments, according to John Paul II, are in some respect signs and means of penance and reconciliation. When we are baptized, our sins are remitted. Confirmation accomplishes a deeper conversion of heart and a more intimate incorporation in the fellowship of the reconciled. The Eucharist, according to the Council of Trent, serves as a remedy for daily and venial faults, but those who are conscious of having committed grave sin may not receive Holy Communion until they have been reconciled with God. Finally, the sacrament of the anointing of the sick involves an acceptance of one's sufferings and death as a penance for sin. Matrimony unites couples in a reconciling unity, and the sacrament of orders equips the Church with pastors to carry on the ministry of reconciliation (RP 27).

The Sacrament of Penance

One of the seven sacraments is called par excellence the sacrament of penance and reconciliation because of the self-accusation of the recipient and the absolution given by the minister. At the present time this sacrament is undergoing a kind of crisis, which was extensively discussed at the synod of 1983. One reason for this crisis is surely the weakened sense of sin, discussed above. Another is the wide-spread impression that one can obtain forgiveness directly from God, even in a habitual way, without recourse to the sacrament, as though reconciliation with God did not involve reconciliation with the Church, the community of reconcili-ation. Further difficulties arise from the manner in which the sacrament is some-times administered, especially when confessors diverge from one another in their moral doctrine (RP 28).

In the face of these difficulties, John Paul II encourages priests not to neglect the confessional. As we have seen in our treatment of priesthood (chapter 6), he regards this as "undoubtedly the most difficult and sensitive, the most exhausting and demanding ministry of the priest, but also one of the most beautiful and con-soling" (RP 29). The new *Ordo paenitentiae* promulgated by Paul VI was designed to make the celebration of this sacrament more meaningful. It placed greater emphasis on the social nature of sin and reconciliation (RP 31, IV). It also provided readings from Scripture that could help to give fresh life to the sacra-ment and prevent it from falling into mere formalism (RP 32). Although the con-fession of venial sins is not strictly required, it is recommended for the sake of obtaining the grace of the sacrament and the spiritual direction that the penitent can receive from it (RP 32).

In its essence the sacrament of penance has two main features. On the one hand it is a judicial act, and on the other hand it is medicinal. In its judicial aspect, this sacrament is a tribunal of mercy rather than of strict and rigorous justice. Unlike the practice in courts of law, sinners who come to this sacrament accuse them-selves and willingly accept the penance imposed upon them. The modern mind is particularly sensitive to the dimension of healing in this sacrament (RP 31, II). The minister acts in the person of Christ the physician of souls (RP 29).

Components and Forms
of the Sacrament of Penance

The sacrament of penance has a number of components that the pope spells out in his apostolic exhortation on the subject.

An examination of conscience is an indispensable condition for the proper reception of the sacrament. Sorrow for sin, or contrition, which is the essential action on the part of the penitent, necessarily includes a resolution of amendment. Confession of sins is required for the sake of the judicial and medicinal purposes of the sacrament, because unless the penitent manifested his or her sins, the con-fessor could not act as judge or administer a salutary penance. From the stand-point of the minister, the essential aspect of the sacrament consists in the absolution. The words of absolution, administered in the name of the triune God and in the very person of Christ, are an effective sign of the intervention of God blotting our the sinner's guilt (RP 29; 31 III). The final phase of the sacrament of penance consists in the satisfaction, often known as the "penance." In making satisfaction the penitent does not pay a price to God for forgiveness, since this has already been freely bestowed. Readiness to make reparation for the evil done, by restoring what has been unjustly taken or giving compensation for any scandal or injury, is a necessary condition for forgiveness itself (DM 14). By acts of satisfaction the penitent also expresses a commitment to begin a new way of life and to enter into closer union with the passion of Jesus. Such penitential acts, moreover, have power to heal the wounds or imperfections inflicted on the spirit by past sinful conduct (RP 31, III).

According to the current Code of Canon Law, the sacrament of penance may be administered in three forms (canons 960–63). The first and ordinary way of administering the sacrament is by individual confession to a priest, who then gives absolution individually. This is the ideal form, because it permits a personal dialogue with the confessor, who can then give appropriate spiritual direction and impose a penance suited to the dispositions of the individual penitent (RP 32; RH 20).

The second form is the reconciliation of a number of penitents at a collective service in which common preparatory acts precede individual confession and individual absolution. Such a communal service may be especially appropriate at certain seasons of the year, such as Advent and Lent. It has the advantage of giving prominence to the corporate dimension of sin and reconciliation. Provided that there is a sufficient supply of confessors and adequate time for individual confessions, this form of the sacrament may be seen as equivalent to the first, rather than as an exceptional procedure (RP 32).

The third form, wholly exceptional but occasionally necessary, is general confession followed by general absolution. This is allowed by canon law only in cases of grave necessity—for example, in a battle or a natural disaster in which a large group of people are in danger of imminent death. Outside of such emergencies, the bishop must judge whether the conditions exist in his own diocese. Canon law, the pope reminds his readers, requires those who receive general absolution to submit their serious sins to the power of the keys in their next confession, which should be made as soon as an opportunity occurs (canon 963; RP 33).

Finally, at the end of his apostolic exhortation the pope considers the case of those who for some reason are excluded from receiving the sacrament of penance. This can occur, for instance, in the cases of divorced and remarried Catholics, or persons living in some other irregular union. Unless they amend their way of life, such persons are not eligible to receive the sacraments since their present relationship contradicts the teaching of Christ and the Church. Nevertheless, they should be treated with mercy and compassion so that they do not feel abandoned by the Church. They should continue to attend Mass and be encouraged to make acts of faith, hope, and charity. But because the Church cannot agree to call evil good, it cannot give these persons sacramental absolution. They must be encouraged to approach the divine mercy in other ways (RP 34; cf. FC 84).

The Church Penitent

As already mentioned, John Paul II maintains that sin, properly speaking, is always the deed of individual persons. But there is a corporate dimension to sin, since all of us are inclined to participate in the sins to which the social structures of our group incline us. The devaluation of life in contemporary society, as we have noted, disposes people to tolerate the killing of the unborn, the weak, and the aged.

Can this kind of structural sin affect the Church? Some would argue that because the Church is the Body of Christ, it is inalienably holy and hence impervious to sin. This is true if one considers the Church simply in its formal elements—its apostolic heritage of faith, sacraments, and ministry. But the Church consists also in a "material" component—namely, its membership. Every individual member is subject to sin, and at certain times groups of members engage in collective actions that are objectively opposed to the gospel and the moral law. Just as a nation can engage in an unjust war, so too the Church can corporately involve itself in wrongful deeds.

John Paul II in his speeches and writings regularly avoids predicating sin of the Church as such, but he repeatedly acknowledges the sins of its members, including popes and bishops.[3] An Italian journalist has collected no fewer than ninety-four statements of John Paul II dealing with corporate misdeeds for which Christians and Catholics must repent.[4] These statements range over a vast territory, including sins against Christian unity, religious wars, the burning of suspected heretics, anti-Semitism, racism, colonial oppression, black and Indian slavery, discrimination against women, and opposition to new scientific discoveries. While we are not in a position to assess the subjective culpability of our predecessors, we may and should acknowledge that some of their acts were objectively wrong. These collective faults, which have tarnished the moral prestige of the Church, require a "purification of memories." To rid ourselves of this

---

[3] John Paul II regularly makes a distinction between the holy Church and her sinful children and almost always avoids speaking of the "sinful Church." But at least one exception may be found. In a speech at Fatima on May 12, 1982, he declared that he had come "as a pilgrim among pilgrims, in this assembly of the pilgrim Church, of the living, holy, and sinful Church"; text in *L'Osservatore Romano* (Eng.), May 31, 1982, p. 8. For additional commentary, see Joseph A. Komonchak, "Preparing for the New Millennium," *Logos: A Journal of Catholic Thought and Culture* 1 (Summer 1997): 34–55, at 44 and 50.

[4] Luigi Accattoli, *When a Pope Asks Forgiveness: The Mea Culpa's of John Paul II* (Staten Island, N.Y.: Alba House, 1998).

heavy historical burden, we must repudiate the attitudes that gave rise to these sins and ask forgiveness from those that have been injured, while at the same time forgiving those who have injured our own religious community.

The approach of the great jubilee of the year 2000 affords an occasion for a collective examination of conscience on the part of the Christian churches. To pass through the Holy Door that will be symbolically opened at St. Peter's on Christmas, 1999, the people of God must purge themselves from this evil heritage.

The pope summed up his thoughts on this theme most fully in an unpublished memorandum sent to the cardinals in the spring of 1994, in preparation for the consistory that met that year.[5] More succinctly he presents the issues in his apostolic exhortation "On the Coming of the Third Millennium." Conversion, he there points out, is the precondition for reconciliation with God on the part of individuals and communities. It is therefore appropriate that, in preparing for the approaching great jubilee, the Church should become more fully conscious of the sinfulness of her children, recalling the time when they have given scandal and counterwitness to the gospel. The Church, incessantly pursuing the path of penance and renewal, encourages her children to purify themselves by repenting their past errors and infidelities, such as actions that have contributed to Christian division, intolerance and violence in the service of truth, and the failure, even today, to carry through the renewal called for by Vatican II (TMA 32–36). As documents on this theme continue to appear, we may expect some further indications of the pope's views on the need for Catholics to repent for past misdeeds, such as those connected with the Inquisition and the Shoah.

Catholic apologists have often sought to justify everything that was done in the name of the Church. Partly for this reason, the Church continues to be blamed for events of the remote past, often committed by persons insufficiently sensitive to the demands of the gospel. To assuage the rancor and resentment, a frank admission of past errors may be the most effective strategy. Evangelization today, in the eyes of John Paul II, requires a new kind of apologetics, marked by humility, honesty, and love toward those who have been injured by the actions of Catholics individually and collectively. The pope's program of ecclesial repentance is thus linked with his call for new evangelization.

CONCLUSION

The themes of sin, suffering, and penance are central to the theology of John Paul II. Sin, he teaches, cannot be understood except in light of the sense of God. The

---

[5] The memorandum, entitled "Reflections on the Great Jubilee of the Year 2000," is twenty-three pages long. Generous quotations from it are given in Accattoli, *When a Pope Asks Forgiveness,* 55-58 and passim.

world today, deluded by secularism, tends to be forgetful of God and hence blind to sin. Yet sin and guilt are constant in human history. The prototypical instances of sin in Genesis (our first parents, Cain, the Tower of Babel) continue to cast light on the human situation. While individual persons are always responsible for sin, the immense social evils of our time exhibit a frightening solidarity in evil.

The pope develops a rich theology of suffering, which he sees as due, in great part, to sin and sinful structures. The terrible wars and conflicts of our time, he maintains, are rooted in selfishness and in unwillingness to forgive. Human pain, weakness, and death evoke not judgment but rather compassion. Through his own example of patient suffering, John Paul II shows how it is possible to engage in a priestly ministry of suffering, uniting one's own afflictions with those of the crucified Lord.

Both sin and suffering, in the theology of this pope, are taken up into the redemptive work of God, who shows himself as the "Father of mercies" in the gift of his own Son. By conducting its ministry of preaching and sanctification, the Church becomes for the world a true sacrament of reconciliation, offering peace and pardon to all. In this perspective the sacrament of penance and reconciliation takes on new relevance. Only a humble and penitent Church, conscious of the weakness of its members, can successfully evangelize the world.

CHAPTER 8

Laity, Family,
Status of Women

⚭

THAT JOHN PAUL II should show particular interest in the themes of this chapter is not surprising in view of the events of his life mentioned in chapter 1. As a boy and young man he was heavily involved in Catholic youth groups, especially in a circle that met at the house of the bachelor tailor, Jan Tyranowski. During his visits to France and Belgium in 1947 he took pains to study movements such as the Young Christian Workers. His assignment as a parish priest from 1949 to 1951 involved chaplaincy duties for university students at Kraków. As a young bishop he continued to work closely with youth groups and young married couples. Much of this experience has fed into his teaching as pope on the laity, the family, and the vocation of women, the three themes for the present chapter.

The primary sources for the pope's theology of the laity will be his apostolic exhortation *Christifideles laici* (1988) and the twenty-six talks on the laity given in general audiences between October 5, 1993, and September 21, 1994, in the course of a series of catecheses on the Church. For the pope's teaching on the family it will be necessary to consult his apostolic exhortation on the family, *Familiaris consortio* (1981), his "Letter to Families" published in 1994, and the 130 general audience talks given from September 5, 1979, to November 28, 1984, which have been collected in English under the title *The Theology of the Body*.[1] John Paul II's teaching on women is most fully set forth in his apostolic letter "On the Dignity and Vocation of Women," *Mulieris dignitatem* (1988) and his "Letter to Women" published in 1995.

The present chapter will not attempt to set forth all aspects of the pope's teaching on the laity. For a fuller picture it will be necessary to take account of the materials in the next three chapters on the order of culture, the economy, and pol-

---

[1] Boston: Pauline Books & Media, 1997. As noted in chapter 1, this volume includes the general audience talks previously published in four volumes: *Original Unity of Man and Woman, Blessed Are the Pure of Heart, The Theology of Marriage and Celibacy*, and *Reflections on "Humanae Vitae"* (Boston: St. Paul Books & Media, 1981–84).

itics—fields that John Paul II sees as primarily the province of lay men and women.

THE LAITY

Definition of Laity

The laity has normally been defined negatively—that is, as those baptized Christians who are not in clerical orders. Some would prefer to say, still negatively, those who are neither in clerical orders nor in the consecrated life of religion. Vatican II tried instead to accent the positive aspects of the lay state. The Constitution on the Church taught:

> The term "lay faithful" is here understood to mean all the faithful except those in holy orders and those belonging to a religious state sanctioned by the Church. Through baptism, the lay faithful are made one body with Christ and are established among the People of God. They are in their own way made sharers in the priestly, prophetic, and kingly office of Christ. They carry out their own part in the mission of the whole Christian people with respect to the Church and the world. . . . It belongs to the laity to seek the kingdom of God by engaging in temporal affairs and ordering them according to the plan of God. (LG 31)

This text, while it retains the negative element of denying what is proper to the clerical and religious states, emphasizes the positive—that is, baptism, participation in the threefold office of Christ, and active presence in the temporal realm.[2] Of these three features the third is the most distinctive. But it must be acknowledged that some lay people are in the service of the Church while some clerics and religious are heavily engaged in secular or temporal activities. Thus, the negative elements of not being clergy or religious seem to be essential for a clear definition of the laity. The lay state deserves full theological consideration, since it is unquestionably God's plan for most of the human race. The positive characteristics of the lay vocation are connected with the gifts and charisms that pertain not so much to the laity as such as to the particular callings of individuals, for example, as spouses, parents, physicians, musicians, or whatever they may be.

John Paul II picks up where Vatican II left off. The baptismal anointing, he says, has a threefold effect. In the first place it recalls the anointing given to kings in the Old Testament, and thus all the baptized receive a share in the messianic royalty of Christ. The laity are especially called to collaborate with Christ in

---

[2] Cf. Joseph Bagiackas, *A Lay Person's Guide to Pope John Paul II's Teaching on the Laity* (South Bend, Ind.: Light of the Nations Press, 1994), 14. Also useful for this chapter are the booklets Dr. Bagiackas has written on *Pope John Paul II's Teaching on the Family* and on *John Paul II's Teaching on the Role of Women*, both published in the same series.

restoring creation to its original value and ordering it according to the plan of God through their work in the world. They share, secondly, in Christ's priestly office insofar as by their baptism they are qualified to participate in the worship of the Church, offering the sacrifice of the Eucharist through the hands of the ordained priest, who effects the holy sacrifice. Thirdly, the laity are called to share in the prophetic mission of Christ, bearing witness to the gospel by word and deed (CL 14). The prophetic ministry of the laity typically takes the form of witness rather than teaching. In any case, official teaching, which establishes or certifies the doctrine of the Church in a binding way, is not within the province of the laity, since it belongs to the apostolic office.

The Universal Call to Holiness

At Vatican II, Bishop Wojtyła enthusiastically greeted the teaching of *Lumen gentium*, chapter 5, on "The Universal Call to Holiness," urging that it should be strengthened by more emphasis on the applicability of the evangelical counsels to all Christians.[3] Perhaps in answer to that suggestion, the Constitution on the Church was amended in 1964 to encourage the practice of the evangelical counsels even by persons who do not have public vows as religious (LG 39). But it does not say that all the people of God are called to the life of the counsels, nor do I believe that the present pope meant to say that they are. Even short of dedicating themselves to the life of the counsels, lay persons are called to exercise the virtues of poverty, chastity, and obedience to legitimate superiors.

John Paul II teaches, most centrally, that all Christians are called to the perfection of charity. This, he points out, is not a simple moral exhortation but a requirement arising from the very nature of the Church as the Body of Christ and the temple of the Holy Spirit. The beatitudes, representing the summit of Christian perfection, are held forth as ideals to which all members of the Church should aspire. Poverty, meekness, and purity of heart are clearly in line with the counsels proposed in the Sermon on the Mount (CL 16).

In a homily at the World Youth Day in Paris on August 23, 1997, the pope gave an eloquent description of the holiness to which all Christians are called by virtue of their baptism:

> Baptism—"mystery and hope of the world to come" (St. Cyril of Jerusalem, *Procatechesis* 10,12)—is the most beautiful of God's gifts, inviting us to become disciples of the Lord. It brings us into intimacy with God, into the life of the Trinity, from this day forward and on into eternity. It is a grace given to the sinner, a grace which purifies us from sin and opens to us a new future. It is a bath which washes and regenerates. It is an anointing which conforms us to Christ, priest, prophet, and king.

---

[3] Intervention submitted in October or November 1963, published in AS II/4, 340–42.

It is an enlightenment which illumines our path and gives it full meaning. It is a vestment of strength and perfection. Dressed in white on the day of our baptism, as we shall be on the last day, we are called to preserve every day its bright splendor and to discover it anew, through forgiveness, prayer, and Christian living. Baptism is the sign that God has joined us on our journey, that he makes our existence more beautiful and that he transforms our history into a history of holiness.[4]

The Secular Character

The Vatican II Constitution on the Church taught that "the secular character is properly and particularly that of the lay faithful" (LG 31). John Paul II explains this as meaning that the laity are to be in the world, but not of it. For the most part they live in the ordinary circumstances of family and social life and in the workplace, and it is in these situations that they are called to fulfill their Christian vocation. They are called to make the gospel present and effective in the worlds of the media, politics, economics, medicine, science, culture, sports, etc. In this way they can be the salt of the earth, the light and the leaven by which the world is sanctified (CL 15).

Not only are they called to sanctify the world; they are also called to sanctify themselves in everyday professional and social life. In order to emphasize the possibility of sanctity in the lay state, the pope beatified two laymen (Lorenzo Ruiz and Giuseppe Moscati) in October 1987, while the Synod on the Laity was in session.[5]

Ministries Open to the Laity

The involvement of lay Christians in the world does not exclude them from active participation in the inner life of the Church itself. In the Church as a communion, all the members share in the divine life according to their particular state and the charisms given to them. The one Holy Spirit is the source of unity and diversity among the members.

Lay persons are eligible to perform certain ministries in the Church that have their foundation in baptism, confirmation, and matrimony. These ministries, according to the pope, ought to be carefully distinguished from those founded on the sacrament of orders. In *Christifideles laici* the pope criticizes certain aberrations with regard to lay ministry. Only in case of real necessity, he says, should

---

[4] John Paul II, "Do You Know What Your Baptism Does for You?" *Origins* 27 (September 4, 1997): 185–88, at 187–88.

[5] John Paul II, "Address to the Curia: A Profile of 1987," *Origins* 17 (January 28, 1988): 573–76, at 575; cf. CL 17.

pastors delegate to lay persons the tasks of presiding over liturgical prayers, distributing Holy Communion, and conferring baptism. The synod assembly, he recalls, called attention to three abuses: an indiscriminate use of the term "ministry" for merely occasional services, the tendency to "clericalize" the lay faithful, and the erection of an ecclesial structure parallel to that founded on the sacrament of orders (CL 23). For these reasons, perhaps, the pope is notably reserved regarding the presence of the laity in the sanctuary or at the altar.

Similar reservations are contained in the "Instruction on the Collaboration of the Nonordained Faithful in Priests' Sacred Ministry," issued by eight congregations and councils of the Holy See, and approved by the pope *in forma specifica*, on August 15, 1997.[6] This document warns against inflations of the concept of ministry to include good works done without any ecclesial mandate. It also forbids the recourse to extraordinary ministers of the Eucharist in cases where priests or deacons are available.

Paul VI in 1972 abolished minor orders and opened up to laymen the nonordained ministries of lector and acolyte. At the synod of 1987 there was some discussion of the criteria that ought to be used in admitting persons to these ministries. Some bishops proposed that women should be eligible. In alluding to this discussion in *Christifideles laici*, the pope observed that a commission was studying the whole question of the increase of ministries entrusted to the lay faithful. In the meantime pastors should see to it that the essential difference between the ministerial priesthood and the common priesthood is respected (CL 23).

In addition to established ministries such as these, the laity receive various charisms from the Holy Spirit. Paul speaks in 1 Corinthians 12 and elsewhere of gifts of wisdom, knowledge, healing, miracle-working, prophecy, speaking in tongues, interpreting tongues, and discerning spirits. Gifts such as these, both extraordinary and ordinary, are bestowed upon lay persons as well as upon the ordained and those in the consecrated life. John Paul II points out that such charismatic gifts are a benefit to the whole Church and should be acknowledged with gratitude, but that claims to charismatic gifts must be carefully discerned. The pastors of the Church have the responsibility to judge the genuineness of charisms (CL 24). The pope's criteria for discerning charisms have already been discussed in chapter 5 in connection with the sense of the faithful.

One place in which the charismatic gifts of the laity can be particularly valuable is the parish. Gifted layman and lay women should be invited and urged to engage in education and evangelization. Their collaboration in parish and diocesan councils should be appreciated and encouraged (CL 25–27).

---

[6] Eight Vatican Offices, "Some Questions Regarding Collaboration of Nonordained Faithful in Priests' Sacred Ministry," *Origins* 27 (November 27, 1997): 397–409. Approval by the pope *in forma specifica* gives a document the same juridical weight as if written by the pope himself.

Free Associations of the Laity

In recent years a large number of new groups and associations of the laity have emerged and have greatly contributed to the renewal of the Church and of society. John Paul II considers them "a providential gift of the Holy Spirit to the Church of our time."[7] To encourage this development, the pope on May 30, 1998, addressed half a million members of new communities and heard testimonies given by the founders of the Focolare Movement, the Neocatechumenal Way, the communities of L'Arche (the Ark), and Communion and Liberation. The pope welcomed these movements as expressions of the unforeseen dynamism of the Holy Spirit, but reminded them that "every charism is given for the common good, that is, for the benefit of the whole Church."[8] Since the institutional and the charismatic aspects are co-essential to the Church's constitution, the authenticity of charisms must be guaranteed, he said, by competent ecclesiastical authority.

In his apostolic exhortation on the laity, John Paul II affirms that lay people are always free to form new communities provided that the proper relationship to ecclesiastical authority is maintained (CL 29). He lays down a variety of criteria for discerning and recognizing lay groups. They must contribute to Christian holiness, profess the faith of the Church, maintain communion with the local bishop, and conform to the Church's apostolic goals. If they engage in the social apostolate, they must, in addition, adhere to the Church's social teaching (CL 30).

Universal Call to the Apostolate

As mentioned in chapter 1, Bishop Wojtyła at Vatican II objected to an early version of the Decree on the Lay Apostolate because it seemed to put the emphasis too exclusively on associations. The apostolate, he said, is a duty of all Christians, including those who do not belong to associations. He also stated that the lay apostolate should not be treated as though it were directed only *ad extra*, toward persons and groups outside the Church. The lay faithful may be called to engage in an apostolate *ad intra*, so as to build up the Church and its members in faith and love.[9]

These themes reappear in *Christifideles laici*. Every disciple, says the pope, is personally called to share in the evangelizing mission of the Church. Evangelization is the most precious service that the Church can render to humanity. It is directed both to the Church itself and to the world. Through evangelization the Church builds itself up as a community of faith and love; it also has a healing and

[7] John Paul II, Ad Limina Address, "The Laity, Their Life and Mission," *Origins* 28 (June 18, 1988): 78–80, at 79.

[8] "This is the Day the Lord has Made!" *L'Osservatore Romano* (Eng.), June 3, 1998: 1–2.

[9] Text in AS III/4, 69–70, 788–89.

elevating impact on society, strengthens the bonds of social unity, and imbues individual lives with a deeper sense of meaning and direction (CL 33; cf. GS 40). Some members of the laity, including even married couples, will be called to go into mission territory in imitation of Aquila and Priscilla (CL 35; cf. Acts 18:1–3, 18, 26; Rom. 16:3–4).

THE FAMILY

Basic Unit of Society

As a personalist, John Paul II is convinced that persons are inherently social; they are called in the innermost depths of themselves to enter into communion with others and to give themselves to others. There is a relationship of interdependence and reciprocity between the person and society. Whatever is done in favor of society redounds to the benefit of the individual while, on the other hand, all that builds up the individual members has a positive impact on the quality of the society (CL 40).

From the beginning God created human beings male and female, in a relation of partnership. The first and most basic expression of the social dimension of the person is the married couple and the nuclear family. The family is the basic cell of society (CL 40; cf. FC 42 and CA 49). It is the place where future citizens are formed, and from it they receive their basic training in virtue. As the larger society becomes more highly structured, people tend to be reduced to a kind of anonymity that prevents them from realizing their dignity. The family is a force that can humanize and personalize society. It can counteract the depersonalizing influences of collective organizations and give individuals a sense of their own uniqueness and unrepeatability. Since the good of society depends on the personal formation and virtue of its members, every attack on the family is implicitly an attack on society itself (CL 40, 43).

In his "Letter to Families" written on the occasion of the United Nations International Year of the Family (1994), John Paul II expresses his concern at the worldwide deterioration of the family. "Unfortunately," he says,

> various programs backed by very powerful resources nowadays seem to aim at the breakdown of the family. At times it appears that concerted efforts are being made to present as normal and attractive, and even to glamorize, situations which are in fact "irregular." Indeed, they contradict "the truth and love" which should inspire and guide relationships between men and women, thus causing tensions and divisions within families, with grave consequences particularly for children.[10]

[10]John Paul II, "Letter to Families" §5; *Origins* 23 (March 3, 1994): 637–59, at 640.

The vigorous participation of the Holy See in the Cairo Conference on Population and Development in 1994 and in the Beijing Conference on Women in 1995 demonstrated the pope's determination to protect the family as the basic cell of society.

Conjugal Union between Spouses

God himself, as Father, Son, and Holy Spirit, is a loving communion of persons. He created human beings to share in this mystery of communion. The conjugal community, even when not blessed with children, is a communion of life and love. Marriage takes on an added dimension in relation to Christ the redeemer. Speaking to a group of American bishops at their *ad limina* visit on September 24, 1983, the pope declared: "Human conjugal love remains forever a great sacramental expression of the fact that 'Christ loved the Church and gave himself up for her' (Eph. 5:25)."[11] Christian marriage is a real symbol of the nuptial union between Christ as Bridegroom and the Church as the Bride for whose sake he sacrificed himself (TB 318–24).

The Church recognizes two ways of realizing the vocation of the human person to love: marriage and virginity or celibacy (FC 11; TB 276–78). Conjugal charity is the specific way in which spouses participate in the charity of Christ (FC 13). The family accordingly has the mission to reveal, safeguard, and communicate interpersonal love, and thereby to actualize in a particular way the love of Christ for the Church (FC 17). It follows that the union between husband and wife, like that between Christ and the Church, is a permanent and exclusive bond between two parties, who mutually give themselves to one another. The institution of marriage is not a regulation imposed from outside to restrict the freedom of the parties, but an intrinsic requirement of the covenantal love it expresses (FC 11). Any union that was not permanent and exclusive would fail to express and foster that type of love.

The Transmission of Life

Sexual union is the preeminent means by which a man and a woman express their total mutual self-giving. Such an expression could not appropriately take place except within the permanent and exclusive commitment of marriage. In his apostolic exhortation on the family John Paul II summarizes very concisely the doctrine of his earlier work, *Love and Responsibility*. He writes:

> Sexuality, by means of which man and woman give themselves to one another through the acts which are proper and exclusive to spouses, is by no means some-

[11]John Paul II, "The Family, Marriage, and Sexuality," *Origins* 13 (October 13, 1983): 316–18, at 318.

thing purely biological, but concerns the innermost being of the human person as such. It is realized in a truly human way only if it is an integral part of the love by which a man and a woman commit themselves totally to one another until death. The total physical self-giving would be a lie if it were not the sign and fruit of a total personal self-giving, in which the whole person, including the temporal dimension, is present: If the person were to withhold something or reserve the possibility of deciding otherwise in the future, by this very fact he or she would not be giving totally. (FC 11)

The pope then goes on, in the same article of *Familiaris consortio*, to show that this total self-giving also corresponds to the demands of responsible fertility. According to God's design, the act of sexual union gives the couple the capacity to cooperate with God in the generation of a new human person (FC 14). Fecundity is the sign and fruit of conjugal love (FC 28). The inherent language of the conjugal act, expressing as it does the total reciprocal self-giving of the husband and wife, is falsified if the couple positively exclude openness to procreation, thus separating the unitive from the procreative meaning of the act (FC 32).

In *The Theology of the Body,* some forty pages are devoted to the exposition and defense of the teaching of Paul VI on marriage in *Humanae vitae.* Whereas Paul VI had expressed the challenge to marital chastity in terms of endurance, John Paul II puts it rather in terms of living out the call to be faithful to the iconography of marriage as a sign of full mutual self-giving. He also goes beyond Paul VI by maintaining that the wrongfulness of contraception stems not only from natural law but also from revelation. When the biblical teaching on marriage and sexuality is taken in its full context, it becomes evident that the precept "belongs not only to the natural moral law but also to the *moral order revealed by God*" (TB 389, italics in original).

At Vatican II Bishop Wojtyła submitted a written intervention in which he maintained that modern scientific knowledge about fertility can serve the purpose of responsible parenthood and be consonant with the dignity of the persons as rational agents.[12] He repeats this in his teaching as pope. Natural family planning, unlike artificial contraception, does not block the natural process within the womb. Instead, the couple waits on God, so to speak, by waiting on nature, which allows for sexual relations that will not result in procreation. Periodic continence during fertile periods requires an exercise of self-control and chastity and helps the spouses to grow in love and responsibility, thus living out their marital relationship in a human and virtuous manner (FC 33; TB 399–401).

Parenthood cannot be restricted to the conception and birth of offspring. Since children require nurture in order to live a full human life, the parents have the responsibility and the right to educate their children, a process that completes pro-

---

[12] Text in AS IV/35, 242–43.

creation (FC 36). Children must be educated in all that is needed for their growth and maturation. This includes, in the case of Christian families, the raising of the children in the faith. "The State and the Church have the obligation to give families all possible aid to enable them to perform their educational role properly" (FC 40).

The Family as Miniature Church

Vatican II said that the family is, so to speak, a "domestic church, in which the parents must be for their children, by word and by example, the first preachers of the faith" (LG 11). John Paul II has frequently repeated the term "*ecclesia domestica*" without adding the qualifier *veluti* ("as it were") used by the council (e.g., CT 68; FC 49, 52; EV 92).[13] Parents, he declares, are the first heralds of the gospel for their children. They become fully parents by communicating not only bodily life but also the life of the spirit (FC 39). It is in the family that human persons are not only inducted into the human community but also, by means of baptism and education in the faith, introduced into God's family, which is the Church (FC 15). By reliving the sacrificial love of Christ the family becomes a saved community and, by communicating that same love, it becomes also a saving community (FC 49). The family is called to be a hearth from which radiate faith and charity, transforming society in accordance with God's plan.

The Rights of the Family

As noted in *Familiaris consortio* the Synod of 1980 proposed the issuance of a Charter of Family Rights (FC 46). Following up on this suggestion, the Holy See drew up such a charter, and released it in November 1983. It included rights such as the following: the right to marry, to have children, to educate children in accordance with the parents' moral and religious convictions, to choose schools for their children, to earn a suitable family wage so that mothers will not be obliged to work outside the home to the detriment of the family; the right to decent housing; and the right to emigrate and immigrate with one's family in cases where persons are compelled to leave their native land.[14]

THEOLOGY OF WOMAN

John Paul II has frequently spoken of the status and rights of women. The document in which he most fully explores the theology of woman is the apostolic let-

---

[13] See also John Paul II, "Letter to Families" §§3, 15; pp. 639 and 649.
[14] Holy See, "Charter of the Rights of the Family," *Origins* 13 (December 15, 1983): 461–64.

ter *Mulieris dignitatem*. The following analysis will be based primarily on this letter.

The Equal Dignity of Women

Following the first creation account, John Paul II frequently quotes the verse, "God created man in his own image; in the image of God he created them; male and female he created them" (Gen. 1:27). Man and woman, he concludes, are equally persons; they are equally created in God's image. The second creation account, in the second chapter of Genesis, represents Adam as having been created first, and Eve as taken from his rib in order to be his helpmate. Adam and Eve together are one flesh. They are called to live in a community of love. Adam was incomplete without Eve, whom he needed as his helper, but he was also needed to help her, because the dependence was mutual. Through their loving union Adam and Eve are called to mirror in the world the communion of love that is in God (MD 6–7). In the communion of marriage both of the spouses are enriched by being welcomed and accepted by the self-giving of the other (TB 69–72).

Only in the third chapter of Genesis, where the penalty of original sin is imposed, do we hear of the domination of the wife by the husband: "He shall rule over you" (Gen. 3:16). Women habitually suffer from the aggressiveness of men, which is common because of the effects of sin. But sin is not the last word. In Christ we have the founding of a new order based on redemption. In his own sacrificial love for the Church he sets an example for husbands. Paul can therefore teach in Ephesians: "Husbands, love your wives, as Christ loved the Church and gave himself up for her" (Eph. 5:25). Husband and wife, according to Paul, are one flesh. Just as no one hates his own flesh, so husbands must cherish their wives. By this love the husband affirms the wife as a person. As reconstituted in Christ, the headship of the husband takes the form not of domination but of loving sacrifice. Even though the husband is the head, the subjection of husband and wife is not one-sided but mutual (MD 23-24). Paul can therefore write to husbands and wives that they should "be subject to one another out of reverence for Christ" (Eph. 5:21).

The Vocations of Motherhood and Virginity

By their physical constitution women are naturally oriented to motherhood—conception, pregnancy, and giving birth. But motherhood should not be understood in merely physical terms. It is linked to the personal dimension of feminine life. The mother is filled with wonder at the mystery of life as it develops in her womb. She has a unique contact with the new human being developing within her. In general it may be said that women are more capable than men are of paying attention to other persons. For this reason the mother makes a special contribution to the education of the child, though the father should make his own contribution also (MD 17–19).

Jesus' doctrine of virginity or celibacy for the sake of the kingdom of God represents a clear innovation with respect to the Old Testament. This vocation is not given to all; it comes through a special grace or calling from God. By freely choosing virginity in accordance with God's call, some women are able to realize their femininity in a way distinct from marriage. It is a special participation in the bridal relationship of the Church to Christ. Like marriage, virginity is a total self-gift, in this case to Christ as Bridegroom. While involving a renunciation of physical motherhood, virginity can open up the possibility of various kinds of spiritual motherhood. Women's religious orders have traditionally served the needy, including the sick, the handicapped, the abandoned, orphans, the elderly, and others on the margins of society (MD 20–21).

Much as he esteems the vocation of motherhood, John Paul II should not be understood as though he wished to resurrect male domination and confine women to the privacy of the home. In his Letter to Women on the eve of the Beijing Conference of 1995 he deplored the marginalization of women in society and called for their full presence and activity in every area of life—social, cultural, artistic, and political. Women, he believes, have a special contribution to make for the sake of peace and reconciliation.[15] Elsewhere John Paul II calls for a "new feminism" that rejects the temptation of imitating models of male domination; one that affirms the true genius of women and overcomes all discrimination, violence, and exploitation (EV 99; VC 58).

Diversity of Roles

John Paul II teaches that the value and dignity of women will be best promoted not by ignoring their differences from men but rather by celebrating and profiting from the diversity. Womanhood, he says, expresses humanity just as much as manhood does, but in a different and complementary way.[16]

At various times John Paul II has addressed the phenomenon of contemporary feminism. In certain expressions this movement tends to disregard what is specific to each sex and even to "masculinize" women, with the result that less respect is accorded to those gifts that are distinctively feminine. He notes with satisfaction, however, that "in the midst of this very situation the authentic theology of woman is being reborn. The spiritual beauty, the particular genius, of women is being rediscovered" (CTH 217).

---

[15] John Paul II, "Letter to Women," *Origins* 25 (July 27, 1995): 137-43.
[16] Ibid., §7, p. 141.

These diverse gifts have their place also in the Church, which in its sacramental life reflects the different roles of the two sexes in salvation history. The priest at the altar, who offers the sacrifice of Christ, is an icon of Christ in his capacity as Bridegroom. The ministerial priesthood is a humble service, oriented toward the growth of the whole People of God in faith and love. Following Hans Urs von Balthasar, the pope holds that the Church lives both by a Petrine principle of apostolic ministry and by a Marian principle of life and fruitful receptivity. Of the two, the Marian principle is primary. The whole purpose of the hierarchical ministry is to form the Church according to the sanctity prefigured in Mary, who is par excellence the type and figure of the Church (cf. MD 27).

Mary as Archetype

In *Mulieris dignitatem* John Paul II calls attention to Mary as the human person most perfectly united to God. By a singular privilege, she who is both virgin and mother, exemplifies the dual vocation of woman. She can help all women to see how the two vocations explain and complete each other. As Spouse of the Holy Spirit, Mary brings forth the Incarnate Word, thus realizing the vocation of physical motherhood in a prototypical way. But her motherhood is also spiritual. As New Eve, she is mother of all those who live by the grace of Christ. Virgins who dedicate themselves to Christ in a bridal relationship are privileged to enjoy a spiritual fecundity that assimilates them to Mary. The Church is most perfectly realized in its highest member, Mary, a virgin who remains faithful to her heavenly Spouse and who becomes a Mother in the order of grace by accepting God's word in faith (MD 20–22).

The Church grows through love, which is the true and final measure of sanctity. In relation to the holiness that is the goal of the Church's existence the hierarchical and sacramental aspects of the Church are secondary and instrumental. Women, since they are by nature especially disposed to love, have a natural affinity with the Church. The Church, typified by Mary as its most outstanding member, is unceasingly grateful for all the fruits of feminine holiness (MD 31).

CONCLUSION

John Paul II's energetic promotion of theology of the laity shows his freedom from every semblance of clericalism. Although he sees the hierarchical priesthood as essential to the Church, he views it as a service for the sake of building up the whole body in holiness. The call to Christian holiness goes out to every baptized Christian, clerical or lay.

Pope John Paul's theology of the laity represents a fresh reading of Holy Scripture in the light of a rich personalist philosophy. He meditates at length on the early chapters of Genesis as well as on the Gospels and Pauline letters. From the original solitude of Adam, he passes on to consider the spousal relationship of Adam and Eve as a reflection of the divine communion of persons. The body, with its sexual characteristics, bears a nuptial meaning, which must be lived out personally through the mutual self-gift of persons. In the perspectives of the New Testament, marriage appears as a sacrament or efficacious sign of spousal relationship of Christ to the Church.

Sexual love, as seen by John Paul II, is a visible expression of the interior moral structure of the human person. Contraception, he contends, violates the true meaning of marital union, as known both by reason and by revelation.

Taking up a hint in Vatican II, the pope describes the Christian family as an *ecclesia domestica*—a church in miniature. Secular society must respect the rights of the family as the basic unit on which its survival and health depend. In the Church and society at large, men and women have equal dignity, but their roles should not be confused, since they have distinct contributions to make.

All the baptized, whether male or female, participate in Christ's threefold office. In ways distinct from the clergy, they are called to worship, to bear witness, and to order creation to its true end. As individuals and in associations, the laity play an indispensable part in evangelizing the worlds of politics, business, science, and culture. In the new communities and ecclesial movements founded in the present century the pope sees a remarkable rediscovery of the laity's conscious and active participation in the mission of the Church.

CHAPTER 9

Theology of Culture

V ATICAN II AND POPE JOHN PAUL II, as we have noted, understand the vocation of the laity as predominantly secular. Lay persons are expected to "engage in temporal affairs and order them according to the plan of God" (LG 31). The meaning of "temporal affairs" is spelled out more concretely in part 2 of the Pastoral Constitution on the Church in the Modern World. The first chapter deals with marriage and the family; the second and third chapters with culture and work; and the last two chapters with politics and international life. Having already discussed marriage and the family in chapter 8, we may in this chapter turn to the sphere of culture.

From his early years Karol Wojtyła, as a poet, dramatist, and philosophy professor in a Communist country with a deeply rooted Catholic heritage, developed a keen interest in the relations between faith and culture. As a young man he wrote poems and plays, using literature and drama as ways of sustaining the national culture and faith-traditions of his people under the brutalities of the Nazi occupation and the oppressive heel of Soviet Marxism.

As a bishop at Vatican II Wojtyła took an active part in the composition of *Gaudium et spes* and submitted a written intervention proposing about a dozen emendations to the draft of the chapter on the Church and culture.[1] Early in his pontificate, in 1982, he set up a Pontifical Council for Culture. In the letter establishing this council he wrote: "Since the beginning of my pontificate I have considered the Church's dialogue with the cultures of our time to be a vital area, one in which the destiny of the world at the end of the twentieth century is at stake."[2]

The teaching of John Paul II on the relationship between faith and culture is scattered through innumerable encyclicals, apostolic exhortations, letters,

---

[1] AS IV/3, 349–50.

[2] Letter to Cardinal Agostino Casaroli, May 20, 1982, establishing the Pontifical Council for Culture, *L'Osservatore Romano* (Eng.), June 28, 1982, pp. 19–20 at 19.

addresses, and homilies, as well as books and articles composed before he assumed the papal office.[3] I shall attempt to synthesize the main points of his thinking under seven headings of my own.

THEOLOGICAL ANTHROPOLOGY

Behind all of the pope's thinking about culture stands the theological anthropology that underlies the Pastoral Constitution *Gaudium et spes*, and is amplified in works such as John Paul II's catechesis on the book of Genesis.[4] Central to this teaching is the idea that every human person is created in the image of God (GS 12) and is therefore endowed with inalienable freedom and personal dignity. As Vatican II had already said, man is the only creature on earth that exists for its own sake (GS 24). The gospel reveals the deepest truth about humanity (GS 41), including the truth that in Jesus Christ God has in some way united himself with every human being (GS 22). In his inaugural encyclical, *Redemptor hominis*, the pope drew the consequence that because everyone is included in the mystery of redemption, all are entrusted to the solicitude of the Church. "The object of her care is man in his unique unrepeatable human reality, which keeps intact the image and likeness of God himself" (RH 13). For this reason the Church professes a universal humanism: no individual or group is beyond her motherly solicitude.

According to Holy Scripture, God created human beings not as isolated individuals but as social beings, destined to live in communion with others. The first community was marked by a difference of gender: "male and female he created them" (Gen. 1:27). Although called to exercise dominion over the rest of creation, human beings were not given arbitrary dominative power. They were obliged to respect the order of creation, the goodness of which God recognized even before the "sixth day," when Adam was formed. People all too easily forget that their power to reshape the world through their own labor is always based "on God's prior and original gift of the things that are" (CA 37). The relationship of men and

---

[3] See the five addresses gathered by Joseph Gremillion in *The Church and Culture since Vatican II* (Notre Dame, Ind.: University of Notre Dame Press, 1985), 187–222. Included are John Paul II's address to the UNESCO General Conference at Paris: "Man's Entire Humanity Is Expressed in Culture" (1980); the speeches to the first three of the annual sessions of the Pontifical Council for Culture (1983, 1984, 1985), and the pope's 1984 Christmas Message to the College of Cardinals, "One Church, Many Cultures."

[4] John Paul II, *Original Unity of Man and Woman: Catechesis on the Book of Genesis* (Boston: St. Paul Editions, 1981), reprinted as part 1 of *The Theology of the Body* (Boston: Pauline Books & Media, 1997). For commentary, see Kenneth L. Schmitz, *At the Center of the Human Drama: The Philosophical Anthropology of Karol Wojtyła/Pope John Paul II* (Washington, D.C.: Catholic University of America Press, 1993), 90-107.

women to the rest of creation is therefore one of responsible stewardship. Without them there would be no one to till the earth (cf. Gen. 2:5–6 as analyzed in TB 27–28 and 40–42).

HUMAN EXISTENCE AND CULTURE

What distinguishes man from every other kind of creature is culture. Plants and animals live but have no culture. Thomas Aquinas, commenting on Aristotle, affirmed that humanity lives by productive skill and intellect ("*Genus humanum arte et ratione vivit*").[5] John Paul II paraphrases this as meaning that "Man lives a really human life thanks to culture. . . . Culture is a specific way of man's 'existing' and 'being.'"[6] Culture is that by which man becomes more human, thereby achieving an increase, not necessarily of having, but of being. As a result of culture man *is* to a greater degree. Culture is *of* man, since no other being has culture; it is *from* man, since man creates it; and it is *for* man, since its prime purpose is to develop man as man.[7]

From this follows the basic norm by which any culture is to be evaluated. Human nature, according to John Paul II, "is itself the measure of culture and the condition ensuring that man does not become the prisoner of any of his cultures, but asserts his personal dignity by living in accordance with the profound truth of his being" (VS 53). In his apostolic constitution on Catholic universities, *Ex corde Ecclesiae*, the pope lists more specific criteria for evaluating a culture: its contribution to the meaning and freedom of the human person, the sense of responsibility, and openness to the transcendent. "To the respect for persons is joined the preeminent value of the family, the primary unit of every human culture."[8] In the end, therefore, it should be asked: Does a given cultural development enhance all the dimensions of human existence, perfecting all the capacities that are distinctively human?

In opposition to the Marxists, John Paul II denies that culture is determined by sheerly economic factors, such as the conditions of production. One of the great weaknesses of Soviet Communism was its dismissal of culture as a mere superstructure. In fact, culture is the self-expression of the human spirit, and is essentially oriented to truth, goodness, and beauty. Although culture is always

---

[5] Thomas Aquinas, commentary on Aristotle, *Post. Analyt.*, n. 1; quoted by John Paul II in UNESCO Address, §6, 189.

[6] Ibid.

[7] Address to Intellectuals and Scientists at Coimbra, Portugal, May 15, 1982, §3; *Origins* 12 (May 27, 1982): 27–29, at 28.

[8] John Paul II, Apostolic Constitution *Ex corde Ecclesiae*, §45; *Origins* 20 (October 4, 1990): 265–76, at 273.

objectified in products of one kind or another, it is also constitutive of the human subject. Whenever we engage in a truly human action (an *actus humanus*, which is consciously willed, as distinct from a mere *actus hominis*, which occurs without thought and volition), we not only produce an external effect but simultaneously modify ourselves. The essence of praxis consists in the self-realization of the acting subject, who at the same time renders the nonhuman environment in some way more human. Praxis, in the sense of action that recoils upon the agent, "provides a basis for speaking of culture as a connatural reality in relation to the human being."[9]

Because culture deals with the human in all its dimensions, it transcends politics and economics, which deal only with inner-worldly activities. Culture is inseparable from religion, inasmuch as God is the author, sustainer, and final goal of human existence. "Religion," says the pope, "often represents the transcendent dimension of the culture itself" (VC 79). And elsewhere he declares: "At the heart of every culture lies the attitude a person takes to the greatest mystery: the mystery of God. . . . When this question is eliminated, the culture and moral life of nations are corrupted" (CA 24).

Like Leninist Communism, National Socialism sought to abolish religion as an independent force and to redefine the human in exclusively this-worldly terms—economic and political. The two systems were alike in subjugating the economic, political, and cultural orders to the power of the totalitarian state. The failure of both systems was, at the deepest level, cultural. By introducing a spiritual void into the heart of human existence, these systems threw the human heart into turmoil, thus sowing the seeds of their own destruction (CA 24).

THE GOSPEL AND CULTURE

The link between the gospel and culture, for John Paul II, comes through humanity, for the gospel, as we read in *Gaudium et spes*, "fully discloses humankind to itself and unfolds its noble calling" (GS 22). Jesus Christ is the truth that liberates men and women from the powers of sin and death. They rise to their full stature through increasingly perfect knowledge of, and adherence to, the truth.[10] The gospel favors the development of culture, and authentic culture, conversely, brings people closer to the gospel.

---

[9] John Paul II, "The Problem of the Constitution of Culture through Human Praxis," in Karol Wojtyła, *Person and Community: Selected Essays* (New York: Peter Lang, 1993), 263–75, quotation from 267.
[10] UNESCO Address, §17, p. 196.

From the very beginning, says the pope, the gospel was engaged with persons. It both drew upon their talents and contributed to their development. Cultures change and advance by assimilating new experiences. All of us are children of the culture in which we were raised, but we become parents of the culture we bequeath to our posterity (FR 71).

The gospel can make a unique contribution to culture because deep in every culture lies an impulse toward its own fulfillment through the reception of revelation, which liberates it from its involvement in sin and ambiguity. Without stripping cultures of their native richness, the gospel calls them to the plenitude of truth. The message of truth incites them to develop in new ways (ibid.).

In many of his speeches and writings, the pope expatiates on the capacity of the gospel, with its orientation toward the authentic well-being of all humanity, to promote and defend human values. In the encyclical *Centesimus annus*, for example, he characterizes the Church's special mission toward cultures:

> The Church promotes those aspects of human behavior which favor a true culture of peace, as opposed to models in which the individual is lost in the crowd, in which the role of one's initiative and freedom is neglected, and in which one's greatness is posited in the arts of conflict and war. The Church renders this service to human society by preaching the truth about the creation of the world, which God has placed in human hands so that people may make it fruitful and more perfect through their work; and by preaching the truth about the Redemption, whereby the Son of God has saved mankind and at the same time has united all people, making them responsible for one another. (CA 51)

It should be evident, therefore, that human culture can always be renewed in the light of a sound anthropology and the principles of the gospel.[11] In explaining the mandate of the Pontifical Council for Culture, the pope declared: "We must make our contemporaries understand that the gospel of Christ is a source of progress and enrichment for all human beings."[12]

Catholic universities, in the thinking of John Paul II, are privileged places for the dialogue between faith and culture. The university helps the Church to come to greater knowledge of cultures and a more accurate assessment of their respective strengths and weaknesses. Conversely, it helps people of different cultures to gain a better understanding of faith.[13] The study of philosophy, because it concerns itself with universal and objective truth, rather than mere appearances, is especially valuable for a fruitful exchange among cultures (FR 69).

---

[11] Address at Coimbra, §7, p. 29.

[12] Address to Pontifical Council for Culture, January 17, 1987; text in *L'Osservatore Romano* (Eng.), February 9, 1987, pp. 11–12.

[13] *Ex corde Ecclesiae* §44, p. 273.

THE CONTEMPORARY CRISIS OF CULTURE

John Paul II agrees with those who discern a certain alienation in modern culture. The achievements of technology and politics, which have erected elaborate new instruments intended for the service of humanity, have taken on a life of their own, enslaving and threatening their own producers (RH 15–16). The power to subdue the earth turns against humanity, inducing suffering and anxiety, as may be seen from the massive poverty of the Third World and the persistent fear of nuclear disaster (RH 16). Speaking to UNESCO in 1980 the pope declared that the future of humanity and the world is threatened because the marvelous results of their researches are being misappropriated:

> Whereas science is called to be in the service of man's life, it is too often a fact that it is subjected to purposes that destroy the real dignity of man and of human life. That is the case when scientific research itself is directed towards those purposes or when its results are applied to purposes contrary to the good of mankind. That happens in the field of genetic manipulations and biological experimentations as well as in that of chemical, bacteriological or nuclear armaments.[14]

John Paul II speaks often of the signs of disintegration in contemporary society. The recent decline of the West in terms of cultural influence, he asserts, "seems to have its basis in a crisis of truth." This is at bottom a metaphysical crisis. "An objective vision of the truth is often replaced by a more or less spontaneous subjective view. Objective morality gives way to individual ethics, where each person seems to set himself up as the norm. . . ."[15]

In his encyclical on faith and reason, the pope directs attention to a variety of currents in modern philosophy that interfere with the quest for wisdom. After brief discussions of eclecticism, historicism, scientism, pragmatism, nihilism, and various forms of postmodernism, he points out how these movements contribute to the contemporary sense of meaninglessness and despair (FR 86–91). "Reason," in its one-sided focus on human subjectivity, "seems to have forgotten that men and women are always called to direct their steps toward a truth which transcends them. Sundered from that truth, individuals are at the mercy of caprice, and their state as persons ends up being judged by pragmatic criteria based essentially upon experimental data, in the mistaken belief that technology must dominate all" (FR 5).

In his encyclical on moral norms, *Veritatis splendor*, John Paul II calls upon the Church to mount a major pastoral effort to clarify the relationship between human freedom and divine law. All around us "the saving power of truth is contested, and freedom alone, uprooted from any objectivity, is left to decide by itself

---

[14] UNESCO Address, §21, p. 198.
[15] Coimbra Address, §6, p. 29.

what is good and what is evil" (VS 84). This moral relativism, in the judgment of the pope, leads to gross violations of human rights and disrespect for human life, especially in the stages before birth and in old age.

In his encyclical "The Gospel of Life," *Evangelium vitae*, the pope remarks that the prevalent scientific and technical mentality gives rise to "a practical materialism, which breeds individualism, utilitarianism, and hedonism." All too often, he says, suffering is regarded as a useless burden, sexuality is depersonalized and exploited, and procreation is avoided (EV 23). This mentality breeds a "culture of death" resembling that described by the apostle Paul in the first chapter of his Letter to the Romans. In proclaiming the "gospel of life" the Holy Father calls for a cultural transformation in which the links among freedom, truth, and life are reestablished.

In his critique of Western societies the present pope speaks frequently of the menace of consumerism, which ensnares people in a web of false and superficial gratifications rather than helping them to express their personhood in an authentic way. Advertising and aggressive marketing, intent upon profits, create artificial human needs that hinder the formation of a mature personality. People lose themselves in the quest for affluence, luxury, amusement, and sensory pleasures, neglecting the quest for truth, beauty, goodness, and communion with others (CA 36). In this way people are alienated from their deepest selves, from their fellow human beings, and from God, their final destiny (CA 41).

This critique of contemporary culture is reinforced in the pope's addresses to the Pontifical Council for Culture. He speaks at one point of the growth of an "anti-culture" that manifests itself in growing violence, murderous confrontations, and the exploitation of instincts and selfish interests.[16] He notes that our world is characterized by clashing ideologies.[17] "Social and cultural transformation, political upheaval, ideological fermentations, religious restlessness, ethical research, all show a world in gestation, which is trying to discover its form and direction, its organic synthesis, and its prophetic renewal."[18] This situation constitutes a challenge and an opportunity for the Church to penetrate the soul of living cultures. "The meeting of cultures is nowadays a privileged area of dialogue between men committed to the search for a new humanism for our time" in which the various cultures can overcome their harmful limitations and open themselves "to him who is their source and end" and whose grace alone can heal the wounds of sin.[19]

---

[16] Address to Pontifical Council for Culture, January 16, 1984, §8; 207–9, at 209.

[17] Address to Pontifical Council for Culture, January 15, 1985, §3, 210–11, at 211.

[18] Address to Pontifical Council for Culture, January 13, 1986; *L'Osservatore Romano* (Eng.), January 27, 1986, p. 3.

[19] Letter to Casaroli, p. 19.

RECIPROCITY BETWEEN
THE CHURCH AND CULTURE

The dependence between the Church and culture is mutual. On the one hand, the cultures of the world need the gospel, which enriches them "by helping them to go beyond the defective or even inhuman features in them, and by communicating to their legitimate values the fullness of Christ" (CA 53). The gospel "does not spring spontaneously from any cultural soil; it has always been transmitted by means of an apostolic dialogue which inevitably becomes part of a certain dialogue of cultures" (CT 53). A culture that has been impregnated with the gospel, sincerely received in faith, becomes capable of expressing and living out the truth and of proclaiming the revealed mystery.[20]

From Paul VI the present pope takes over the idea of an evangelization of cultures. The gospel, he maintains, is creative of culture, as may be seen from the great masterpieces of art, music, and literature that emerged from Christian Europe.[21] The past contributions of the gospel to the cultures of the Western world are capable of being matched in other regions in the future, as the pope has explained in his pastoral visits to Asia, Africa, and other continents. Their cultures, as the pope seems to view them, could be vastly enriched by the transcendent values that the gospel can supply.

While human cultures depend on the gospel for their purification and enrichment, the gospel, conversely, depends on culture. The Church has need of culture in order for it to manifest the unsearchable riches of Christ and "to progress towards a daily more complete and profound awareness of the truth, which has already been given to her in its entirety by the Lord" (FC 10). "The synthesis between culture and faith," writes Pope John Paul II, "is not just a demand of culture, but also of faith. . . . A faith that does not become culture is a faith that has not been fully received, not thoroughly thought through, not faithfully lived out."[22] The Church relies on culture for its ability to express and communicate the truth of the gospel. The Church "has used in her preaching the discoveries of various cultures to spread and explain the message of Christ to all nations, to probe it and more deeply understand it, and give it better expression in liturgical celebrations."[23] Only at its peril can faith seek to insulate itself from culture: "A faith that places itself on the margin of what is human, of what is therefore cul-

[20] Homily at Cartagena, Columbia, July 6, 1986, §7; text in *L'Osservatore Romano* (Eng.), September 8, 1986, p. 6.

[21] UNESCO Address, §10, p. 192.

[22] Discourse to Participants in the National Congress of the Movement of Cultural Commitment, January 18, 1982, *L'Osservatore Romano* (Eng.), March 8, 1982; quoted in Letter to Casaroli, p. 19.

[23] Coimbra Address, §5, p. 29.

ture, would be a faith unfaithful to the fullness of what the word of God manifests and reveals, a decapitated faith, worse still, a faith in the process of self-annihilation."[24]

INCULTURATION

At various times since the beginning of his pontificate John Paul II has used the term "inculturation," which, though a neologism, "expresses very well one of the elements of the great mystery of the Incarnation."[25] Speaking to the members of the Pontifical Biblical Commission, the pope meditated on God's mysterious plan to transmit his transcendent and absolute message in the fragility of particular human languages from Abraham to the seer of the Apocalypse. Among the vessels of clay that God deigned to use, the pope reckons the human language and experience of the Mesopotamians, the Egyptians, the Canaanites, the Persians, and the Hellenistic writers of the New Testament.[26]

John Paul II returns to the theme of inculturation in his encyclical on Cyril and Methodius, the apostles of the Slavs. While incarnating the gospel in the cultures of Slavic peoples, they introduced these cultures into the life of the Church. Reflecting on this achievement, the pope remarks that for the fullness of catholicity, every culture must play its part in the universal plan of salvation. But in order to play that part, the cultures must remain open and alert to the other churches and traditions, maintaining the universal Catholic communion (SA 54). Recalling the relationship between Byzantium and Rome in the first millennium, John Paul II frequently remarks that the Church then breathed with two lungs, and that it must learn to do so once again (UUS 54).

The principle of inculturation has great significance for missiology, as the pope explains in his visits to Zaire, Kenya, India, and elsewhere. To the aboriginal peoples of Australia he declared in November 1986: "You do not have to be divided into two parts. . . . Jesus calls you to accept his words and his values into your own culture" (quoted in UUS 19). The apostolic exhortation on the Church in Africa calls attention to the need to avoid syncretism and mandates study commissions to examine in depth all the cultural aspects of problems concerning marriage, the veneration of ancestors, and the spirit world from the theological, sacramental, and liturgical points of view (EA 64).

---

[24] John Paul II, *Ex corde Ecclesiae* 44, p. 273, quoting from an address to Catholic intellectuals at Medellín, Columbia, July 5, 1986.

[25] Address to Pontifical Biblical Commission, April 26, 1979; *Origins* 9 (May 24, 1979): 15–16, at 15.

[26] Ibid.

There is of course an inbuilt danger in inculturation. It can adulterate the gospel by interpreting it in terms of the ideas, values, and behavioral patterns of people still in need of evangelization. Recognizing this danger, the pope points out that the gospel can build only on authentic human values, and that it inwardly transforms even these values by integrating them into Christian faith (RMis 52). He lays down two criteria for sound inculturation: compatibility with the gospel and communion with the universal Church (FC 10). Speaking at Cartegena in Columbia in 1986, he declared: "The closer a particular church is to the universal Church . . . 'the more will this church be able to translate the treasure of faith into the legitimate variety of expressions of the profession of faith.'"[27]

In an address to a meeting of cardinals he cautioned that emphasis on special experiences in different sociocultural contexts must respect the necessity of being "in tune with those which other Christians, in contact with different cultural contexts, feel called to live in order to be faithful to demands arising from the one single and identical mystery of Christ."[28] Catholics all over the world must be able to recognize one another as worshiping the same God and as united by the same Spirit of Christ. The Apostolic See, according to the pope, has a special responsibility to serve the Church's universal unity. The Church must therefore provide commonly shared standards of belief and conduct. Solicitude for unity among all the churches therefore gives rise to a daily tension in the life of every pope.[29] No abstract formula can resolve that tension. Often enough, a balance between conflicting goods must be worked out pragmatically. The bishops of the region, according to John Paul, have the major responsibility for mediating between the concerns of the universal and the local church.[30]

In his encyclical on faith and reason John Paul II spoke at some length of the inculturation of the faith in India today. He acknowledges the value of the ancient religions and philosophies of India, which manifest the quest of the human spirit for liberation. Christianity may enrich its thought by drawing from this heritage elements compatible with its own faith. But the legitimate defense of the uniqueness and integrity of Indian thought must not fall into the excess of allowing that culture to close in upon itself, so that it affirms itself only in opposition to other traditions. Christianity, for its part, must retain what it has providentially gained from its inculturation in the Greco-Roman world, passing on the benefits of that experience as it encounters other cultures (FR 72).

[27] Cartegena Address, §11, quoting Paul VI, *Evangelii nuntiandi*, 64; text in *L'Osservatore Romano* (Eng.), September 8, 1986, p. 6.

[28] John Paul II, "One Church, Many Cultures," Annual Christmas Address to the College of Cardinals, Vatican City, December 21, 1984, §4, p. 215.

[29] Ibid. §6; pp. 217-18.

[30] Address to Bishops of India, New Delhi, February 1, 1985, §5; *Origins* 15 (February 20, 1986): 587-91, at 589.

APPLICATIONS TO THE UNITED STATES

In his speeches to American bishops on their quinquennial visits to Rome, and on his several trips to the United States, the pope has had occasions to comment on the cultural situation of this nation, as he sees it. He has made it abundantly clear that he supports the ethical and spiritual concerns that influenced the founding fathers. Political freedom, he holds, can provide opportunities for people to exercise their generosity and responsibility to one another as children of God and brothers and sisters in a common humanity.[31]

In his visit to the United States and Canada in the autumn of 1987, the pope spoke frequently of the reconciling power of Christ, which enables people of diverse races and cultures to live together in mutual love and respect. He gave addresses aimed specifically at African-American, American Indian, and Hispanic Catholics. Then on September 16, in Dodger Stadium, Los Angeles, he spoke at some length of ethnic diversity. After observing that many Catholics in California had imported their faith together with their specific cultural traditions, he went on to say:

> As a result, the Church in California, and particularly the Church in Los Angeles, is truly catholic in the fullest sense, embracing peoples and cultures of the widest and richest variety.
>
> Today in the Church in Los Angeles, Christ is Anglo and Hispanic, Christ is Vietnamese and Irish, Christ is Korean and Italian, Christ is Japanese and Filipino, Christ is Native American, Croatian, Samoan, and many other ethnic groups. . . . And the Church, with all her different members, remains the one Body of Christ, professing the one faith, united in hope and in love.[32]

This hymn to diversity was qualified by the pope's realization that where diversity is cultivated without mutual love and respect, it can easily lead to the kind of violence that has more than once erupted in Los Angeles itself, both before and after the pope's visit of 1987.

At a later point in the same address John Paul II alluded to the problem of consumerism, which has been one of his major concerns. He stated:

> The Church faces a particularly difficult task in her efforts to preach the word of God in all cultures in which the faithful are constantly challenged by consumerism and a pleasure-seeking mentality, where utility, productivity, and hedonism are exalted while God and his law are forgotten. In these situations where ideas and behavior directly contradict the truth about God and about humanity itself, the Church's wit-

---

[31] See, for instance, his remarks to President Ronald Reagan on September 10, 1987; *Origins* 17 (September 24, 1987): 238–39. This theme will be taken up in chapter 11, below.

[32] "The Ethnic Universality of the Church," *Origins* 17 (October 15, 1987): 305–9, at 307.

ness must be unpopular. She must take a clear stand on the word of God and proclaim the whole gospel message with great confidence in the Holy Spirit.[33]

Still more sharply focused were the reflections on American culture embodied in the pope's response to Archbishop Rembert Weakland in their dialogue in Los Angeles on September 16, 1987. Archbishop Weakland had declared: "The Church in the United States of American can boast of having the largest number of educated faithful in the world."[34] To this the pope replied that in that case the Church should be in a position to exercise great influence upon American culture. Then he asked:

> But how is the American culture evolving today? Is this evolution being influenced by the gospel? Does it clearly reflect Christian inspiration? Your music, your poetry and art, your drama, your painting and sculpture, the literature you are producing— are all those things which reflect the soul of a nation being influenced by the spirit of Christ for the perfection of humanity?[35]

The pope went on to assert that it is above all for the laity, once they have been inspired by the gospel, to bring the gospel's uplifting and purifying influence into the world of culture. He did not give a judgment about how well the American laity are fulfilling their mission. He left the answers to his own questions open. Christian writers and teachers, in particular, must ask themselves whether they are making a positive contribution toward the synthesis of faith and culture, or, on the contrary, perpetuating that unhealthy cleavage which Paul VI memorably described as "the drama of our time."[36]

CONCLUSION

In his esteem for culture, as in other aspects of his thinking, Pope John Paul II shows himself to be a humanist and a personalist. His enthusiasm for literature and the arts reflects his own youthful career as a poet and dramatist.

Distancing himself from the individualistic existentialism of Kierkegaard and Sartre, Wojtyła insists that the human person flourishes only in reciprocity with others. He favors communities in which people interact to build a common culture. He borrows and corrects certain themes in Hegel in order to show how cultural productivity reflects the dynamism of the human spirit in its movement toward the Absolute, and in so doing fortifies the very movement it expresses.

---

[33] Ibid., 308–9.
[34] "Meeting with United States Bishops," *Origins* 17 (October 1, 1987): 255–67, at 262.
[35] Ibid., 263.
[36] Paul VI, Apostolic Exhortation *Evangelii nuntiandi* (1975), §20.

As a believer, John Paul II is convinced that culture, at its best, brings people into confrontation with the encompassing transcendent mystery. If culture seeks to bracket out the deepest dimensions of life, it becomes anemic and decays. Religion and culture grow together. Just as culture requires religion to rise to its full stature, so religion becomes sterile and withers unless it finds cultural self-expression. By fostering artistic and intellectual achievement, religion identifies itself with the beautiful and the true, which are always reflections of the divine. A religion that cultivates all these dimensions of reality is more attractive, more credible, and more influential than one that defines itself as a special function or department of life.

John Paul II welcomes the achievements of science and technology to the extent that they can serve the authentic growth of men and women. But, like Max Scheler and other personalists, he is on guard against forms of technology that could dominate and enslave the human spirit. Just as he has in the past deplored the hegemony of political interests in totalitarian states, so today he warns democracies against embracing a purely economic model of productivity and consumption. Neither politics nor economics, he insists, must be allowed to become supreme. The cultural order is more fundamental than either of them since, unlike them, it deals with the meaning of human existence as a whole. And culture, as already mentioned, attains its summit when it encounters the transcendent. In a sense, therefore, Wojtyła might be able to agree with Paul Tillich's dictum: "Religion is the substance of culture and culture the form of religion."[37]

---

[37] Paul Tillich, *Systematic Theology* 3 (Chicago: University of Chicago Press, 1963), 248.

CHAPTER **10**

Economic and Social Order

∞

THEOLOGY OF WORK

JOHN PAUL II, THOUGH HIS LIFE has been primarily devoted to the service of the Church, is not a stranger to the world of work. As a young man he was forced to do hard manual labor in a chemical plant during the Nazi occupation. In the course of his doctoral studies he visited France and Belgium, where he became interested in the Young Christian Workers (JOC) and the worker-priest experiment. As a professor he specialized in social ethics. Pursuing this field of specialization during the council, he took an active part in the composition of the Pastoral Constitution on the Church in the Modern World. Subsequently, as a cardinal and as pope, he became a key supporter of the shipyard workers at Gdansk and the spiritual father of the Solidarity movement headed by Lech Walesa.

The pope's theology of work and the economy, as of many other subjects, is in strict continuity with Vatican II. He draws frequently on the Pastoral Constitution *Gaudium et spes*, especially the third chapter of part 1, dealing with human activity throughout the world (§§33–39), and the third chapter of part 2, on economic and social life (§§63–72). His own book *The Acting Person* provides the dynamic personalist perspective for his elaborations on these sources. As pope he has issued three important social encyclicals: *Laborem exercens* (1981), *Sollicitudo rei socialis* (1987), and *Centesimus annus* (1991). The first and third of these encyclicals were composed to commemorate the ninetieth and hundredth anniversaries, respectively, of Leo XIII's great encyclical *Rerum novarum* (1891). All three of John Paul II's social encyclicals contain important passages dealing with work and the economy.

Although he sometimes makes rather detailed applications to technical economic and social questions, John Paul II insists that Catholic social teaching is not ideology. Founded as it is on the Christian doctrine of God, humanity, and nature, it pertains to the field of theology. Proclamation of this social doctrine is an inte-

130

gral part of the Church's evangelizing mission (SRS 41; CA 5). The specific competence of the Church, according to the pope, is not to propose particular social and economic systems but to lay down principles and criteria that can direct work toward the authentic progress of society, safeguarding the dignity and rights of all persons, including very specifically those who work.

Work in Relation to Creation, the Fall, and Redemption

The theology of work may be considered in relation to the creation, the Fall, and the redemption. In his exposition the pope turns in the first place to the opening chapters of Genesis, which in his view set forth a kind of proto-gospel of work. The paradigm for all work is given in the divine activity of creation. God toils for six days, at the end of which he enjoys a Sabbath rest.

The creation accounts in Genesis, according to John Paul II, constitute the first "gospel of work" (LE 25; DD 10). They are intended to instruct us about our own activity. Among all visible creatures, only human beings were created to the image and likeness of God, as sharers in his sovereignty. Human work is therefore a participation in, and prolongation of, the creative activity of God. The Father, even when he enters into his Sabbath rest, in some sense continues to work throughout history, as Jesus indicated when he said, "My Father is working still, and I am working" (John 5:17; DD 11).

God intends that human beings should be his fellow workers. Without human activity there would be no one to till the earth (TB 28, 39; cf. Gen. 2:5–6).[1] Man, according to Vatican II, is the only creature in the visible world that exists for its own sake; others are for the sake of man (GS 24; cf. RH 13; SR 114; CA 32). In the original blessing pronounced at the moment of creation, humanity is given dominion over all other creatures on earth (Gen. 1:26–28). Invested though they are with dominion over the rest of creation, human beings did not receive arbitrary dominative power. They are obliged to respect the order of creation, the goodness of which God recognized even before the "sixth day," when Adam was formed. "The dominion granted to man by the Creator is not an absolute power, nor can one speak of a freedom to 'use or misuse,' or to dispose of things as one pleases" (SRS 34). People too easily forget that their power to reshape the world through their own labor is always based "on God's prior and original gift of the things that are" (CA 37). The relationship of men and women to the rest of creation is therefore one of responsible stewardship.

---

[1] For commentary, see Kenneth L. Schmitz, *At the Center of the Human Drama: The Philosophical Anthropology of Karol Wojtyła/Pope John Paul II* (Washington, D.C.: Catholic University of America Press, 1993), 96–97.

The nature of work has been affected by the Fall. Work has become difficult, onerous, often painful, and even at times dangerous. The earth brings forth thorns and thistles; man lives by the sweat of his face (Gen. 3:17–19; LE 9; 27). Human activity is weighed down by the slavery of creation to corruption (Rom. 8:21–22). Work consequently assumes a penitential aspect.

Another effect of sin is concupiscence, which involves an inordinate desire for riches, pleasures, and esteem. This leads easily to the kind of consumerist culture that is rampant in the affluent societies of our time. The senseless destruction of the environment, which unfortunately is widespread in our day, is rooted in the anthropological error by which man regards his own desires as the norm, setting himself up in place of God and forgetting his mission to be a cooperator with God in the management of creation (CA 37).

John Paul II describes the devastating effects of consumerism in many of his encyclicals (RH 16, DM 11, SRS 28, and CA 36 and 41). In the consumerist culture, he says, the market is flooded with luxury goods that are acquired for purposes of amusement or as status symbols. The rich are surfeited by a super-abundance of possessions and enslaved by the tasks of protecting and managing their wealth. Meanwhile the poor are left in dire misery. The Church has a prophetic charge to give a voice to the poor and a conscience to the rich and powerful.

Work should be understood not only with reference to creation and the Fall but also with reference to the redemption (LE 26). Christ the Son of God became a worker, a carpenter, and by the labor of his hands at Nazareth he ennobled the dignity of work (SR 303; cf. Vatican II, GS 67). By painful toil endured in union with the Crucified, we can take up our cross and follow the Master. "The Christian finds in human work a small part of the cross of Christ and accepts it in the same spirit of redemption in which Christ accepted his cross for us" (LE 27). As the cross contains the seeds of the resurrection, so the labor of the human family prepares for the final advent of the kingdom of God.

Work as Transitive
and Intransitive Action

With the help of his philosophy of human action, John Paul II points out that work, like any human activity, has two aspects, transitive and intransitive.[2] Transitive action is that which terminates in an external product—for example, a pot or pan, a car or a garage. The purpose of transitive action is to make the world a fitter place for human habitation, and in that sense to "humanize" the world.

---

[2] Karol Wojtyła, "The Problem of the Constitution of Culture Through Human Praxis," in Karol Wojtyła, *Person and Community: Selected Essays* (New York: Peter Lang, 1993), 263–75, at 266.

Because the world was created for the sake of humanity, production is not in itself an act of violence against creation. The world and nature have a certain readiness to be put at the disposal of humanity. Transitive action, however, goes awry when the world is polluted, when its resources are depleted, when its natural beauty is defaced. Care of the environment is a moral responsibility. The world was created not simply to be used through transitive activity but also to be contemplated and appreciated—activities that are intransitive.[3]

The intransitive aspect of human action—that which remains in the agent as subject—is the second dimension. Even when we work on external matter, something of our labor remains within us. We are transformed by what we do. Through our action we shape ourselves into what we in fact become.

In Wojtyła's personalist perspective the intransitive dimension is more important than the transitive, because personal subjects are more important than things, including the products of their labor. The pope's foremost concern is with what people do to themselves by acting. The tendency to subordinate persons to things, which is a mark of contemporary consumerist societies, is shared in varying degrees by Western liberalism and by Chinese and Soviet Marxism. These ideologies, though in some respects opposed to each other, are alike in giving primacy to material goods on the ground of their superficial attractiveness and utility (LE 13).

Marxist theory depicts the human person as a product of praxis, which is said to recoil upon the agent and shape the latter's consciousness (LE 13).[4] In opposition to dialectical materialism John Paul II holds that industry and culture are not determined by simply economic factors, such as the conditions of production. As the self-expression of the spirit, human activity is essentially related to truth, goodness, and beauty. Although work and culture are always objectified in products of one kind or another, human activity, as an actualization of the subject, is perfective of the agent. The essence of praxis consists in the self-realization of the acting subject, who at the same time renders the nonhuman environment in some way more human. Praxis must therefore be understood as proceeding from the human subject and perfecting it, rather than as degrading the person and turning the agent into a mere product.[5]

Personalist Principles

In accordance with his personalist humanism John Paul II insists on the priority of labor over capital (LE 12). By this he means not that laborers are to be preferred to capitalists, but that the persons involved in the production process are more

---

[3] Ibid., 270–71.

[4] Marxist theory on this point is well expounded by Rocco Buttiglione, *Karol Wojtyła* (Grand Rapids, Mich.: Eerdmans, 1997), 292–305.

[5] John Paul II, *Person and Community*, 266-67.

important than the impersonal instruments they use (factories, machines, laboratories, computers, and the like). The deep chasm between capitalists and workers that existed at the time of Leo XIII no longer obtains in most parts of the world (LE 7; CA 4–5). The historical antagonism is being progressively transcended. Many workers share in the tasks of management and enjoy some measure of ownership. The task of management can itself be considered as a form of labor.

Labor, while it should ideally redound to the benefit of the laborer as an individual, has larger purposes. It is intended also to benefit the family, the nation, and the universal human community. Opposing the unbridled thirst for profits and power, John Paul II calls for a theology of development that takes account of the whole human person and every person. Authentic development, he maintains, must respect the cultural, transcendent, and religious dimensions of human life (SRS 46; CA 29). In light of these broadly humanistic goals it is possible to correct some of the errors of what the pope calls "economism"—a view that evaluates enterprises only in terms of productivity and profits (LE 13).

Following a long Catholic tradition, John Paul II favors the institution of private property as a natural right, but he also notes, as did Leo XIII, that the use of private property must be subordinated to the common good (LE 14; CA 30). In *Centesimus annus* John Paul II notes that in older economies the possession of tangible property was the primary basis of wealth. In the modern world the decisive factor is increasingly man himself, with his knowledge and technical skills (CA 31–32). Human resources, developed through interaction among persons, are more important today than physical property, which can usually be replaced in case of loss.

Technology is a great ally of human progress, since it renders work more efficient and less onerous. But it has a shadow side. It diminishes the personal satisfaction that laborers have often felt in their own products. Sometimes, too, technology makes workers the slaves of the machines they use. New technological advances often cause unemployment or, at best, require difficult retraining (LE 5).

Modern trade unions, the pope recalls, grew up in the struggle of workers to protect their rights against exploitative entrepreneurs and owners. But the history of such organizations goes back to the medieval guilds of artisans, which had much broader purposes, involving solidarity, support, and mutual benefit. If unions are to be of value today, they must overcome their tendency to serve as weapons in a class struggle; they must not take on the characteristics of political parties struggling for power or allow themselves to succumb to the class egoism that they deprecate in the capitalist class. They cannot be denied the right to strike, but strikes should be seen as a last resort and should not be abused in ways detrimental to the common good (LE 20).[6]

[6] The role of unions and other teachings of the encyclical are clearly set forth in Robert A. Destro,

While calling attention to problems such as those here mentioned, John Paul II denies that it is the Church's proper task to prescribe concrete solutions. Real and effective solutions "can arise only from within the framework of different historical situations through the efforts of all those who responsibly confront concrete problems in all their social, economic, political, and cultural aspects as these interact with one another" (CA 43). Every effort should be made to organize society in such a way that work is available for all who wish and need to work. The right to work must not be systematically denied (CA 43).

Theology of Leisure

Work, fruitful though it be, is not the goal of human existence. Inasmuch as work is for human beings, not they for it (LE 6), work must be understood in relation to leisure. John Paul II's thought on this matter is most thoroughly expounded in his apostolic letter, "The Day of the Lord," issued on Pentecost Sunday, 1998.[7]

Even on the purely humanistic level, cycles of work and rest are built into the natural order (DD 65). Intense application is normally followed by rest and recreation. By the precept of the Sunday observance, the Church lightens the burdens of servants and laborers and protects them from being abused (DD 66).

Rest, however, should not be a merely negative thing. Rather than degenerate into emptiness and boredom, it should be an affirmation of human dignity and contribute to personal growth (DD 68). It should be a time to cultivate family life, social relationships, cultural pursuits, and the enjoyment of the glories of nature (DD 52, 67).

On a higher level, observance of the Sabbath raises our minds beyond all creation to the contemplation of the Creator. God sets the example by taking the first Sabbath to contemplate the beauty of the world he has made (DD 11). In honoring God's rest, we are able to discover our dependence on the Creator and in so doing to achieve better understanding of our true condition (DD 61, 65).

In the Decalogue we are commanded to remember the Sabbath day and keep it holy (Deut. 20:8; DD 13, 62). We sanctify it by taking time to praise God and give thanks for his blessings (DD 16). Under the Mosaic Law the Sabbath day celebrated not only the gifts of creation but also the liberation given in the exodus (Deut. 5:15; DD 12, 17). The Christian Sunday observance goes a stage further by celebrating the liberation from the more radical evil of sin achieved for the whole human race through Christ's resurrection from the dead (DD 63). By its selection

---

"*Laborem exercens*," in *A Century of Catholic Social Thought,* ed. George Weigel and Robert Royal, (Washington, D.C.: Ethics and Public Policy Center, 1991), 145–61, esp. 149–50.

[7] John Paul II, "Observing and Celebrating the Day of the Lord," *Origins* 28 (July 30, 1998): 133–51.

of Sunday, Christianity recalls the day when Christ rose from the grave and entered into his Sabbath rest (Heb. 4:9-10; DD 8). Each Sunday also evokes the creation of light, which the first creation narrative situates on the first day (Gen. 1:3; DD 18, 24). Christ is the true light, the sun that knows no setting (DD 27, 37).

For the Church, Sunday has added significance as the day appointed for the regular assembly of the faithful, when they recall their identity as a people brought into unity by God, the *ekklesia* (DD 31). From another angle, Sunday may be seen as the eighth day, prefiguring the final consummation (DD 26, 37–38). By our Sunday worship we renew our energies and anticipate the final Sabbath rest of the people of God, "for whoever enters God's rest also ceases from his labors as God did from his" (Heb. 4:10; LE 25). By keeping Sundays holy the Church bears witness to its eschatological hope (DD 75).

Having this deep religious significance, Sunday must not be allowed to be swallowed up into vacuous weekends, in which people engage in frivolous or even morally questionable forms of entertainment (DD 4, 82). It should be the animating force of the entire week, the soul of the other six days (DD 83). Time given to God in prayer and worship is not lost (DD 7).

SOCIAL ORGANIZATION

Christian Responsibility

As a Pole living through the horrors of the Second World War, the Nazi occupation, and the disastrous consequences of the Yalta conference, Wojtyła became acutely conscious of violations of the rights of nations and of the devastations wrought by tyranny and war. Such calamities, he believes, have their ultimate root in human sinfulness, and more specifically in the inordinate appetite for possessions, power, and status. To prevent the inequities that breed violence and war, spiritual remedies are essential. The Church therefore has a right and a duty to use her influence on behalf of peace and justice. The quest for human rights, if it is not to bring about new conflicts, must itself be animated by the spirit of the gospel. The Church's religious mission, as noted by Vatican II, equips her with "a function, a light, and an energy that can serve to structure and consolidate the human community according to divine law" (GS 42). The "widest sphere of Christian responsibility," having to do with the promotion of peace and international community, is dealt with in the final chapter of *Gaudium et spes* (SR 305).

Building on texts such as this, Cardinal Wojtyła in *Sources of Renewal* proclaimed that economic cooperation is a basic tool of national communities and international institutions (SR 306). "The Council," he wrote, "emphasizes the value of the constructive presence of the Church in the international community, helping to strengthen peace throughout the world and to lay a solid foundation for the construction of fraternal union among all men by proclaiming the divine and natural law" (SR 307). As pope, Wojtyła has continued to speak of the spirit and structures needed if human and social development are to proceed according to the divine plan.

Socioeconomic Systems

On various occasions John Paul II has given some broad principles regarding the kinds of system that would be most compatible with the principles of natural law and revelation. He clearly rejects the Marxist ideology, which depends on a radically false anthropology and leads to class struggle, the "dictatorship of the proletariat," and the concentration of power in the hands of an oppressive elite (LE 11). But he is equally critical of "capitalist neo-liberalism," which, as he puts it, "subordinates the human person to blind market forces and conditions the development of peoples on those forces. From its centers of power, such neo-liberalism often places unbearable burdens upon less favored countries."[8]

Capitalism, however, can be admissible if one means by it "an economic system which recognizes the fundamental and positive role of business, the market, private property and the resulting responsibility for the means of production as well as free human creativity in the economic sector" (CA 42). The pope praises the free market as "the most efficient system for utilizing resources and effectively responding to needs" (CA 34). While asserting this much, he acknowledges that the mechanisms of the market often fail to take care of individual needs. State intervention may be needed to provide for such cases, to preserve the common good, and to safeguard the natural and human environments (CA 40).

Responsibility for securing human rights in the economic sector, according to the pope, belongs in part to the state but "it cannot mean one-sided centralization by the public authorities." Individuals, free groups, and local work centers and complexes must exercise their initiatives (LE 18). In the "welfare state" personal initiative is crushed and inefficiency abounds. At this point reference is made to the "principle of subsidiarity," according to which "a community of a higher order should not interfere in the internal life of a community of a lower order, depriving the latter of its functions" (CA 48). The family and other intermediate structures can frequently care for the needs of individuals who would otherwise be "suffocated between two poles represented by the state and the marketplace" (CA 49).

[8]John Paul II, "Homily in Havana's Plaza of the Revolution," §4; *Origins* 27 (February 5, 1998): 545-48, at 547.

International Solidarity

In his speeches and encyclicals John Paul II calls attention to urgent problems that cut across the boundaries of individual nations, such as care for the environment, international peace, the arms race, refugees, terrorism, and the marginalization of whole subcontinents in the spheres of economic and human development (LE 17; SRS 22–26; CA 58). He expresses his conviction that an adequate response to these problems requires the action of international agencies. Just as structures below the national state are needed for the protection of individuals, so also it is necessary, in the current phase of increasing globalization, to have effective international structures.

The Church's "preferential option for the poor" must be understood in a global context. In the past the Church, following the example and teaching of Jesus, has shown its love for the poor by personal care of individuals and by running charitable institutions. In our day these remedies no longer suffice. Since poverty is assuming massive proportions in spite of technological and economic progress, internationally coordinated measures on a global scale must be taken while there is still time to avert tragic crises (CA 57).

The increasing globalization of the economy can sometimes be degrading and impoverishing for needy and dependent nations, but it can also be beneficial if guided by the virtue of solidarity, with the realization that the goods of creation are divinely intended for all (SRS 39; CA 58). The "virtue of solidarity" in this context means "a firm and persevering determination to commit oneself to the common good; that is to say, to the good of all and of each individual, because we are *all* really responsible *for all*" (SRS 38).

In the past such solidarity has been conspicuously absent. The history of Europe, as seen by John Paul II, is marked by terrible events incompatible with the true spirit of humanity. In cruel wars "millions of people have been murdered because of their race, their nationality, their convictions, or simply because they were in the way."[9] As shown by persecutions and genocides, "the general acceptance of legitimate plurality on the social, civil and religious levels has been arrived at with great difficulty."[10] It is imperative to renounce the intransigent nationalism, selfish ambitions, and racist ideologies that have repeatedly led to oppression and war.[11] In a speech to UNESCO in 1980 the pope declared:

[9] John Paul II, "The Heart of Europe," speech at Vienna, September 10, 1983, §3; *Origins* 13 (September 29, 1983): 267–70, at 268.

[10] John Paul II, Visit to the Synagogue in Rome, April 13, 1986, §3; *Origins* 15 (April 24, 1986): 729–33, at 731.

[11] John Paul II, "Message Marking the 50th Anniversary of the War's End in Europe," May 16, 1995; *Origins* 25 (June 1, 1995): 33–39, at 36–37.

> Referring to the origins of your Organization, I stress the necessity of mobilizing all forces which direct the spiritual dimension of human existence, and which bear witness to the primacy of the spiritual in man . . . in order not to succumb again to the monstrous alienation of collective evil, which is always ready to use material powers in the exterminating struggle of men against men, of nations against nations.[12]

Respect for the inalienable rights of the human person, John Paul II believes, is the key to a more promising future. In his address to the General Assembly of the United Nations in New York in October 1979, he resoundingly affirmed his support for the Universal Declaration of Human Rights, describing it as "the basic inspiration and cornerstone of the United Nations organization."[13] He gave a detailed list of universally recognized human rights, which, he said, "concern the satisfaction of man's essential needs, the exercise of his freedoms and his relationships with others; but always they concern man, they concern man's full human dimension" (§13). Violation of such rights is, in the pope's view, "a form of warfare against humanity" (§16).

In his next visit to the United Nations General Assembly, on October 5, 1995, John Paul II returned to the theme of the rights of individuals and nations. He condemned exclusive nationalism and called for an ethic of solidarity. He appealed to the United Nations to "rise above the cold status of an administrative institution and to become a moral center where all nations of the world would feel at home and develop a shared awareness of being, as it were a 'family of nations.'"[14]

In this and similar addresses John Paul II has made it clear that faith and theology are not simply the private concern of persons who happen to belong to a certain religious group. They are public matters that the world ignores at its peril. Vatican II, in words quoted by Cardinal Wojtyła, addressed its teaching on the community of nations to a universal audience:

> Drawn from the treasures of the teaching of the Church, the proposals of this Council are intended for all men, whether they believe in God or whether they do not explicitly acknowledge him; they are intended to help them to a keener awareness of their own destiny, to make the world conform better to the surpassing dignity of man, and to meet the pressing appeals of our times with a generous and common effort of love. (GS 91; quoted in SR 309)

In this spirit John Paul II, speaking to the United Nations in 1995, expressed

---

[12] John Paul II, "Man's Entire Humanity Expressed in Culture," Address to UNESCO, Paris, June 2, 1980, §4; in *The Church and Culture since Vatican II,* ed. Joseph Gremillion (Notre Dame, Ind.: University of Notre Dame Press, 1985), 187–97, at 188-89. A different translation from the French original appears in *Origins* 10 (June 12, 1980): 58–64, at 60.

[13] John Paul II, "The U.N. Address," §9; *Origins* 9 (October 11, 1979): 257–66, at 260.

[14] John Paul II, "The Fabric of Relations among Peoples," §14; *Origins* 25 (October 19, 1995): 293–99, at 298.

his hope that God's loving care for all creation, as revealed in Jesus Christ, would put an end to hatred and intolerance and promote the solidarity of the entire human family. As we come to the close of the second Christian millennium, he declared, the peoples of the world must unite in a common effort to build a civilization of love, a true culture of freedom worthy of the human person. More succinctly, the pope said in another context: "Peace bears the name of Jesus Christ."[15]

CONCLUSION

The views of John Paul II on work, leisure, and the socioeconomic order are of a piece with his teaching on culture. He consistently opts for a personalism that contemplates human beings as free and responsible subjects, socially related to one another in community and ordered toward God as their final end. He is deeply conscious of the effects of sin, which lead us into conflict with ourselves, with one another, and with God. But he is even more conscious of the redemptive grace of Christ, which liberates us from the burden of sin and redirects us toward our true goal.

The pope stands firmly in the tradition of Catholic social teaching from Leo XIII through Vatican II and the recent popes. He defends private property and economic initiative against all forms of totalitarian socialism. In *Centesimus annus* he comes close to endorsing free-market capitalism, but even in this encyclical he is on guard against individualistic liberalism. He recognizes the necessity of state control to prevent wealth and power from falling into the hands of a privileged class or privileged nations. The Church, he believes, has an indispensable role in making people aware of their inherent dignity and their eternal destiny. If its voice is heard, the Church can make a unique contribution toward fashioning a civilization of peace and love.

[15] John Paul II, Closing address at Assisi, October 27, 1986, §4; *Origins* 16 (November 6, 1986): 370–71, at 370.

CHAPTER 11

The Free Person in a Free Society

PERSONAL FREEDOM

V ATICAN II's PASTORAL CONSTITUTION on the Church in the Modern World has five chapters. We have already dealt with the themes of the first three and the fifth: those on culture, the family, the economy, and the international community. It remains for us to discuss how John Paul II has responded to the concerns of the chapter on the political community, in which the council addresses the questions of human rights, the common good, civil liberty, and Church–state relations. Before plunging directly into social and political aspects it will be helpful to sketch the main lines of Wojtyła's analysis of human freedom in relation to conscience and the law of God. Vatican II dealt with this personal aspect of freedom in the first chapter of *Gaudium et spes* and in its Declaration on Religious Freedom, *Dignitatis humanae*.

The Concept of Freedom

The word has different though analogous meanings at the natural and the personal levels. At the lowest level, that of nature, freedom means only the absence of physical constraint. A balloon rises freely when nothing obstructs it; a stone falls freely when nothing impedes it. A dog is free if it is let off the leash so that it can follow its impulses. To be free, in this sense, is to act according to an inner inclination. To be unfree is to have that inclination frustrated.

At a higher level, distinctive to persons, freedom demands, in addition, the absence of psychological compulsion. My freedom as a person is diminished to the extent that instinct or passion compels me to act in certain ways, for example, to flee from danger or flinch with pain.

If my motives could never transcend my individual self-interest or the collective self-interest of my group, I could never be psychologically free. I could always be manipulated and compelled to act in specific ways by fear of punishment or hope of reward. Just as animals can be drawn or driven by the dangling of a carrot or the wielding of a whip, so a child can be induced to behave in certain ways by the prospect of gratification or the fear of pain. Unless we were able to escape from the determinism of instinct or appetite, we could always be forced to act by promises and threats.

One of the benefits of training and discipline is to enhance our zone of inner freedom. By education and exercise we develop the motivation and character that enable us to resist physical and especially psychological pressures. Some learn to go for long periods without sleep, to abstain from food, or to endure intense physical pain without abandoning their resolve. Such heroic persons have greater freedom than others. They have a larger zone of inner self-determination.

In determining my own course of action, I cannot dispense with motives. If choices were completely arbitrary, freedom would be meaningless and in the last analysis impossible. In my free actions I follow what I apprehend as good and worthy of being chosen, but the choice is not forced upon me. I consent to the attraction because my reason approves of it. In acting freely I experience myself as the source of my own activity and as responsible for the results.

In *Veritatis splendor* the pope quotes St. Gregory of Nyssa on the royal dignity that pertains to those who have this kind of dominion over themselves. "The soul shows its royal and exalted character . . . in that it is free and self-governed, swayed autonomously by its own will. Of whom else can this be said, save a king?" (VS 38).[1] According to the pope, freedom does not attain this royal dignity until it rises to the level of making choices that perfect the dynamism of the human spirit toward the divine, following motives that solicit, but do not coerce, its free adherence. To this effect the pope quotes from Vatican II: "God willed to leave them [human beings] in the hands of their own counsel (cf. Sir. 15:14), so that they would seek their Creator of their own accord and would freely arrive at full and blessed perfection by cleaving to God" (GS 17; VS 38).

The moral law, as known to reason, does not constrain us; it leaves us physically and psychologically free either to obey it or not. But if we reject the true good, we yield to the passions and instincts of our lower nature and thereby undermine our authentic freedom. To act freely against the truth is to erode freedom itself.

Freedom and Truth

The rootedness of freedom in truth has been a constant and central theme in the writings of John Paul II. As a young bishop at Vatican II he made two speeches and three written interventions on the subject of religious liberty, and in each case

---

[1] The quotation is from Gregory of Nyssa, *De hominis opificio*, chap. 4 (PG 44:135–36).

he emphasized the importance of getting beyond mere tolerance and promoting adherence to the truth as the norm of freedom. The earlier drafts of the Declaration on Religious Freedom in his judgment failed to bring out the connection with truth. This theme should not be skirted, he said, "for freedom on the one hand is for the sake of truth and on the other hand it cannot be perfected except by means of truth. Hence the words of our Lord, which speak so clearly to everyone: 'The truth will make you free' (John 8:32). There is no freedom without truth."[2]

This same theme permeates Wojtyła's teaching as pope. In his first encyclical, *Redemptor hominis*, he quotes again the words of Christ, "You will know the truth, and the truth will make you free." He adds: "These words contain both a fundamental requirement and a warning: the requirement of an honest relationship with regard to truth as a condition for authentic freedom, and the warning to avoid every kind of illusory freedom, every superficial unilateral freedom, every freedom that fails to enter into the whole truth about man and the world" (RH 12).

As has already been noted, we possess this freedom only when we go beyond individual and collective selfishness and reach out to that which reason perceives to be objectively good and true. Our freedom is not diminished but expanded and fulfilled when we employ it to achieve what is truly good. In *Veritatis splendor* the pope quotes from Vatican II to the effect that when we act through conscious and free choice, as our dignity requires, we are prompted personally from within, and not determined by external pressure or blind impulse (VS 42; cf. GS 17).

John Paul II's philosophy of freedom runs counter to the value-free concept so prevalent in contemporary culture, perhaps especially in the United States. Many people today would say that freedom and truth are wholly separable, since anyone is free to affirm the truth and abide by it, to ignore the truth, and even to deny it and act against it. If freedom were bound by truth, they ask, how could it be freedom? In the course of his discussion of freedom and law in *Veritatis splendor* the pope answers by insisting that it is in cleaving to the truth that we are, as Christ taught, made truly free. He rejects a whole series of ethical systems that propose novel criteria for the moral evaluation of human action. Despite their variety, he declares, systems such as utilitarianism, pragmatism, proportionalism, and consequentialism are at one in minimizing or even denying the dependence of freedom upon truth (VS 34; cf. 74–75).

Freedom and Generosity

In an important paper on *The Personal Structure of Self-Determination*, Cardinal Wojtyła makes a further inference, based on the relational character of the person. Every person, he maintains, is both a being willed by God for itself and at the

[2]AS III/2, 530–32, at 531.

same time a being turned toward others. To be isolated from others is a form of self-imprisonment. We become most truly human in the measure that we go out of ourselves and give ourselves for the sake of others. This "law of the gift," as the pope calls it, is inscribed in the dynamic structure of the person as fashioned in the image of the divine. He confirms this insight by quoting from Vatican II: "The human being, who is the only creature on earth that God willed for itself, cannot attain its full identity except through a disinterested gift of self" (GS 24). The citizen serves the common good out of a free commitment or devotion. Those who love God serve him freely, and in giving that service they enhance their freedom.

Obedience to the truth that comes from God should not be regarded as a form of heteronomy or self-alienation, as though God were a hostile power imposing terms on humanity as a defeated enemy. His love proceeds from pure benevolence toward his creatures. By embracing God's will for me I follow my own deepest vocation. By submitting to God's law, I fulfill the law of my being as a creature made to the image and likeness of God, who is present in my inmost depths (cf. VS 41).

The supreme exemplars of freedom, for John Paul II, are the martyrs—men and women so committed to the known good that they stand up under pressures that would be too great for others. Given the choice between denying their principles and losing their lives, they freely accept death and thereby give witness to the sovereignty of truth. Jesus, who freely laid down his life for our sakes, sets the pattern for martyrs (VS 90–94).

The martyrs are exceptional cases. For the theology of freedom it is important to recognize that the freedom with which we are born is frail and limited. John Paul II compares it to a seed that must be cultivated. Some degree of freedom is constitutive of human nature, but because of original sin we are inclined to prefer limited and ephemeral goods to those that are pure and abiding. We are even tempted to assert our freedom against our Creator, as if freedom could exist apart from God who rules our destinies. But Christ the Redeemer helps to liberate us from this illusion. As Paul writes in Galatians 5:1, "For freedom Christ has set us free." Because Christ is the truth, it is also true to say, according to the passage already quoted, that the truth sets us free (John 8:32; VS 86).

Freedom and Law

By the law of the covenant, Christ brings his people out of bondage and unites them to himself. The Sinai Covenant of the Old Testament has been perfected by the new law of the gospel, which Scripture describes as an interior law "written not with ink but with the Spirit of the living God, not on tablets of stone, but on tablets of human hearts" (2 Cor. 3:3, quoted in VS 45).[3]

---

[3] In VS 45 the pope refers also to Jer. 31:31–33, Rom. 8:2, Gal. 5:6, and 2 Cor. 3:17.

As a new and interior law the gospel teaches us both by enlightening our minds and by instilling a love and affection for the truth (VS 45). The divinely given attraction toward the true goal of human existence, which is none other than God himself, does not impede our freedom of choice, since it inclines us to the very thing that right reason would select. The inner instinct of grace heals our rebellious wills and inclines us to do as God wills. In so doing it removes an obstacle to freedom—our innate tendency to pursue the immediate and apparent good rather than the ultimate and true good. The divine attraction brings us closer to the final condition of the blessed in heaven, who cannot do other than love God but who do so freely because they see how lovable God is (VS 23–24).

Freedom and Conscience

In speaking of the interior law of the gospel we begin to touch on the theme of conscience. Some thinkers today depict conscience as a supreme tribunal that dispenses us from the control of truth and law, substituting for these principles purely subjective criteria such as sincerity, authenticity, and being at peace with oneself (VS 32, p. 53). In opposition to this view, John Paul II shows in *Veritatis splendor* that conscience is an act of intelligence guided by objective norms. His treatment of the point follows closely the lines of Paul in Rom. 2:14–16 (VS 54–57; cf. GS 16). Conscience, so considered, is an unwritten law, inscribed by God in the human heart. The pope quotes Bonaventure to the effect that conscience is a herald or messenger sent into the world by God to relay his commands (VS 58). Without this divine mandate conscience would have no binding force.

John Paul II's treatment of conscience is very similar to that of John Henry Newman in his *Letter to the Duke of Norfolk*. Like Newman, he denies that conscience is a power that exempts us from all higher authority and authorizes us to do what we please. On the contrary, it is a stern monitor that requires us to seek out what is truly good. Far from dispensing us from authority, it impels us to seek out the best authoritative guidance we can get. The pope quotes Newman to the effect that "conscience has rights because it has its duties" (VS 34).[4] The freedom of conscience is, as the pope expresses it, freedom in the truth, but never freedom from the truth (VS 64).

Freedom and Vocation

Although we are not at liberty to act in defiance of the divine law, that law allows for a great variety in the choice of vocations—whether to be a carpenter or a

---

[4] The reference is to Newman's "Letter to the Duke of Norfolk," §5, "Conscience," reprinted in *Newman and Gladstone: The Vatican Decrees*, ed. Alvan A. Ryan (Notre Dame, Ind. University of Notre Dame, 1962), 130.

lawyer, married or celibate, etc. God invites us to make creative decisions, consonant with the moral law. The first chapter of *Veritatis splendor* is an extended meditation on the call of the rich young man in Matthew 19. John Paul II calls attention to the distinction between the fulfillment of the commandments, which is required by everyone for the sake of salvation, and the counsels, whereby some are exhorted to seek a higher perfection. God may invite us, without compelling us, to go beyond what sheer conformity to the law requires. Obedience to the commandments is required of every human being as a condition for salvation; some individuals receive, over and above the commandments, a particular vocation whereby they are invited to follow freely what God offers to them as the path to a more perfect freedom. Presumably the rich young man could have saved his soul by continuing to observe the precepts of the Decalogue, as he had been doing for years, but he was anxious to do more. When he learned what was needed for him to be perfect, however, he did not have the inner freedom from attachments that was needed to follow the higher call (VS 16–18; cf. Church 555–58).

Religious Freedom

John Paul II strongly affirms the duty of every human being to search for religious truth and to adhere to it once that truth becomes known. At the same time he insists, as did Vatican II in its Declaration on Religious Freedom, that the search must be a free one. No one can be forced to accept the truth of faith. It belongs to the very nature of the act of faith that it be free (DH 10). The pope recognizes, however, that the freedom of religion has not always been respected, even by rulers professing the Catholic faith. History is full of examples of attempts to make conversions by the sword, even though theologians have frequently protested against these methods (CTH 190–92). Adherents of practically all religious faiths, Christian or non-Christian, Protestant, Catholic, and Orthodox, were guilty of similar excesses. Only fairly recently has the doctrine of religious freedom won general recognition in Western society (TMA 35).

THE FREE SOCIETY

Human Rights

In his political philosophy John Paul II, following the lead of Vatican II and recent popes, professes a robust doctrine of human rights. As a young priest in Poland he was convinced that this theme enabled Christians to call attention to major weaknesses in the philosophy of Marxism. Ontologically, Wojtyła maintains, the right to freedom accrues to human beings because of their rational nature, which makes them inherently capable of deciding for themselves in the light of conscience.[5] The inherent dignity of the human person is the presupposition of any and all rights. In *Love and Responsibility* Wojtyła sets forth what he calls the "personalistic principle," to the effect that the only suitable attitude toward persons is one of love.[6] Every person has a right not to be treated by others as a mere object of pleasure or convenience (CTH 201).

In the light of revelation, John Paul II solidifies and expands the basis for human rights. Their obligatory character, he argues, arises because the dynamism of human nature, with its freedom and rationality, is not a mere accident of nature but reflects the eternal law of God, from which all moral obligations derive. Only God, the supreme good, constitutes the unshakable foundation and essential condition of morality (VS 99).

The transcendent dignity of the human person derives most fundamentally from being created as a visible image of the invisible God. More than this, we are "redeemed by the blood of Christ, and made holy by the presence of the Holy Spirit" (VS 10). Our human dignity is fully revealed in Christ, whose sacrifice eloquently expresses how precious we are in the eyes of the Creator. Tarnished by sin, our dignity is definitively restored through the cross and shown forth in the resurrection (cf. RH 10).

Among human rights, first place should no doubt be accorded to the right to life, which is the principal theme of the long encyclical *Evangelium vitae*. Here the pope teaches that because human life has a sacred and inviolable character, it is always gravely immoral to destroy innocent human life. He then applies this general principle with special emphasis to two cases: abortion and euthanasia, both of which he brands as heinous crimes. In his discussion of abortion he warns against experimentation on embryos (EV 63), and in treating euthanasia he rejects the legitimacy of suicide and physician-assisted suicide (EV 66). He admits that in self-defense it may sometimes be necessary to kill aggressors (EV 55) and he concedes, very reluctantly, that capital punishment can be warranted when there is no other way to protect society against criminals. But he adds that "as a result of steady improvements in the organization of the penal system, such cases are very rare if not practically nonexistent" (EV 56).

Human rights, according to John Paul II, do not derive from positive law, either human or divine, but are inscribed in the very nature of reality. When we are forbidden to murder, commit adultery, steal, bear false witness, and the like, these negative rules, according to the pope, "express with particular force the ever

[5] Karol Wojtyła (John Paul II), *Love and Responsibility* (New York: Farrar, Straus, Giroux, 1981), 21–24.

[6] Ibid., 41.

urgent need to protect human life, the communion of persons in marriage, private property, truthfulness, and people's good name" (VS 13).

The Transcendent Ground
of Political Freedom

The Second Vatican Council in its Pastoral Constitution on the Church in the Modern World put the Catholic Church on record as opposing totalitarian and dictatorial regimes (GS 75) and as favoring forms of government that allow "the largest numbers of citizens to participate in public affairs with genuine freedom" (GS 31; cf. 35). As a proponent of the council's teaching John Paul II has been consistently favorable to free and participatory societies.

During his visits to the United States the pope has taken the occasion to comment on his enthusiasm for the Declaration of Independence and on the moral and spiritual principles underlying the Constitution. At a meeting with President Reagan on September 10, 1987, he recalled how the American Constitution, whose bicentennial was then being celebrated, testified to the connection between freedom and truth:

> The only true freedom, the only freedom that can truly satisfy is the freedom to do what we ought as human beings created by God according to his plan. It is the freedom to live the truth of what we are and who we are before God, the truth of our identity as children of God, as brothers and sisters in a common humanity.[7]

The most complete expression of the pope's thinking on democracy is found perhaps in *Centesimus annus*, where he points out that authentic democracy is possible only on the basis of a correct conception of the human person. Human rights cannot be secure unless they are founded in God the Creator. If all human beings are created equal, and are entitled to life, liberty, and the pursuit of happiness, this is because God has made them to his own image and likeness. Without this transcendent grounding, human rights would not be inviolable (CA 44). Yet this transcendent basis is widely questioned today. He writes:

> Nowadays there is a tendency to claim that agnosticism and skeptical relativism are the philosophy and the basic attitude which correspond to democratic forms of political life. Those who are convinced that they know the truth and firmly adhere to it are considered unreliable from a democratic point of view, since they do not accept that truth is determined by the majority or that it is subject to variation according to different political trends. (CA 46)

---

[7] John Paul II, "The Miami Meeting with President Reagan," *Origins* 17 (September 24, 1987): 238–39, at 238.

To this the pope responds: "If there is no ultimate truth to guide and direct political activity, then ideas and convictions can easily be manipulated for reasons of power. As history demonstrates, a democracy without values easily turns into open or thinly disguised totalitarianism" (ibid.).

In *Evangelium vitae* the pope carries this critique of majoritarian democracy and ethical relativism to greater lengths. Democracy, he declares, may not be idolized. As a system of government, it is only a means to an end. Its moral value is not automatic, but depends on conformity to the moral law to which it, like every other form of human behavior, must be subject. Democracy stands or falls with the values it embodies and promotes, such as respect for inalienable human rights and for the common good (EV 70).

If the state is entitled to legalize the direct killing of innocent human beings on the basis of a majority vote, law becomes an instrument of injustice and loses its power to oblige in conscience. Conscience, in fact, demands disobedience to laws that seriously violate innate human rights, such as the right to life, which is most fundamental.

> The basis of these values [true rights] cannot be provisional and changeable "majority" opinions, but only the acknowledgement of an objective moral law, which, as the "natural law" written in the human heart, is the obligatory point of reference for civil law itself. If, as a result of a tragic obscuring of the collective conscience, an attitude of skepticism were to succeed in bringing into question even the fundamental principles of the moral law, the democratic system itself would be shaken to its foundations, and would be reduced to a mere mechanism for regulating different and opposing interests on a purely empirical basis. (EV 70)

The criterion of majority voting, according to the pope, is unreliable because the most powerful members of society, through their control of the media of communication, are often in a position to maneuver the votes, manipulate the opinion polls, and shape the formation of a majority consensus. To use an example that the pope does not use: Hitler may have had the support of the majority of the German people, but this does not justify his measures against the Jews and his war crimes.

Conscientious Disobedience

Toward the end of the third chapter of *Evangelium vitae* John Paul II speaks of the problems faced by Catholics in a society that condones or even requires abortion, euthanasia, and the like. He writes:

> Laws that authorize and promote abortion and euthanasia are radically opposed not only to the good of the individual but also to the common good; as such they are completely lacking in authentic juridical validity. . . . Consequently, a civil law authorizing abortion or euthanasia ceases by that very fact to be a true, morally binding civil law. (EV 72)

In the following paragraph he goes on to say that there is no obligation in conscience to obey such laws; instead there is a grave and clear obligation to oppose them by conscientious objection. He compares such laws to the law of Pharaoh commanding that all newborn males of Hebrew parentage be put to death. The midwives, fearing God, refused to obey that law, and thereby saved the life of Moses. Their heroic conduct illustrates the general principle that in case of conflict, God rather than human authorities is to be obeyed (EV 73).

Because laws authorizing crimes against human life are intrinsically unjust, we are forbidden to obey them, to vote for them, or to campaign in favor of them. Yet there are difficult cases, in which a person must decide whether to support a law that restricts abortion to certain cases rather than allowing it across the board. John Paul II teaches that to support the more restrictive alternative would not amount to unjust cooperation, but that politicians supporting laws that legalize abortions in certain cases should make their opposition to abortion known, so as to avoid scandal (ibid.).

The pope then goes into a discussion of the general principles governing cooperation. He makes the standard distinctions between formal and material cooperation, and between immediate and remote material cooperation. This is not the place in which to delve into these fine and technical distinctions. It may be worth mentioning that he treats immediate material cooperation as tantamount to formal cooperation. One never has the right to participate directly in the act of killing an innocent human being on the pretext that some human authority permits or requires it. Each person must take responsibility for his or her own actions (EV 74).

Political and Social Rights

The right to life, which is the central theme of *Evangelium vitae*, is in the pope's view only the first and most fundamental of many human rights. Repeatedly in his writings John Paul II refers with approval to the Universal Declaration of Human Rights that was adopted by the United Nations in 1948. In his address to the United Nations in 1979 he enumerated, among human rights that are universally recognized, "the right to life, liberty, and the security of the person; the right to food, clothing, housing, sufficient health care, rest and leisure; the right to freedom of expression, education, and culture; the right to freedom of thought, conscience, and religion." The list, too long to be quoted here in its entirety, ended with the "right to political participation and the right to participate in the free choice of the political system of the people to which one belongs."[8]

All these lists of human rights are abstract. The pope clearly recognizes that philosophical and theological principles cannot automatically be translated into

[8]Address to United Nations General Assembly, §13; *Origins* 9 (October 11, 1979): 257–66, at 262.

positive law or judicial practice. The talents of statesmen and jurists are needed to determine the respective responsibilities of the state and of private agencies in securing these rights, and the extent to which a given right—for example, the right to education or to free expression—can be positively implemented in a given situation. In the personalist framework of Wojtyła's thought, the social nature of human beings is not completely fulfilled by the state. According to the principle of subsidiarity, intermediary groups, such as the family, the neighborhood, and private voluntary agencies, should be relied on to the extent possible (CA 13, 48). The state does not have a responsibility to solve every social problem or prosecute every moral evil (CA 11). So far as possible, the state refrains from intervening in the private sector, which lies beyond its ordinary competence. Not every moral right, therefore, can be translated into a legal right. Conversely, one may have a legal right to perform a certain action without having a moral right to do so.

Relations between Church and State

In its Pastoral Constitution *Gaudium et spes* and its Declaration on Religious Freedom, *Dignitatis humanae*, Vatican II renounced any claims that the Church might have made to enjoy a privileged status as the religion of the state. While allowing for a diversity of Church–state relationships, it insisted on the universal human right to worship according to one's conscientious convictions (DH 6). The state was seen as having a limited competence that did not extend to deciding questions of religious truth or enforcing adherence to the true religion (GS 74-75). The state and the Church were seen as having different spheres of competence and disposing of different sets of means. The state, responsible for the peace, prosperity, and good order of the civil community, has the right to use coercive power when necessary to avoid serious evils. The Church, which is responsible for proclaiming the truth of the gospel to all and for administering the means of salvation to its own faithful, uses only the power of the word of God and of persuasion. In the words of John Paul II, "The Church addresses people with full respect for their freedom. Her mission does not restrict freedom but rather promotes it. *The Church proposes; she imposes nothing*" (RMis 39).

Following Vatican II, John Paul II describes the state and the Church as two relatively independent societies, whose concerns at certain points intersect. The members of both institutions will be best served if the two cooperate harmoniously without seeking to perform each other's tasks (SR 416–17). The Church has the right to insist on its freedom to preach the gospel, administer the sacraments, and exercise pastoral care over its members. As the pope told the bishops of Cuba, the Church, when it asks for religious freedom, "is not asking for a gift, a privilege or a permission dependent on contingent situations, political strategies or the will of the authorities. Rather she demands the effective recognition of an inalienable right."[9] All citizens have the right and duty to seek the truth about God and to profess their faith. The state, therefore, may not enforce atheism or discriminate against citizens on the ground of their religion. The Church, for its part, teaches its members to serve the common good of the secular society, to perform their civic duties, and to obey just laws (RH 17).

In the course of history the proper distinction between the spiritual and the secular powers has not always been respected by the one or the other. On his visit to the Parliament of Europe, the pope deplored what he called "integralism":

> Our European history clearly reveals just how often the boundary between "what belongs to Caesar" and "what belongs to God" has been overstepped in both directions. Medieval Latin Christianity—just to take an example—despite the fact that it evolved the natural concept of the Sate, harkening back to the great tradition of Aristotle, fell into the integralist trap of excluding from the temporal community all those who did not profess the true faith. Religious integralism, which does not distinguish between the spheres of influence of faith and civil life, and which is still practiced today in other parts of the world, would seem to be incompatible with the spirit of Europe as it was forged by the Christian message.[10]

On various occasions the pope alludes to the principle "*cuius regio eius religio*" as a particularly noxious violation of religious freedom, leading to forced conversions or cruel expulsions inflicted on Protestants and Catholics, depending on the principality in which they found themselves.[11] It is unjust for the state to demand that members of the civic community profess the faith of their secular ruler. The bitter conflicts resulting from integralism in its various forms can only be resolved by a better theology of ecumenism and interfaith relations, the theme of our next chapter.

CONCLUSION

Karol Wojtyła, as a personalist moral theologian, has thought long and deeply about human dignity and freedom. He attaches great importance to the capacity

[9] John Paul II, "Remarks to the Nation's Bishops," January 25, 1998, §3; *Origins* 27 (February 5, 1998): 562–64, at 563.

[10] John Paul II, "The United Europe of Tomorrow," Strasbourg, October 11, 1988, §10; *Origins* 18 (October 27, 1988): 330–32, at 332.

[11] See, for example, the remarks of John Paul II at his meeting with the evangelical community in Salzburg, Austria, on June 26, 1988, and his remarks at his general audience of July 5, 1995, on his return from Slovakia. These remarks are quoted in Luigi Accattoli, *When a Pope Asks Forgiveness* (Staten Island, N.Y.: Alba House, 1998), 149 and 148 respectively.

of persons to make their own decisions without external coercion. But he is no libertarian. For him freedom is not an end in itself but a means to attain what is truly and intrinsically good. Freedom, he holds, destroys itself when it pits itself against the true and the good. But when it adheres to the known good in the face of pressures to forsake it, freedom realizes itself most strikingly, as in cases of martyrdom.

Obedience to conscience, far from constricting freedom, allows it to achieve its true purpose. The Church has gradually advanced in its appreciation of freedom of conscience. Although in the past force has sometimes been used in the service of religious truth, the Church of our day proclaims that adherence to the faith must necessarily be free.

John Paul II has been an ardent apostle of human dignity and human rights. He maintains that in any and all circumstances the human person must be treated with respect as a creature made to the image and likeness of God, redeemed by the blood of Christ, and called to share forever in the blessedness of the triune God.

From the basic dignity of the human person John Paul II concluded to the inviolability of innocent human life. He strongly opposes abortion, euthanasia, and suicide. Rights and duties are, in his view, correlative. The biblical prohibitions against murder, adultery, theft, and false witness, therefore, may be seen as the reverse side of the right to life and the rights of married love, personal property, and a good reputation.

Because he anchors human rights firmly in the natural law, the pope effectively guards against spurious rights to do what is morally wrong. Because he adheres to the principle of subsidiarity, he does not allow the doctrine of rights to justify an omnicompetent welfare state.

John Paul II is favorable to democracy in the sense that he welcomes the full participation of citizens in public affairs. But he also insists that principles of justice and morality cannot be settled by majority vote. Individuals and societies are obliged to conform to the moral law as known through right reason and clarified by revelation, not to twist truth and morality to their own preferences.

Building as he does on the achievements of Vatican II, John Paul II holds for a clear distinction between the competences of Church and state. He recognizes that the state, because of its strictly temporal mission, has no authority to adjudicate questions of religious truth or to suppress religious error, except insofar as aberrations disturb civil peace and public order. Conversely the Church, with its purely spiritual mission, lacks any mandate to impose truth by force. The Church is content to live in a free society that grants equal protection to different religions, provided that it enjoys the freedom to carry on its evangelizing mission. The gospel must be preached in its fullness. Because it has implications for the order-

ing of human society, the Church, according to John Paul II, can make a distinctive contribution to the promotion of a civilization of peace and love.

On all these points, the pope stands in perfect continuity with Vatican II, John
XXIII, and Paul VI. He consistently upholds the conciliar teaching against any
resurgent integralism on the one hand and against relativistic agnosticism on the
other.

CHAPTER 12

Ecumenism
and the Religions

⌒⌒

THE RELATIONSHIP OF CHRISTIANITY to other religions got off to a negative start in the early centuries, which were marked by hostile confrontations first with Judaism and then with the Hellenistic religions. Then came the struggles against heresy, in which the Catholic authors depicted dissident groups in wholly pejorative terms. The Reformation spawned defensive and polemical attitudes that became deeply ingrained in the Catholicism of the next few centuries. But with Vatican II the official attitude of the Catholic Church underwent a decisive change, anticipated by private theological initiatives in the preceding fifty years. In its Decree on Ecumenism and its Declaration on Non-Christian Religions the council took a predominantly positive stance. Without denying or trivializing the existing differences, the council proposed to emphasize, as far as possible, the common elements and to increase the measure of agreement through honest and respectful dialogue.

Karol Wojtyła as a bishop participated eagerly in this shift of attitude. During his stay in Rome as a bishop at the council, he is reported to have said in conversation with a close friend:

> The prime objective in his [Pope John's] mind was that of Christian unity, and we have already come a long way in that direction. The Church feels as never before that what unites Christians is stronger than what divides them. It has recognized the Christian values in other churches, has accepted its share of blame and responsibility for our divisions. The longing for [Christian] unity is accompanied by a longing for unity among the whole human race. The new conception of the [Church as the pilgrim] "people of God" has thrown fresh light on the old truth about the possibility of salvation outside the limits of the Church.[1]

---

[1]Karol Wojtyła, in conversation reported by Mieczyslaw Malinski, quoted by George H. Williams, *The Mind of John Paul II* (New York: Seabury, 1981), 168.

Although these may not be the exact words used by Bishop Wojtyła, all the elements in this quotation ring true. In the first part of this chapter we shall see how as pope he has toiled for Christian unity, and in the second part, how he has promoted a Christian universalism that is intended to contribute to solidarity among men and women of all religious persuasions.

ECUMENISM

The Priority of Ecumenism

Since the beginning of his pontificate John Paul II has formally committed himself to ecumenism as one of his highest pastoral priorities.[2] Vatican II, he declares, has irreversibly expressed the Catholic Church's commitment to the ecumenical movement. His lengthy encyclical on ecumenism, *Ut unum sint*, is the first encyclical dedicated to Christian unity since Vatican II.

Here and there in his writings John Paul II gives many reasons for his emphasis on ecumenism. Five may here be mentioned. The first is that Jesus Christ, on the night before his passion, prayed that all his disciples might be one, as he and the Father are one, so that their wonderful union might bring the world to believe. Since Christ wills this visible unity, the pope observes, it cannot be seen as impossible, as merely optional, or as marginal to the mission of the Church. Ecumenism is a permanent and essential priority in the calling of all Christians.[3]

A second motive for ecumenical commitment derives from the fact that the movement, according to Vatican II, has been stirred up by the Holy Spirit (UR 1). It is therefore a holy cause that claims the allegiance of all the faithful.

The movement is, in the third place, grounded in the very nature of the Church, which is solemnly charged to bring the gospel to all humanity. The mission of the Church, like that of Christ, is universal. The disunity of Christians gravely damages the effectiveness of Christian witness. It is a scandal that deters people from believing the gospel.

A fourth motive is the evident benefit that ecumenism confers on the churches, as shown from past experience. In his encyclical *Ut unum sint*, the pope has a chapter of some forty pages describing some of the gains already achieved. The universal brotherhood of Christians, he says, has become a firm ecumenical conviction (UUS 42). Significant convergences have been attained in the biblical and

---

[2] John Paul II, Address to the Roman Curia on June 28, 1985, §10; *Origins* 15 (July 18, 1985): 125–28, at 128.

[3] John Paul II, Allocution at Meeting with the Armenian Patriarch, Chnork Kalustian, on November 29, 1979; John Paul II, *Addresses and Homilies on Ecumenism 1978–1980*, ed. J. B. Sheerin and J. F. Hotchkin (Washington, D.C.: United States Catholic Conference, 1980), 68–70, at 69.

liturgical areas. Many common statements have been issued expressing the grow-ing doctrinal rapprochement. Even short of achieving full mutual recognition and communion, the churches have been able to collaborate in many practical areas.

Fifthly, the pope maintains that our ecumenical efforts have special urgency as the second millennium of Christianity nears its end. In his apostolic letter on preparations for the coming jubilee the pope notes that for a worthy celebration of that occasion it is important that Christians be able to show themselves more closely united than they have been in the past (TMA 45).

Goals of Ecumenism

Debates have arisen regarding the aims of the ecumenical movement. In 1995, in the course of an official visit to the Holy See, the general secretary of the World Council of Churches, Konrad Raiser, declared that the churches should deliber-ately ignore the old disputes about doctrine and devote themselves to the new questions revolving about peace, justice, and the protection of the environment.[4] Rejecting the goal of structured unity sealed by agreed doctrinal formulations, Raiser proposed what he called "a much more dynamic understanding of unity—unity as process."[5]

John Paul II, however, is unwilling to settle for unity as a mere process or a simple coalition for secular objectives. Ecumenism, he holds, is aimed at the full unity in faith and love, in life and work, of all who confess the one Lord Jesus Christ.[6] He repeatedly declares that the ultimate goal of the ecumenical move-ment is to reestablish full visible unity among all the baptized (UUS 77). On occa-sion he speaks of organic unity,[7] "constituted by the bonds of the profession of faith, the sacraments, and hierarchical communion" (UUS 9).

Ecumenical Strategy

In his ecumenical theology John Paul II favors what might be called a *communio* model. The objective is not uniformity or absorption but fullness of commu-

---

[4] Konrad Raiser, "Thirty Years in the Service of the Ecumenical Movement: The Joint Working Group between the Roman Catholic Church and the World Council of Churches," conference given at the Centro Pro Unione, Rome, April 4, 1995; *Centro Pro Unione Semi-annual Bulletin* 48 (Fall 1995): 2–8.

[5] Konrad Raiser, Interview for *Radio Vaticana*, as published in their *Radiogiornale* of April 10, 1995; quoted by Edward Cardinal Cassidy, "That They May Be One: The Imperatives and Prospects of Christian Unity," unpublished address of September 16, 1995.

[6] John Paul II, Address to Delegates of National Ecumenical Commissions, November 23, 1979; *Addresses and Homilies,* 52–56, at 53.

[7] John Paul II, Address at Ecumenical Gathering at Nairobi, Kenya, May 7, 1980; *Addresses and Homilies*, 103–5, at 104.

nion—that is to say, shared life in the one holy catholic and apostolic Church, expressed by a common celebration of the Eucharist (UUS 78). The Latin term *communio*, like the Greek *koinōnia*, is used to express something more than mere human fellowship; it is a mysterious gift bestowed by Christ on his Church, transcending all the human causes of division. Wherever there is Christian faith or sacramental life a measure of *communio* is already present. All who believe in Christ and are baptized in his name exist in a profound, even if still imperfect, communion, thanks to the active presence of the Holy Spirit in one and all. The ecumenical process is a movement from the partial communion already enjoyed toward the perfect communion to which we aspire. The first stage of the process consists in recognizing and manifesting the incomplete fellowship that now unites us.[8]

This partial communion is made up of many elements. The vast majority of Christians believe in one God, Father, Son, and Holy Spirit. Practically all Christians baptize in the name of the triune God. They share identical, or almost identical, Scriptures and recite many of the same prayers, including the "Our Father." For the most part, Christians accept early creeds such as the Apostles' Creed and that of Constantinople (often called the Nicene Creed). Building on common elements such as these, the churches can converge toward ever fuller communion in the Lord.

Spiritual Ecumenism

Having glanced at the goal and the basic strategy, we may now turn to the means or methods. John Paul II gives pride of place to spiritual ecumenism, whereby Christians dispose themselves for what God may be pleased to do through them. The first requirement of the ecumenist, according to the pope, is interior conversion, which issues from faithfulness to the Holy Spirit.[9] As he said at Canterbury during his pastoral visit to England in 1982: "Still, such hopes and programs will be of no use at all if our struggle for unity is not rooted in our union with God."[10]

Jesus, the pope recalls, began his mission with the call to "repent and believe in the gospel" (Mark 1:15; UUS 15). Ecumenical progress has often been impeded by arrogance and presumption, leading the parties to condemn one another (UUS 15). Not infrequently intolerance and violence have marked the relations between

---

[8] John Paul II, "Letter to Joint Working Group," *Addresses and Homilies*, 10.

[9] John Paul II, Address to U.S. Ecumenical Leaders, October 7, 1979; *Addresses and Homilies*, 43–46, at 46.

[10] John Paul II, address at Canterbury, quoted by Jan Cardinal Willebrands, "John Paul II and the Search for Full Unity among Christians," *John Paul II: A Panorama of His Teachings* (Brooklyn, N.Y.: New City Press, 1989), 48–64, at 56.

separated communities. For these attitudes and actions it is necessary for all to repent (TMA 35).

Personal and collective repentance must be accompanied by prayer, another essential element of spiritual ecumenism. Such prayer, united with Christ's own prayer to the Father that his disciples might be one, reminds us that Christian unity is ultimately a gift of God for which we can only ask, placing our confidence in him alone.[11]

Of special value, according to John Paul II, is the prayer in which separated Christians come together in the name of their Lord. The united prayer of Christians is an invitation to Christ himself to visit the community of those who call upon him, relying on his promise: "When two or three are gathered in my name, there am I in the midst of them" (Matt. 18:20; UUS 21). The pope rejoices in the observance of the Week of Prayer for Christian Unity which is held either in January or in the time around Pentecost in many parts of the world (UUS 24). Individual prayer for unity, even by cloistered religious, can also be very efficacious (UUS 27).[12]

Dialogue

The next major component of the pope's strategy, second only to spirituality in its importance, is dialogue. The two means, indeed, are not fully distinct, for prayer itself is a dialogue with God, and in any truly Christian dialogue God must be present as an invisible partner. When not restricted to the merely human or horizontal level, encounters among Christians can become what John Paul II, like Paul VI before him, calls a dialogue of salvation. Such a dialogue takes account of the divine redeemer, who is himself our reconciliation (UUS 35).

As a personalist philosopher, John Paul II has over the years had a keen interest in dialogue, which he views as an indispensable means toward human self-realization. In a certain sense, we become the persons that we are by dialogue with other persons. By encountering them in mutual address, we learn to recognize them as partners and to overcome feelings of isolation, antagonism, and conflict. All who enter into ecumenical dialogue must presuppose in their partners a sincere desire for reconciliation and unity in the truth (UUS 29). When we undertake

[11] John Paul II, Address for Week of Prayer for Unity, January 17, 1979; *Addresses and Homilies*, 5–9, at 6.

[12] On January 24, 1983, in the course of the Week of Prayer for Unity, John Paul II beatified a Sardinian Trappestine nun, Maria Gabriella of Unity, who died in 1939, having offered her life, hidden though it was from the gaze of human eyes, for the cause of Christian unity. Her example, the pope remarks in UUS 27, reminds us that there are no special times or places required for ecumenical prayer. It can be conducted even by those who are not in personal contact with Christians of traditions other than their own.

dialogue with these dispositions, we gain a new perspective on reality, obtain new insights, and find ourselves personally transformed.

In the footsteps of Paul VI, who wrote eloquently on dialogue in his first encyclical, *Ecclesiam suam*, John Paul II views dialogue as a key to ecumenical advancement as well as to relationships within the Church. Like Paul VI, he is convinced that strictly theological dialogue, in order to be successful, must be preceded and accompanied by a dialogue of charity, in which the parties who have been estranged resume living in cordial personal relationships. Just as Paul VI cultivated personal relationships with Patriarch Athenagoras and Archbishop Ramsey, John Paul II attaches great importance to his face-to-face meetings with the subsequent patriarchs of Constantinople and Archbishops of Canterbury, as well as with other ecumenical leaders. He regularly sends messages to the heads of the other churches and Christian communities at Easter time; he keeps them informed about important decisions being made, and documents being prepared, in the Catholic Church.[13]

Turning to theological dialogue, John Paul II expresses his confidence that it can resolve many of the issues that have separated Christians in the past. But at the same time he recognizes the danger of hasty harmonizations that could lead to merely apparent solutions that would conceal rather than resolve the real differences.[14] He is on guard against any reductionism that would achieve agreement through doctrinal compromise (RH 6). In an address to the Roman curia on June 28, 1980, he declared that "the union of Christians cannot be sought in a 'compromise' between the various theological positions, but only in a common meeting in the most ample and mature fullness of Christian truth."[15]

The Church, as the trustee of revealed truth, simply lacks the authority to bargain away any part of the divinely given deposit of faith. The only unity worth having is a unity in the truth. As we read in *Ut unum sint*: "The unity willed by God can be attained only by the adherence of all to the content of revealed truth in its entirety. In matters of faith, compromise is in contradiction with God who is truth" (UUS 18). Dialogue therefore consists not in doctrinal dilution but in a mutual exchange in which the communities enrich one another, enabling each to grow into the plenitude of divine truth, and thereby to advance along the path that God has marked out for them. In testifying to the truth as we have come to know it, we perform a service of love, helping others to grow into Christ the head, even as we are helped by them (UUS 87). Truth and love are in no way contrary to each other; they grow together. To quote from the pope again: "Love increases by

[13] Willebrands, "John Paul II and the Search . . . ," 63.

[14] John Paul II, Address to West German Bishops, November 17, 1980; *Addresses and Homilies*, 154–55, at 154.

[15] John Paul II, Address to the Roman Curia, June 28, 1980, §17; *Addresses and Homilies*, 126–30, at 130.

means of truth, and the truth draws near to the person by the help of love."[16] Ecumenical dialogue requires of the theologians who undertake it a great maturity and certainty in the faith professed by the Church, and a particular fidelity to the teaching of the magisterium, which authoritatively declares the faith of the Church.[17]

In seeking to find one another in the fullness of revealed truth the partner churches are summoned to an examination of conscience. Loyalty to the truth can lead them not only to challenge others but also to undertake a sincere reappraisal of their own heritage. They must have the humility to acknowledge and correct any false interpretations of the deposit of faith and to move beyond partial and culturally conditioned misreadings of the Christian heritage. Dialogue can especially help the participants to transcend the distortions that have come about as a result of the controversies and polemics of the past.

In his encyclical on ecumenism John Paul II proposes a list of topics that he considers especially important for ecumenical dialogue. The list includes the relationship between Scripture and tradition, the Eucharist as sacrifice and real presence, the ordained ministry, the teaching office of the Church, and Mary as mother and type of the Church. He also welcomes the recommendations of the Fifth World Conference on Faith and Order, held at Salamanca in 1994, to begin a new study of the universal ministry of Christian unity. At Geneva in 1984 he acknowledged that while the bishop of Rome is the visible sign and guarantor of ecclesiastical unity, the exercise of papal primacy has been marked by painful memories, for which he expressed sorrow to the extent that he and his predecessors have been responsible (UUS 88). He freely confessed the sense of personal weakness and the need for divine mercy and forgiveness that the popes must feel before the high responsibilities of their office. He found comfort in the Lord's gentleness in dealing with the failures of Peter himself (UUS 4 and 92). In a surprising gesture that has aroused considerable discussion, John Paul II has asked the leaders of the other churches and their theologians to assist him in finding ways of exercising the primacy so that it will better serve the unity of the whole flock of Christ (UUS 95-96). He cannot of course renounce anything that is essential to the Petrine office, but he seeks advice in conducting the office entrusted to him.[18]

[16] John Paul II, *Insegnamenti* V/2; quoted by Willebrands, "John Paul II and the Search . . . ," p. 55.

[17] John Paul II, *Insegnamenti* III/1, p. 1892; quoted by Willebrands, "John Paul II and the Search . . . ," p. 55.

[18] Patriarch Bartholomew of Constantinople, speaking at Zurich on December 14, 1995, responded to the pope's invitation. He made it clear that according to his own understanding of the Orthodox position, all bishops are equally successors of all the apostles. Rome, he said, exercises a legitimate role of supervision but not of government. The text of this response is found in *Istina* 41 (April–June 1996): 184–87. As the editors of *Istina* note, it appears difficult to reconcile this Ortho-

Cooperation

In addition to spiritual ecumenism and dialogue John Paul II recognizes a third ingredient in ecumenism, practical cooperation. This consists in the first place in common witness and proclamation of the Christian faith. Although we fall short of the perfect union to which we are called, "we can and must immediately reach and display to the world our unity in proclaiming the mystery of Christ, in revealing the divine dimension and also the human dimension of the redemption" (RH 11). In proclaiming Christ to the world, the pope believes, we set in clearer light the dignity of each human being and the exalted destiny to which all are called.

Not only can Christians of different communities testify together to Jesus as Lord and to the triune God; they can also collaborate to some extent in religious instruction. In his apostolic exhortation on catechesis, *Catechesi tradendae*, the pope remarks that in situations of religious plurality, it may be opportune to have certain experiences of ecumenical collaboration, but these are necessarily limited, since doctrinal divergences still exist and since it is important for Catholics to be initiated into the ecclesial life of their own Church (CT 33).

Collaboration extends not only to the fields of witness and doctrine but also to social action. Frequently in his speeches and writings John Paul II quotes from Vatican II the statement, "Cooperation among all Christians vividly expresses that bond which already unites them, and sets in clearer relief the features of Christ the Servant" (UR 12, quoted in UUS 40). Cooperation among Christians is not only a means of helping those in need; it is also a form of witness and a means of evangelization (UUS 40). In addressing the many ills that afflict our world, such as hunger, drugs, and unemployed youth, the collaborative action of Christians is a way of bearing joint witness to Christ and the gospel.[19] There is hardly a country in the world, the pope declares, in which the Catholic Church is not cooperating with other Christians in working for social justice, human rights, development, and the relief of need.[20]

---

dox position with the dogmatic teaching of Vatican I and Vatican II, especially in light of the *nota praevia* appended to the Vatican II Constitution on the Church (ibid., 187–89).

In an interview for the Polish Catholic periodical *Tygodnik Powszechny* the secretary general of the World Council of Churches, Konrad Raiser, said that the key obstacle for Christian unity was the doctrine of Vatican I that the pope has universal jurisdictional power and that his *ex cathedra* decisions are infallible. See Catholic News Service dispatch of July 8, 1996.

On December 2–4, 1996, the Congregation for the Doctrine of the Faith held a symposium on "The Primacy of the Successor of Peter," the acts of which were published in October 1998 with a final statement in which the Congregation for the Doctrine of the Faith summarized the essentials of Catholic teaching on the primacy. The final statement is reprinted in *Origins* 28 (January 28, 1999): 560–63.

[19] John Paul II, Address to Roman Curia, June 29, 1985, §9, p. 128.

[20] John Paul II, Address to Delegates of National Ecumenical Commissions, p. 54.

In several of the talks given in the course of his visit to Ireland in 1979 John Paul II emphasized the importance of the united service of Christians to defend spiritual and moral values and to oppose violence, especially in Northern Ireland. All Catholics, especially the bishops and other clergy, have a responsibility to be ministers of peace and reconciliation.[21]

Priorities within Ecumenism

The present pope gives special emphasis to relationships with the Orthodox and other ancient churches of the East, because the prospects of union with them are far greater, at least from the theological point of view, since many of these churches have retained the apostolic faith, a true Eucharist, and a valid apostolic ministry.[22] Indeed, they may be said even today to be in almost full, though still imperfect, communion with the Catholic Church.[23]

The pope's interest in the East does not come simply from the fact that he is a Slav, but as a Slav he feels a special affinity with the nations of Eastern Europe, many of which are predominantly Orthodox. Early in his pontificate, in 1980, he bestowed on Cyril and Methodius, the Greek missionaries who evangelized the Slavs in the ninth century, the title of copatrons of Europe together with St. Benedict, who had already been named patron of Europe by Paul VI. In 1985 John Paul issued the encyclical *Slavorum apostoli*, honoring Cyril and Methodius for their inculturation of the faith in Eastern Europe. In 1988 he published an apostolic letter, *Euntes in mundum,* celebrating the millennium of the baptism of St. Vladimir of Kiev, and followed up this letter with a message to Ukrainian Catholics in which he insisted that the existence of Eastern Catholic Churches is not an obstacle but in many ways an aid to ecumenical contacts with the Orthodox.[24] As has been mentioned in chapter 9, he likes to say that Christianity must learn again to breathe with its two lungs, the Western and the Eastern.[25]

In 1995 the pope wrote an apostolic letter, *Orientale lumen,* in which he again expressed his profound appreciation for the heritage of Eastern Christianity. After

[21] John Paul II, Address to Representatives of Other Christian Churches in Dublin, September 29, 1979 (*Addresses and Homilies*, 38), and Address to Irish Bishops, Dublin, September 30, 1979 (ibid., 40–41).

[22] John Paul II, Homily in the Church of the Holy Spirit, Istanbul, November 29, 1979; *Addresses and Homilies*, 63-68, at 66.

[23] John Paul II, Address for the Week of Prayer for Unity, 1979, p. 8.

[24] John Paul II, "Message to Ukrainian Catholics," §6 quotes Vatican II, UR 14 and 17, and adds that the council does not see in these Oriental Catholic Churches "an obstacle to full communion with our Orthodox brethren" but on the contrary a means of promoting the visible unity of the whole Church. See text in *Origins* 17 (May 5,1988): 816–18, at 817–18. The text of *Euntes in mundum* is in *Origins* 17 (March 31, 1988): 709–18.

[25] E.g., John Paul II, Address to Roman Curia on June 28, 1980, §14, p. 127; also UUS 54.

reviewing many of the characteristic themes and emphases of the Oriental theology he expressed his own "holy nostalgia" for the centuries in which the East and West had lived together in full communion of faith and charity. The disruption of that communion, he said, "has deprived the world of a joint witness that could perhaps have avoided so many tragedies and even changed the course of history."[26] As the dawn of the new millennium turns our eyes toward the East, he reflected, we have special reason to renew our efforts to give united witness in order that the voice of Christ may be more credibly heard by those who are thirsting for the word of God.

These letters have been accompanied by dramatic gestures, such as the pope's visit to Patriarch Dimitrios of Constantinople in 1979 and Dimitrios's return visit to Rome in 1987. On this latter occasion the pope and the patriarch together recited the Nicene-Constantinopolitan Creed according to the original Greek text. In June 1995 Patriarch Bartholomew, the successor of Dimitrios, visited Rome and issued with John Paul II a joint declaration affirming their prayerful commitment to work for mutual forgiveness between the churches and the eventual restoration of full communion.[27]

It seems clear that before full reconciliation can be achieved on the theological level the dialogue of charity must make further advances. As the pope and Patriarch Dimitrios of Constantinople noted in their joint declaration, the relationships are burdened by painful memories from the past. There is need of what John Paul sometimes calls a "healing of memories" or a "purification of the collective memory of our churches."[28]

The pope has frequently indicated his conviction that the theological issues between the Eastern and Western churches can be resolved by dialogue provided that there is a spirit of pardon and an earnest desire for reconciliation.

It will probably not be easy for theologians to arrive at mutually acceptable interpretations of the doctrines by which the Orthodox and Catholic churches have been divided over the past thousand years, such as the procession of the Holy Spirit and the pope's universal primacy of jurisdiction. But some encouragement may be drawn from the way in which the patriarchs of several ancient Oriental churches, Coptic Orthodox and Syrian Orthodox, have in recent years signed declarations affirming their acceptance of the christological faith of the great councils. By means of a modern hermeneutics of unity, it may be possible in the course of time to arrive at mutually acceptable formulations of doctrines disputed between the Orthodox and Catholic churches.

---

[26] John Paul II, Apostolic Letter *Orientale lumen*, §28; *Origins* 25 (May 18, 1996): 1–13, at 12.

[27] John Paul II and Bartholomew I, Joint Declaration; *Origins* 25 (July 27, 1995): 148–49, at 148.

[28] Joint Declaration of John Paul II and the Ecumenical Patriarch Dimitrios I, November 30, 1979; text in *Addresses and Homilies*, 81–83, at 82.

More difficult in some ways have been the relations between the Catholic Church and the churches springing from the Reformation of the sixteenth century. But in his visits to England and Germany the pope has done a great deal to build common ground with Anglicans and Lutherans, for example. In 1982 he prayed together with the primate of the Anglican communion at Canterbury cathedral. In a trip to Germany in 1980, the 450th anniversary of the Augsburg Confession, the pope affirmed that his hope for unity was spurred by the finding of the German Catholic bishops that the Augsburg Confession represents "not simply a partial consensus on some truths but rather a full accord on fundamental and central truths."[29] As of this writing, efforts are being made to frame a joint declaration by Lutherans and Catholics, to be issued by the member churches of the Lutheran World Federation and the Holy See, expressing the substantive agreements between the two communions on the nature of justification as a free and unmerited grace, received in faith.[30]

A major obstacle to progress in relations with the Anglicans, Lutherans, and most Protestants has been the decision of these churches to ordain women to the pastoral office, including in some cases the episcopate. Paul VI and John Paul II pleaded with the archbishops of Canterbury not to take this step, since it would gravely impair relations of Anglicans with Roman Catholics and with the Orthodox, as well as the other ancient churches of the East. As the pope and Archbishop George Carey acknowledged in their meeting on December 5, 1996, no solution has as yet been found for this difficulty.[31] It would appear that the churches which ordain women have, on the whole, a more functional and less sacramental concept of ministry than those that do not. The sacramental vision is strictly bound to the action of Christ in instituting the ministry as interpreted in the unbroken tradition of the centuries. The functional vision is open to adaptations that seem to be dictated by social exigencies.

Conclusion

John Paul II has not attempted to make any radical innovations in his ecumenical theology. He has built faithfully on the teaching of the Second Vatican Council

[29] John Paul II, Address to Evangelical Church Members, November 17, 1980; *Addresses and Homilies*, 157–60, at 158.

[30] The text of this Joint Declaration, as approved by the Council of the Lutheran World Federation, may be found in *Origins* 28 (July 16, 1998): 120–27, together with an official Catholic response, pp. 130–32.

[31] John Paul II at his meeting with Archbishop Carey of Canterbury said that the disagreement about conferring priestly ordination on women "puts into clear relief the need to reach an understanding of how the church authoritatively discerns the teaching and practice which constitute the apostolic faith entrusted to us." See *Origins* 26 (December 19, 1996): 437, 439, at 439. See also the Common Declaration issued by the two prelates (ibid., 442).

and that of Paul VI. But he has made some clear advances in systematizing the whole program of ecumenism and in deepening the motivation behind it. By showing that the quest for unity is grounded in the unalterable will of Christ for his Church, the present pope makes it clear that ecumenism does not depend on prospects of visible success, but that it is to be pursued in all times and places, even in the face of indifference and hostility. He has outlined a strategy that can guide the efforts not of Catholics alone but of all Christians. Aware of the difficulties of the enterprise, he has warned against facile accords based on compromise. Thanks to his insistence on the fullness of revealed truth he has given respectability to ecumenism in circles that have tended to dismiss it as a form of reductionism. His eager participation in the dialogue of charity, especially in his relations with the churches of the East, has minimized the tensions that have been unavoidable, especially in the countries of the former Soviet Union. In the course of time, the pope's courtesy toward the Orthodox may lead to the restoration of full communion which has thus far proved unattainable.

The program of John Paul II has a strength and solidity that derive from faith alone. He makes it clear that Christian unity, if it ever comes about, cannot be a human achievement but only a gift of God. For this reason he keeps the primary emphasis on spiritual ecumenism and prayer. The most effective ecumenism is that which cultivates patience, humility, and fervent trust in the Holy Spirit, who enables us to hope against hope and to leave the future in the hands of God, the sole master of our destinies.

THE RELIGIONS

Starting Point in Vatican II

Vatican II, in its Declaration on Non-Christian Religions, *Nostra aetate*, acknowledged the importance of the coming great dialogue among world religions. It was, I believe, the first council in history to speak of these other faiths in positive terms. In a crucial paragraph it stated:

> The Catholic Church rejects nothing that is true and holy in these religions. She looks with sincere respect upon those ways of conduct and of life, those rules and teachings which, though differing in many particulars from what she holds and sets forth, nevertheless often reflect a ray of that Truth which enlightens all men. Indeed, she proclaims and ever must proclaim Christ, "the way, the truth, and the life" (John 14:6), in whom men find the fullness of religious life, and in whom God has reconciled all things to himself (cf. 2 Cor. 5:18-19). (NA 2)

Other important passages dealing with the religions may be found in the Constitution on the Church and in the Decree on the Church's missionary activity.

While adopting a basically positive view of the religions, the council did not clearly state that they are supernaturally revealed or that they are means of salvation for their members, but it did assert that salvation is possible for those who profess religions other than Christianity (LG 16; AG 7).

In treating the religions, as in most other matters, John Paul II is very much the man of Vatican II. So far as I can determine, he makes no doctrinal moves that clearly go beyond the council, but he does give an interpretation of the council that, at least in its emphasis, is original. He insists on the universal relevance of Christianity, and hence its relevance to all the religions. He refuses to settle for a relativistic pluralism. Humankind, he declares, has only one origin and one destiny. Created in the divine image, all men and women are called to understand themselves in relation to Christ, the universal Savior.

Christological Perspective

As in other areas of theology, John Paul II is strongly christological in his theology of the religions. He picks up from Vatican II the patristic theme that "seeds of the Word" (*semina Verbi*) are present in all the religions, and hence that all of them have a common soteriological root (RH 11; RMis 28; CTH 81; cf. Vatican II, AG 11 and 15). The infinite source of all grace and life has been made manifest in Jesus Christ. Although persons of good will can attain salvation without knowing Christ or actually joining the Church, no one can be saved without Christ and without being oriented to the Church. The Church has a divine mandate laid upon it to preach the Gospel to all. Catholic Christianity with its unique doctrinal and sacramental heritage remains the ordinary means of salvation in God's plan.[32] The task of the Church is to help members of all religions to overcome their errors and limitations, and to recognize that Christ is the completion of all that is good and salvific in their teaching and practices.[33]

Dialogue

In *Redemptoris missio* John Paul II teaches that interreligious dialogue is part of the Church's evangelizing mission. By dialogue he understands a process of mutual instruction and enlightenment. True interfaith dialogue does not arise

---

[32] John Paul II, Letter to Federation of Asian Bishops' Conferences, 1990; *The Christian Faith in the Doctrinal Documents of the Catholic Church,* ed. Josef Neuner and Jacques Dupuis (New York: Alba House, 1996), §1053.

[33] Address to Roman Curia, December 22, 1986; *Origins* 16 (January 15, 1987): 561-63, at 561–62.

from self-interest, but is demanded by deep respect for all that the Spirit has wrought in the various religions. Through dialogue the Church seeks to uncover and cultivate the "seeds of the Word" and the rays of truth that are to be found among all peoples and in all religious traditions.

In his discussions of dialogue the pope frequently repeats that doctrinal compromise must be avoided. As he puts it in *Redemptoris missio*: "Those engaged in dialogue must be consistent with their own religious traditions and convictions . . . knowing that dialogue can enrich each side. There must be no abandonment of principles or false irenicism" (RMis 56).

This kind of dialogue is illustrated in *Crossing the Threshold of Faith*, which contains short chapters on different religions—African and Asian animism, Chinese Confucianism and Taoism, Buddhism, New Age Gnosticism, Islam, and Judaism. While he has words of praise for all these religions (except perhaps New Age), he is also critical of them. He is quite candid in declaring that he finds Buddhism too negative in its attitude toward the world (pp. 85–89) and that Islamic fundamentalism violates the principles of religious freedom (p. 94). He is notably cordial in his treatment of Judaism, but he insists that the covenant with Israel still awaits completion by the New Covenant (pp. 99–100).

Prayer

In the earlier treatment of the Holy Spirit we have already alluded to the connection between the Holy Spirit and prayer. The pope's devotion to the prayer to the Holy Spirit given to him by his father has already been noted in chapter 2. In saying that prayer as a child, he observes, he came to understand the meaning of the words of Christ to the Samaritan woman about the true worshipers, who worship God in the Spirit and in truth (John 4:23; CTH 141-42). The pope says that the Holy Spirit, as the breath of divine life, makes itself felt in prayer. And he adds: "Wherever people are praying in the world, there the Holy Spirit is, the living breath of prayer" (D&V 65). It is this realization that has prompted the pope to organize two important summits of prayer for members of all religions, held at Assisi. In his address to the Roman curia of December 22, 1987, the pope reflected on the Assisi day of prayer for peace on October 27, 1986. Referring to the statements of Paul in Rom. 8:26–27 about how the Holy Spirit intercedes for us with unutterable groanings when we do not know how to pray as we ought, the pope concluded: "We can indeed maintain that every authentic prayer is called forth by the Holy Spirit, who is mysteriously present in the heart of every person." In praying one submits totally to God and recognizes one's own poverty in rela-

[34]John Paul II, Address to the Roman Curia; *Origins* 16 (Jan. 15, 1987): 561–63, at 563.

tion to him. Prayer is therefore an important means of realizing God's plan for humanity.[34]

Cooperation for Peace and Justice

The vast potential of the religions for peace and justice is recognized in many writings of John Paul II. In several of his social encyclicals he appeals to leaders of the great religions to offer joint witness to their common convictions concerning the dignity of humanity, created by God. The various religions, he believes, can play a preeminent role in preserving peace and in building a city worthy of man (SRS 47; CA 60). At the interreligious prayer meetings at Assisi he was confirmed in his conviction that peace and religion go hand in hand. In one of his reflections on the Assisi meeting of October 27, 1986, he declared: "Religions worthy of the name, the open religions spoken of by Henri Bergson,[35] are not just projections of human desires but an openness and submission to the transcendent will of God which asserts itself in every conscience." Thanks to their spiritual vision of man, these religions are capable of respecting fundamental human rights. A religious and ethical vision, according to the pope, can overcome the instincts of aggression and xenophobia and avert the tendency to violence and terrorism. Universal human solidarity requires an ethic of transcendence, founded on the divine will as manifested in authentic religion.[36]

Conclusion

In his theology of the religions, as in his ecumenism, Pope John Paul II is guided by his conviction that trinitarian Christocentrism is the true universalism. Because of his conviction that all human beings are called to grow into union with God through Jesus Christ, and that the Holy Spirit is prompting every man and woman to seek the truth that is present in the living Christ, we need not resign ourselves to an unreconciled pluralism or an amorphous syncretism. The Church, as the universal sacrament of salvation, must perseveringly seek to overcome all disruptive differences. The fullness of truth as given in Jesus Christ is not a barrier to dialogue and cooperation. On the contrary, that truth alone gives hope and promise of success in all our ecumenical and interreligious endeavors.

[35] John Paul II is presumably referring to Henri Bergson, *The Two Sources of Morality and Religion* (French original, 1932; English translation, New York: Henry Holt, 1935). Bergson contrasts static religions with dynamic religions, closed societies with open societies.

[36] John Paul II, Address to Diplomats, §§6–8; *Origins* 16 (January 29, 1987): 592–96, quotation from §6, p. 594.

CHAPTER 13

Eschatology and History

∽

IN THE CHRISTIAN THEOLOGICAL perspective history is essential but is not the ultimate horizon. Time is encompassed by eternity. All history begins, unfolds, and reaches completion through the action of the triune God, who is the same yesterday, today, and tomorrow, without beginning and without end. Time, on the contrary, has a beginning, a middle, and an end.

In every historical action of God, all three divine persons are involved. Creation is not the work of the Father alone, but of Father, Son, and Holy Spirit. The incarnation is not the work of the Son alone, but also that of the Father who sends him and of the Holy Spirit by whom he is conceived. When the Spirit descends upon the Church, the Father and the Son are at work in sending the Spirit. The sending of the Spirit marks what one may call the beginning of the end-time. The Spirit is the pledge, the first installment (*arrabon*) of the promised inheritance of everlasting glory (Eph. 1:13–14; Spirit 428).

ESCHATOLOGY

The Concept

Eschatology is the doctrine of the end-time, in which the fullness of salvation is accomplished (SR 161). Although this consummation is brought about by all three divine persons, John Paul II attributes it particularly to Christ. "The eschaton," he writes, "is effected not by the world or by man but by Christ. It is Christ who makes all things subject to the Father. And this 'making subject' is inseparable from his own filial 'submission' to the Father, as the Apostle teaches us (1 Cor. 3:23)." Christ subjects himself and all creatures to the Father, so that God may be all in all (SCdn 177; cf. 1 Cor. 15:27–28).

John Paul II acknowledges that there has been a certain decline in eschatological consciousness in the past generation or two. The malaise produced by recent wars, totalitarian dictatorships, and grinding poverty, together with the exhilarating prospects of technological progress, has drawn our attention away from ultimate realities. We are tempted to fall into a certain "horizontalism" in which the idea of salvation becomes secularized (RMis 11). Most of our contemporaries are therefore less concerned with ultimate reality than were previous generations (CTH 178, 183).

In answer to complaints that eschatology may now be considered irrelevant, the pope replies that many still sense that there must be someone who in the end will be able to speak the truth about the good and evil people have done and to award fitting recompense. They feel that there must be One who knows us completely, judges us justly, and determines the outcome of our lives (CTH 184).

The traditional doctrine of eschatology, as it has developed since the Middle Ages, focuses on the final outcome of individual human lives, including death and what comes after death— judgment, heaven, hell, and purgatory. Retreats and missions that focused on these themes were regularly preached until very recently and may well return to favor. Although these spiritual exercises did not do justice to all aspects of biblical revelation, they had a solid scriptural foundation and exerted a profoundly personal pastoral appeal. Many were brought to conversion and confession by meditation on these themes (CTH 179).

Death and Judgment

Death in its negative aspect is the deprivation of earthly life brought about by the dissolution of the body. Considered as a biological happening, death is inevitable; it is something that human beings share with all visible creation. Nevertheless, as Vatican II noted, "man, bearing in himself the seed of eternity, which cannot be reduced to mere matter, rebels against death" (GS 18; SCdn 159). Every human person in a mysterious way reaches out toward the promise of new life given in Christ.

Personalist philosophy, to which the pope adheres, tends to emphasize the positive aspect of death. The believer can accept death as the wages of sin and welcome it as the door to eternal life. To die in the Lord is to experience death in whatever form it comes to us as a supreme exercise of obedience (EV 67). Dying, understood in this way, is an act. Even though we do not choose our own death, we to some degree choose the manner of that death. Normally the manner of our death will be a ratification of the choices we have made in the course of our life (SCdn 161). The "final option" made at death should not be depicted as a completely new choice unrelated to the way we have already chosen to live (cf. RP 17).

Christ came into the world not to judge it but to save it (John 3:17; 12:47; cf. D&V 27). There are some, however, who reject the offer of eternal life. God's love does not deprive the creature of its freedom. The Son, as decreed by the Father, will judge those who say no to God's offer of love (John 5:22; SCdn 178). Jesus tells us that the Holy Spirit, when he comes, will convince the world of sin, of righteousness, and of judgment (John 16:8). In a lengthy commentary on this text John Paul II interprets it as meaning that the Spirit disposes us to recognize that the world has fallen into the bondage of sin, that it is moving toward final judgment, and that Christ's judgment on it is righteous (D&V 27–48; cf. SCdn 178–79).

Jesus in the Gospels speaks of blasphemy against the Holy Spirit as a sin that will not be forgiven (Matt. 12:31 par). Theologians over the centuries have speculated on the meaning of this saying. According to John Paul II the final and unforgivable sin consists in a radical refusal to accept the forgiveness that God offers in Christ—a refusal whereby one condemns oneself to judgment (D&V 46).

Heaven and Hell

Jesus came that we might have life and have it abundantly (John 10:10). Human life is intended to lead to that unending personal communion with the Father to which we are called in the Son by the power of the Holy Spirit (EV 1). Blessedness consists in a sharing in the trinitarian life of God, the supreme *communio personarum* (SCdn 178).

Glory is the irradiation of the divine goodness into the whole of reality (SC 181). Alluding to a famous passage from Irenaeus, John Paul II affirms that the glory of God is man fully alive (SCdn 173, 181).[1] Those who rise to eternal life will receive a participation in Christ's own resurrection, conforming them fully to him (SR 182). Eternal life and the resurrection should therefore be understood christologically, in terms of the movement of the world to its final goal in the risen and glorified Christ.

Hell too belongs to the mystery of the final consummation (SCdn 177). As the opposite of communion, it consists in separation from God and isolation. John Paul II recognizes that the doctrine of eternal punishment has seemed problematic and disturbing to many great thinkers, including Origen, Bulgakov, and Hans Urs von Balthasar (and he might have mentioned John Henry Newman). But the councils have clearly rejected Origen's theory of *apokatastasis*, according to which everyone would be saved in the end, so that there would be no eternal hell. The words of Jesus in the Gospels, as John Paul II understands them, make it undeniable that some will go to eternal punishment (CTH 185; cf. Matt. 25:46). This must be so because God, besides being love, is also justice (SCdn 180–81). Revelation, however, does not tell us who or how many will be lost, and the

---

[1] The allusion is to St. Irenaeus, *Adversus haereses* IV.20:5–7; PG 7:1035.

Church has wisely refrained from teaching that any particular individual, even Judas, is in hell (CTH 186).

Purgatory

The meaning of Purgatory, according to John Paul II, has to be understood in relation to the absolute holiness of God, which man has to approach by being perfected in Christ (SCdn 170). Many theologians explain Purgatory in terms of the debt of temporal punishment incurred by sinners. But John Paul II makes little use of these primarily juridical categories. As a personalist he prefers to interpret Purgatory by reference to the spiritual preparation needed for entrance into beatifying union with the living God (SCdn 170). "God who is love," he writes, "judges through love. It is love that demands purification, before man can be made ready for that union with God which is his ultimate vocation and destiny" (CTH 187). Drawing on the thought of an author very dear to him, the pope identifies the purifying fire of Purgatory with what St. John of the Cross called "the living flame of love" (SCdn 171). The souls in Purgatory are already filled with light, certitude, and joy, because they know that they belong forever to God (Spirit 430).

Eschatology of Church and World

From the Middle Ages until very recently theology has concerned itself primarily with the individual aspects of eschatology and with the "last things" we have just discussed. But Vatican II, building on biblical and early patristic sources, retrieved the ecclesial and cosmic dimensions of eschatology which, as John Paul II acknowledges, were only faintly present in the preaching of recent generations. The ecclesial aspect of eschatology is treated in a highly biblical way in chapter 7 of *Lumen gentium*, "The Eschatological Nature of the Pilgrim Church" (CTH 181–82).

Communal or ecclesial eschatology does not exclude but rather includes the eschatology of the individual person, since there are basic links between the community and the individual (SR 183). The Church in its earthly pilgrimage is tending toward the fullness of the communion of saints, which will be attained through full union of the members of the Church with one another and with their head, the risen and heavenly Christ (SR 184). Eschatology must therefore be Christocentric as well as ecclesial (CTH 185).

Christ is the "firstborn of all creation" (Col. 1:15), for he is the incarnation of the Word through whom all things were created. Thanks to him, the eternal Logos, the world of creatures appears as a "cosmos," an ordered universe. And it is this same Word who, by taking flesh, renews the cosmic order of creation. The Letter to the Ephesians speaks of the purpose of God to set forth in Christ "a plan for the

fullness of time, to unite all things in him, things in heaven and things on earth"
(Eph 1:9-10; cf. TMA 3).

"The eschatology of the Church is at the same time the fulfillment of the world,
a great cosmic consummation" (SR 186). That fulfillment cannot occur except in
Christ, the *Christus consummator*, who is the head of the Church as well as of creation. The glory of God, which is the end of all creation, includes both the salvation of human beings and the renewal of the world in Christ (SR 187-88).
According to the Christian idea, individuals are not saved from a world that is
doomed to destruction. Rather, they are saved in and with the world, which Christ
loved and came to redeem. We look forward confidently to "a new heaven and a
new earth" (Rev. 21:1; DM 8; RMis 59).

THEOLOGY OF HISTORY

History and Eschatology

Salvation reaches its fullness at the end of time, the eschaton, but it does not occur
without preparation. It begins through God's saving action in history. In view of
the history of redemption or salvation, it is possible to speak of a "partially realized eschatology," although John Paul II does not, so far as I know, use this pre-
cise term. "Eschological salvation," he writes, "begins even now in newness of
life in Christ" (RMis 20). The eschatological renewal of the world continues in
the Church (SR 186). The liturgy, when properly performed, conveys a prelude of
the perfect song of praise that will be sung by the heavenly Church (SR 187–88).

Viewing the course of human events from the standpoint of faith, John Paul II
sketches the elements of a rich theology of history. God makes his personal
entrance into history through the twofold mission of the Word and the Holy Spirit.
In these two interlocking phases of salvation history God's action, while fully preserving its divine transcendence, takes place within time and in the sight of human
eyes, thereby becoming a part of human history (SR 156–57).

Centrality of Christ

Salvation history, like Christian eschatology, has a Christocentric structure. In the
incarnation God enters history in a definitive manner. The Lord to whom all ages
belong, the Alpha and the Omega, plunges into the midst of history, making the
love of the Father visible (TMA 10; D&V 49, 54).

Paul calls the moment of the incarnation "the fullness of time" (Gal. 4:4; D&V
49). All history can be computed as being before or after this unique event. It represents the fullness because time is fulfilled by the entrance of eternity into it

(TMA 9). In Jesus Christ time becomes, so to speak, a dimension of God, who sanctifies it from within (TMA 10). Because the fullness of truth and grace are made present in him, Christ is the center, the focal point, and the goal of human history (TMA 59, quoting GS 10).

Centrality of the Holy Spirit

The mission of the Word can never be separated from that of the Holy Spirit. The incarnation itself has a pneumatological aspect because it was brought about by the power of the Holy Spirit, who overshadowed Mary and made her fruitful (D&V 49). John Paul II even asserts that because it constitutes the climax of the divine self-communication, the incarnation is "the greatest work accomplished by the Holy Spirit in the history of creation and salvation" (D&V 50). In this connection the pope recalls that according to Thomas Aquinas the hypostatic union is the supreme grace and is the source of every other grace (ST 3.2.10–12; 3.6.6; 3.7.13; cf. D&V 50).

In his encyclical on the Holy Spirit the pope points out that the Hebrew term "Messiah," means Christ, that is, the Anointed One. The anointing in question is that of the Holy Spirit. Thus, Peter can say in a sermon in Acts that "God anointed Jesus of Nazareth with the Holy Spirit and with power" (Acts 10:38; cf. D&V 15). Conscious of his role as the Christ, the Anointed One, Jesus could apply to himself the words of Isaiah: "The Spirit of the Lord God is upon me, because the Lord has anointed me to bring good tidings to the afflicted . . " (Isa. 61:1–2; Luke 4:18–19; cf. D&V 16). This prophecy, according to John Paul II, is fulfilled in Jesus because he possesses the fullness of the Spirit (D&V 18). Not only is Jesus conceived by the power of the Spirit; he is sent on mission by that same agency, and it is by the power of the Spirit that he casts out demons (Matt. 12:28; cf. Jesus 193).

The Church in History

Thanks to the Holy Spirit, the divine life that is in Jesus becomes disseminated to the furthest reaches of human history. Christ becomes the head of regenerate humanity, and more specifically of his communal body, which is the Church. Paul speaks of Jesus as the firstborn of many brethren, who are adopted children of the Father. This adoption is attributed to the Holy Spirit, who is sent into our hearts and who testifies within us that we are children and heirs of God (Rom. 8:14–15; cf. D&V 52).

The sending of the Spirit upon the Church is the work of the glorified Christ, together with his Father. In his discourse at the Last Supper, Jesus explained that it was necessary for him to depart in order that the Spirit might come (John 16:7;

D&V 61). After his resurrection Jesus was able to breathe on the disciples and say, "Receive the Holy Spirit" (John 20:22; D&V 24). Because the function of the Spirit is to bear witness to Christ, the sending of the Spirit forms part of the mission of the Word himself. By means of the mission of the Holy Spirit, Jesus comes into the midst of his people in a new way and remains with them to the end of the age (John 14:18; Matt. 28:20; cf. D&V 61).

Like Jesus himself, the Church becomes part of human history, rather than remaining above or outside history. According to Vatican II, the Church shares in the humanization of the world, contributing to the better ordering of a society built on freedom and communion (GS 39–40; SR 169–70). The gospel of Christ is the strongest safeguard of human dignity and freedom (SR 170). As it experiences itself amid the vicissitudes of history, the Church learns of its own need for the maturing influence of centuries. As it strives to come to terms with its own historicity, the Church becomes aware of its obligation to update and renew itself. Pope John XXIII and Vatican II popularized the notions of updating (*aggiornamento*) and adaptation to the times (*renovatio accommodata*) (SR 173). The Church, as John Paul II depicts it, does not move through history desperately clinging to a vanishing past. Rather, it confidently looks forward to the goal of human history, where Christ is seated at the right hand of God. Christ's redemptive action orients the world, through the Church, to an ultimate fulfillment that exceeds the possibilities of secular progress and depends on saving action of God. The Church bears witness to the divine values that are proper to the kingdom of God (SR 176–77).

Already in its pilgrim state the Church cherishes its bonds with the Church of glory and with the Church that is undergoing final purification in Purgatory (SR 182). Especially in its sacred liturgy the pilgrim Church celebrates its mysterious union with the saints in heaven and joins in their unending hymn of praise (SR 188). The temporal and the eschatological dimensions of the Church therefore interpenetrate. Thanks to the gifts of the Word and the Spirit, the eschaton is already operative in the Church and in the world.

Universal Action of the Spirit

All grace is mediated by Jesus Christ, in whom the love of God becomes tangibly and irreversibly present in history. As universal redeemer, Christ is the center of the universe and of its history (RH 1). But through the mediation of the Spirit, the loving mercy of God becomes available to those who do not enter into contact with Christ either through immediate personal contact or through the visible ministrations of the Church. In this connection the pope turns again to a favorite biblical text, "God is Spirit and those who worship him must do so in spirit and truth"

(John 4:25). He interprets this text as meaning that all who worship in the Spirit and in truth belong to Christ and are linked in some way with Christ and the Church (D&V 53–54).

Even though the identity of the Holy Spirit as a distinct divine person was not disclosed until the establishment of the New Covenant, the Spirit was at work from the beginning of time, and especially in the economy of the Old Covenant, influencing those who believed in the future coming of Christ (D&V 53). We must cast our gaze still further, recalling that according to Vatican II the Holy Spirit, in a manner known only to God, offers everyone the possibility of being associated in a salvific way with the Paschal mystery (GS 22; D&V 53). The redemptive activity of the Holy Spirit has been exercised at every place and time according to God's eternal plan. But human history is not simply a history of grace and salvation. The grace of God, though offered to all, does not prevent them from sinfully resisting and opposing the Holy Spirit (D&V 55). In the contemporary world the signs and symptoms of sin and death are virtually omnipresent (D&V 57). As a negative sign of our times, the pope speaks of "alarming symptoms of the 'culture of death,' which is advancing above all in prosperous societies" (EV 64).

Time Redeemed

In his apostolic letter on the Sunday observance, *Dies Domini* (1998), John Paul II meditates on time and history in the context of the liturgy. Already in the first chapters of the narrative of Genesis, the labor of God terminates in God's Sabbath rest, which confers meaning on time (DD 60). The meaning of time is fully disclosed in Christ, who is both the Lord of time and, in his earthly life, its center (DD 74). The Sunday liturgy proclaims that time, seen in Christ, "is not the grave of our illusions but the cradle of an ever new future" (DD 84). Time is not an endless repetition, as in the "myth of the eternal return," but an arrow pointing forward to Christ's return at the Parousia (DD 75).

The Church in its liturgy celebrates what Rabbi Abraham Heschel calls "the sacred architecture of time" (DD 15).[2] In the great feasts of the year we recall and reexperience the saving acts of God. In this sacred sequence Sunday has a special place. It gathers up the meaning of the Jewish Sabbath, when God rested from his work, and celebrates the entrance of Jesus into God's Sabbath rest (DD 18, 24). As the "eighth day," Sunday foreshadows the eternal day when the Sun of Justice will have no setting (DD 26, 37). In the Eucharist, which is celebrated with special solemnity on Sundays, we recall the Paschal mystery and await with eager

---

[2] The pope here refers to Abraham J. Heschel, *The Sabbath: Its Meaning for Modern Man* (22nd printing [New York: Farrar, Straus & Young, 1995], 3–24).

expectation the fulfillment of our hopes and the glorious return of Christ (DD 38). In its liturgical context Sunday therefore discloses the meaning of time in Christ as the Alpha and the Omega, the beginning and the end (DD 74).

The Meaning of Advent

God, in his providential government of the universe, sees to it that the entrance of the Son into human history does not take place in an abrupt way, without suitable preparation. The fullness of time cannot occur except as the fulfillment of prior aspirations and intimations. As we read in the Pastoral Constitution on the Church in the Modern World, Christ the Lord is the focal point of the desires of history and of civilization, the fulfillment of the longing of the ages (GS 45; SR 177). He is the divine answer to the yearning of all the world's religions (TMA 6). The books of the Old Testament stand as a permanent witness to the careful divine pedagogy by which the patriarchs and prophets disposed the People of God to look forward to the coming Redeemer (TMA 6). On the very eve of the public ministry of Jesus, John the Baptist was divinely sent to proclaim the one who was to come, "the Lamb of God who takes away the sin of the world" (D&V 19). By giving his life in witness to truth and justice, John became "the forerunner of the Messiah by the manner of his death" (VS 91).

Each year the Church prepares for the feast of Christ's birth by remembering the ways in which God prepared the Jews through types and prophecies. In a special way it celebrates John the Baptist as a patron of the Advent season. Without imitating the great severity of John the Baptist, the Church continues to treasure his memory. Recalling how the Baptist moved the Jews of old to repent and recognize the Lamb of God who would take away their sins (Luke 3:1–7; John 1:29), the Church exhorts all who practice injustice to repent and strive for holiness (TMA 19).

From the writings of John Paul II, however, it is clear that for him the primary patroness of Advent is the Blessed Virgin Mary. During the Marian Year of 1986-1987, celebrating the 2000th anniversary of Mary's birth, he issued the encyclical *Redemptoris mater*, in which he described Mary as the "morning star" (*stella matutina*), whose appearance, like the dawn, announces the proximity of Christ, the "Sun of Justice" (*Sol Justitiae*), before he rises visibly over the horizon (RMat 3). Throughout the years from 1986 to the end of the century, Mary's presence on earth is to be gratefully recalled. Just as the Blessed Virgin carried the Christ-Child in her womb before his birth, so the second millennium, in its final years, bears within itself the seeds of the millennium now waiting to be born.

Already in 1983, in a bull proclaiming a holy year, John Paul II called upon Mary to inspire in the hearts of Christians the same sentiments with which she awaited the birth of the Lord in the lowliness of our human nature.[3] Every Christian, he said, is invited to look forward to this great jubilee with the deep faith, humility, and confidence in God that characterized the Virgin Mother in her days of expectancy.[4]

In every Advent season we seek to dispose ourselves to receive in a new and more abundant way the grace of the Nativity. In addition, each Advent prefigures the definitive coming of Christ, before whom we shall have to render an account of our lives. With hope in his mercy we join in the prayer of the Church, "Come, Lord Jesus!"

Looking forward with special eagerness to the advent of the third millennium, John Paul II asks the faithful to enter into the unceasing prayer of the Bride of Christ, expressed in the words of the book of Revelation, "The Spirit and the Bride say to the Lord Jesus Christ: Come!" (Rev. 22:17; D&V 66). This prayer, rich in eschatological significance, is capable of giving fullness of meaning to the celebration of the great jubilee we are now approaching. The Church wishes to prepare for this jubilee in the Holy Spirit, just as did the Virgin of Nazareth in whom the Word became flesh (D&V 66).

The Meaning of Jubilees

As is evident from the weekly observance of the Sabbath and the annual observance of feasts in the liturgical year, the Church respects the measurements of time: hours, days, years, and centuries. The recurrence of commemorations is an occasion for experiencing more profoundly the proper grace of the events that are being recalled, as we do annually in following the liturgical cycle of seasons and feasts (TMA 16). In both secular and religious life it has become common to celebrate the twenty-fifth and the fiftieth anniversaries of marriage or birth, baptism or ordination as silver and golden jubilees. The sixtieth anniversary is known as the diamond jubilee (TMA 15).

This practice is an inheritance from the Old Testament, in which every seventh year was marked as a sabbatical year and every fiftieth as a jubilee year. According to the prescriptions in the Mosaic Law, jubilee years were hallowed in a special way, by leaving the earth fallow, by releasing slaves, and by cancelling debts. Although it does not seem that these regulations were exactly carried out in actual practice, they remained operative as hopes and ideals, and as such they have inspired Christian social teaching, which has striven to give hope to the marginalized and the oppressed and to build justice and mercy into the laws of nations

---

[3] John Paul II, Papal Bull *Aperite portas Domini* §9, *Origins* 12 (February 10, 1983): 564–68, at 566.

[4] Ibid.; cf. D&V 51.

(TMA 12–13). Reflecting on the Old Testament prescriptions regarding the remission of debts, the pope asks whether the great jubilee of the year 2000 might not be an appropriate time for "reducing substantially, if not canceling outright, the international debt which seriously threatens the future of many nations" (TMA 51).

Preparations for the Year 2000

When John Paul II was elected pope in 1978, his friend and mentor Cardinal Stefan Wyszynski of Warsaw told him, "If the Lord has called you, you must lead the Church into the third millennium."[5] The pope has taken this mandate to heart. His first encyclical began with a statement that the Church is already in a season of Advent, preparing for the great jubilee of the year 2000 (RH 1). More recently, he has spoken of the preparations for this celebration as "a hermeneutical key for my pontificate" (TMA 23).

In his apostolic letter *On the Coming of the Third Millennium*, John Paul II presents the whole history of the Church since the 1950s as a providential preparation for this great jubilee. Vatican II, he believes, offered the needed orientations by calling the Church to a new era of missionary proclamation, of dialogue with the great world religions, of ecumenical efforts for Christian unity, and of involvement in the causes of peace, human rights, and solidarity among peoples. "No council," he writes, "has ever spoken so clearly about Christian unity, about dialogue with non-Christian religions, about the specific meaning of the Old Testament and of Israel, about the dignity of each person's conscience, about the principle of religious liberty, about the different cultural traditions within which the Church carries out her missionary mandate, and about the means of social communication" (TMA 19). As the new millennium approaches, the Church is summoned to an examination of conscience regarding its fidelity to the council and to repentance for the past sins of Christians against the ideals held forth by Vatican II, including the unity of Christians and religious freedom (TMA 33–35). The examination of conscience should not, however, be confined to the past. "On the threshold of the new millennium Christians need to place themselves humbly before the Lord and examine themselves on the responsibility which they have for the evils of our day" (TMA 36).

The pope has made very specific proposals regarding the last three years of the present millennium. He has asked for a series of continental synods, including the 1997 Synod for the Americas, which had as its theme: "Encounter with the Living Jesus Christ: The Way to Conversion, Communion, and Solidarity in Amer-

---

[5] John Paul II is quoted as having stated this in May 1994. See the marginal commentary on *Tertio millennio adveniente* in *Origins* 24 (November 24, 1994): 404.

ica" (TMA 38).[6] This special assembly was held in the Vatican from November 16 to December 12, 1997.[7]

John Paul II has also indicated themes for the universal Church during the last three years of the second millennium. The year 1997 was to be devoted especially to the theological virtue of faith, with a focus on Jesus Christ and on a renewed appreciation of the sacrament of baptism (TMA 40–43). In 1998 the theme shifted to the virtue of hope, with a focus on the Holy Spirit, on the sacrament of confirmation, and on the charismatic gifts that the Spirit distributes in the Church (TMA 44–48). In 1999 the central theme becomes God the Father and the theological virtue of charity which should bring about union among all human beings, especially those who worship the one Father by adherence to monotheistic religions, such as Christianity, Judaism, and Islam. The sacramental focus in 1999 should be on penance and reconciliation (TMA 49–54).

In these three years, respectively, a prominent place is to be given to Mary under each of three different aspects: as the Mother of the Son, the Spouse of the Holy Spirit, and the most favored daughter of the Father.

The jubilee year 2000 is to be celebrated by an international eucharistic congress in Rome (TMA 55). John Paul envisages also the possibility of simultaneous celebrations in the Holy Land and in local churches throughout the world. "It would be very significant," he writes, "if in the Year 2000 it were possible to visit the places on the road taken by the People of God of the Old Covenant" in the Holy Land (TMA 24). He is anxious to have the ecumenical and universal character of the great jubilee reflected by a meeting of all Christians, which would also be open to representatives of other religious who might wish to share the joy of the disciples of Christ (TMA 55). These recommendations make it evident that the pope is concerned to avoid the danger that the jubilee could increase the tensions and rivalries among religions and among Christian bodies. He is convinced that the plan of God requires universal solidarity among all peoples of the world.

CONCLUSION

Although Karol Wojtyła has always insisted on the objectivity of truth, he is not less solicitous to take account of the subjectivity of those who receive it. This attention to the personal subject makes him sensitive to the times and cultures in which revealed truth is accepted and professed. With his feeling for the concrete,

[6] The final message may be found in *Origins* 27 (January 1, 1998): 461–66. The Post-Synodal Apostolic Exhortation *Ecclesia in America* was released on January 22, 1999.

[7] For an account of this assembly, see Richard John Neuhaus, *Appointment in Rome: The Church in America Awakening* (New York: Crossroad, 1999).

he brings out the dramatic and narrative aspects of theology and proposes an intriguing theology of time, of history, and of eschatology.

The drama of God's unfolding revelation involves, at each stage, reciprocity between the divine subject who acts and a human subject or community that responds. The divine action proceeds from all three divine persons, each making his own distinct contribution to an effect that belongs indivisibly to them all. At the human level the drama involves a response that engages the freedom of individual persons in community. They respond within the range of possibilities offered by their particular relationship to the stages and events of salvation history.

These salvific events have meaning and value not only for the immediate recipients but for others who learn of them through testimony and tradition. Recollected in faith and reenacted in the liturgy of the People of God, they continue to inspire and nourish subsequent generations. The biblical concept of memorial (*anamnesis*) prepares for the Christian understanding of sacraments as means of grace. John Paul II dwells particularly on the celebrations of Sundays, holy seasons, anniversaries, and jubilees.

The period between Christ's Ascension and his Parousia is distinguished by the anticipated presence of the eschaton in time. The Holy Spirit, the eschatological gift par excellence, directs the Church in its progressive assimilation of the legacy of Christ—the threefold deposit of faith, sacraments, and ministry. At different stages of history, the Spirit gives particular impulses through the "signs of the times." In our survey of Wojtyła's ecclesiology (chapter 4) we have noted how Vatican II in his estimation represents a new breakthrough in the self-consciousness of the Church and in the maturation of faith. Having described the Church's free appropriation of its faith in *Sources of Renewal*, the pope in his more recent writings ponders the vocation of the Church on the eve of the great jubilee of the year 2000. He is convinced that, with suitable preparation, the coming millennial celebration can be a special moment of grace—in technical language, a *kairos*—for the Church in its service to the human family.

CHAPTER 14

Summing Up

∽

WOJTYŁA'S THEOLOGICAL PERSPECTIVE

A S WAS NOTED IN CHAPTER 1, Karol Wojtyła's theological achievement is not primarily in the field of academic research and abstract theory. He has not had the leisure to plumb the depths of the patristic and medieval tradition, like Henri de Lubac or Yves Congar, or to construct a tightly knit and original synthesis, like Paul Tillich and Karl Rahner. Nor has he undertaken to compose a multivolume theological summa like those of Thomas Aquinas, Karl Barth, and Hans Urs von Balthasar. Wojtyła, however, cannot be excluded from the company of academic theologians. Besides writing two scholarly dissertations, he published, as a professor, hundreds of articles dealing principally with moral theory.

The literary output of this pope, like that of Leo the Great, Gregory the Great, and other great patristic popes and bishops, has been primarily that of a pastor. In positions of ecclesiastical leadership he has tirelessly explained the teaching of the Church on a vast range of topics and brought it to bear on current issues in the Church and in the world. As an official teacher he deliberately avoids trying to settle open questions that are legitimately disputed in the schools. As a pastoral leader he tends to avoid technical disquisitions on the fine points of speculative theology and to focus his attention on matters of immediate devotional or practical relevance. It is in these areas that his major contribution is to be found.

As bishop and pope, John Paul II has been extraordinarily faithful to the agenda set by Vatican II. To situate the council in perspective, he draws on the perennial Catholic tradition, as well as on personalist phenomenology, which provided much of the philosophical background for the council. His work is further enriched by his personal prayer and worship and by his broad interests in literature, science, politics, and social studies. So prolific and many-faceted is his theological output that it almost defies reduction to any kind of schematic unity.[1]

Difficult though the task of synthesis may be, the challenge can be met to some degree. John Paul II does have a central vision and message that students of his thought should be able to articulate. One of his salient convictions is that Christ transcends all ethnic and cultural barriers and is a bearer of reconciliation and mutual understanding among all peoples. As a Slav born and nurtured in Poland, who is at home likewise in the West, Wojtyła sees himself as providentially designated to bring about better communication between Eastern and Western cultures. While avoiding the extremes of Polish Messianism, he is conscious of fulfilling in some ways its prophetic image of the "Slavic pope" in whom the Christian people of Eastern Europe would find a voice.[2]

Wojtyła identifies his particular mission not only geopolitically but also chronologically. He situates his pontificate historically between Vatican II and the end of the millennium. The advent of the third millennium, he says, is a hermeneutical key for his entire pontificate. Vatican II, in his view, providentially prepared the Church for the last decades of the second millennium. It marks a vital stage in the growth of the Church's self-awareness and in the maturation of its faith. Just as human beings come of age by understanding what and who they are, and freely living out their own identity, so the Church comes of age by discovering, freely embracing, and living out its own vocation in Christ.

John Paul II is no restorationist, hankering after the simplicity of an earlier age. He is convinced that the Church is led by the Holy Spirit to develop its teaching in organic continuity with the past, to address the problems of the day, and to influence the shape of things to come. Theology, in his view, should be attuned to the present age. In his own work he shows a keen awareness of contemporary developments in science, culture, and social organization. He seeks to assess the signs of the times in the light of the gospel and Catholic tradition.

With his excellent credentials in philosophy and systematic theology, Karol Wojtyła makes use of a vast panoply of sources. Whenever the subject matter allows, he draws by preference on Holy Scripture. Encyclicals such as *Veritatis splendor* and *Evangelium vitae* are remarkable because the chapter and section headings are, for the most part, biblical quotations. Previous popes and councils have not been inclined to have so much recourse to the Bible for their moral and social doctrine.

[1] Among previous efforts to synthesize the theological teaching of John Paul II, the essays in *The Thought of John Paul II*, ed. John M. McDermott (Rome: Editrice Pontificia Università Gregoriana, 1993) are worthy of recommendation. See especially Gerald A. McCool, S.J., "The Theology of John Paul II," pp. 29–53, the response of John M. McDermott, pp. 55–68, and the further reflections of Joseph Murphy, pp. 123–58.

[2] On Polish Messianism and its influence on Wojtyła, see George H. Williams, *The Mind of John Paul II* (New York: Seabury, 1981), 42–47.

Wojtyła's anthropology, including his theology of the body, is developed from biblical sources, especially the early chapters of Genesis with their two contrasting creation stories. His trinitarian theology is strongly biblical. In *Dives in misericordia*, dealing with God the Father, he includes a lengthy discussion of the Hebrew terms for "mercy" (DM 4). The Christology of *Redemptor hominis* owes much to the Gospel of John. In his encyclical on the Holy Spirit, *Dominum et vivificantem*, he delves deeply into the discourses of Jesus at the Last Supper, as given in the Fourth Gospel. In his exhortation on penance he makes a highly creative use of Lukan parables such as that of Lazarus and the rich man (DM 5–6; cf. Luke 15:11–32). In his encyclical on faith and reason, he devotes a lengthy section to the testimony of Hebrew wisdom literature (FR 16–20).

It is sometimes objected that this pope does not profit sufficiently from modern biblical scholarship. Apart from occasional excursions into source criticism and word studies, this may be conceded. His reason is, perhaps, that he does not seem to restrict the freedom of scholars by endorsing in official documents the hypotheses of any one school.[3]

John Paul II, however, cannot be fairly taxed with fundamentalism. In an important address on "The Interpretation of the Bible in the Church" he insists on the importance of interpreting the texts in their literary and historical context, neglecting none of the human aspects of language. He also supports the recent tendency in hermeneutical philosophy to interpret each text as part of the biblical canon and to be attentive to the contributions of patristic exegesis.[4] In the same address he encourages biblical scholars to be open to a multiplicity of approaches and to pray to the Holy Spirit for the light to discern the word of God in the texts. The message of the Bible needs to be "actualized," he says, in ever new situations.

As a devout believer and a priest, Karol Wojtyła makes extensive use of spiritual writers and of liturgy as theological sources. We have had several occasions to comment on his indebtedness to St. John of the Cross and St. Louis Grignion de Montfort. As an example of his use of liturgy, we might recall his discussion of the Anaphora of St. John Chrysostom and the Greek and Russian icons in his encyclical on Mary (RMat 32–33). The same encyclical concludes with a beautiful meditation on the ancient hymn *Alma Redemptoris mater* (RMat 51–52).

John Paul II shows himself to be thoroughly grounded in the writings of the Fathers, both Eastern and Western. He or his collaborators enrich his writings with an amazing multitude of apt patristic citations. He also draws extensively on the writings of the medieval Scholastics and accords particular authority to

---

[3] For the objection and the response, see Terrence Prendergast, "'A Vision of Wholeness': A Reflection on the Use of Scripture in a Cross-Section of Papal Writings," in *The Thought of John Paul II*, 69–91.

[4] John Paul II, "On the Interpretation of the Bible in the Church," in *The Interpretation of the Bible in the Church* (Vatican City: Libreria Editrice Vaticana, 1993), 7–21.

Thomas Aquinas as "an authentic model for all who seek the truth" (FR 78). He praises St. Thomas especially for his engagement in dialogue with the Arab and Jewish thought of his time, for seeking the truth wherever it might be found, and for achieving harmony between faith and reason (FR 43–44).

With his high confidence in the traditional teaching of the Church, John Paul II carefully aligns his doctrine with the magisterium. He adheres staunchly to the Christology of the ancient councils, to the teaching of Trent on the sacraments, that of Vatican I on faith and on papal primacy, and that of Vatican II on themes such as religious freedom and relations with the modern world. In his teaching on human rights and the social order, he maintains continuity with earlier popes such as Leo XIII and John XXIII.

With these methodological prenotes, we may proceed to summarize some of the leading ideas that have been expounded in the preceding chapters.

TOWARD A SYNTHESIS

Personalist Anthropology

In 1968, shortly after being named a cardinal, Karol Wojtyła wrote to his friend Henri de Lubac:

> I devote my very rare free moments to a work that is close to my heart and devoted to the metaphysical sense and mystery of the PERSON. It seems to me that the debate today is being played on that level. The evil of our times consists in the first place in a kind of degradation, indeed in a pulverization, of the fundamental uniqueness of each human person. This evil is even much more of the metaphysical order than of the moral order. To this disintegration, planned at times by atheistic ideologies, we must oppose, rather than sterile polemics, a kind of "recapitulation" of the inviolable mystery of the person.[5]

Permeating all the pope's work is his anthropology. He understands human existence in personalist and dynamic terms. The person, in his view, is a self-constituting agent, the free and responsible subject of its own activity. Activity, as Wojtyła understands it, can be either transitive or intransitive. In its transitive or transient aspect it produces an effect outside the agent, and in its intransitive or immanent aspect it remains within, and modifies, the person who acts. As a personalist, Wojtyła attaches primary importance to the intransitive. The most important thing, for him, is what the action does to the acting subject.

John Paul II is outstanding for his insistence on human dignity and human rights. We have seen how he grounds these convictions in the creative and redemptive action of God as well as in his analysis of the dynamics of the human

---

[5] Henri de Lubac, *At the Service of the Church* (San Francisco: Ignatius, 1993), 171–72.

psyche. He emphatically maintains that since we constitute ourselves by our own actions, we must be free.

Freedom, according to Wojtyła, is not to be understood primarily in terms of indifference, as in the Molinist system. Rather, he adheres to the Augustinian and Thomistic tradition in which freedom is understood as a voluntary commitment to the true and the good. Sin, as the turning away from the true and the good, is the abuse of freedom. By a responsible use of our own freedom we make ourselves the kind of persons that we are.

At Vatican II Wojtyła was already a strong champion of the doctrine of religious freedom. It is a cardinal feature of his thinking that people ought to be free to follow their conscience, which impels them to seek the truth and to live according to what they perceive as true. In the depths of their conscience all men and women hear the summons to a higher life and the call to union with the divine. Wojtyła insistently proclaims that coercion should never be used to inhibit or constrain the inner dynamics of personal decision and growth. He discountenances violence even, or perhaps especially, when it is used in the service of religious truth.

Persons exist in community. They grow through mutual interaction and wither in isolation. Having been created in the image of the triune God, they are essentially social beings, called to loving communion with one another. They come to themselves by relating to others in loving service and dialogue. They can, however, abuse their freedom and act selfishly against others. In so doing they sink below the level of their own humanity and denature themselves. Self-love is the root of all sin for, as Augustine taught, the love of self leads to a contempt for God. The world into which we are born is deeply marked by sin and the effects of sin. It is riddled with fear, hatred, and conflict. It is a world in desperate need of redemption.

Christology

The appearance of Jesus Christ on this planet is not a mere accident. "Through the Incarnation," writes John Paul II, "God gave human life the dimension that he intended man to have from his first beginning" (RH 1). As Son of God, Jesus reveals the Father's character as merciful love; as perfect man, he also reveals humanity to itself. He is the norm by which the Christian life, and indeed all human life, is to be judged. God does not come into the world in order to crush or diminish human freedom but to guide and direct freedom to its proper goal. Jesus offers himself to all as the way, the truth, and the life. He is the truth that sets us free.

Jesus Christ, the supreme exemplar of human perfection, gave himself totally for the redemption of every man and woman and for the renewal of the whole world. The Christocentrism of John Paul II is coupled with a boundless universalism. Christ in his concrete uniqueness is the center of the universe, the goal of human history, and the focus of each individual's personal quest for salvation.

In relation to redeemed humanity, Jesus has a threefold office as prophet, priest, and king. He is the teacher, sanctifier, and ruler of those who follow him, and in this way he becomes their unique savior. Every human being is called to pass through the Paschal mystery in order to achieve the goal of redemption. It is a universal law of human nature that by generously giving ourselves, we fulfill ourselves at the deepest level. Suffering, accepted as a participation in the sufferings of the God-man, can be redemptive. This pope does not simply theorize about suffering; in his own endurance of pain, adversity, and illness, he offers an example of suffering patiently accepted.

Trinity

Christocentric though his theology surely is, John Paul II avoids Christomonism. The prime instance of personal life, he insists, is to be found in the divine Trinity. The three persons in the godhead have a purely relational existence; they are defined by their mutuality.

Christology itself should therefore be trinitarian. John Paul II regularly speaks of Jesus Christ in relation to the other two divine persons. As the eternal Logos, he owes his entire being to the Father, from whom he proceeds, and as man he perfectly carries out his mission from the Father who sent him into the world. He was conceived by the Holy Spirit, who thereafter inspires his prayer and empowers him for mission. Offering himself up as bidden by the Spirit, Jesus gives his life away, and by this sacrifice makes his life fruitful for others. After totally surrendering himself into the hands of the Father, the risen Lord is able to join the Father in sending the Holy Spirit to carry on his own mission. The Holy Spirit universalizes the work of Christ and brings it home to every individual, enabling them to find their true destiny in Christ.

Mariology

John Paul II is keenly conscious of the singular role of the Blessed Virgin Mary, who holds a unique place in the history of human redemption. Just as Jesus was totally receptive in relation to his Father, so she is the model of creaturely receptivity and obedience, as is indicated by her words, "Behold the handmaid of the Lord" (Luke 1:38). In her total self-giving to God, she embraces virginity, but that sacrifice renders her not sterile but fruitful; it qualifies her to be the mother of the Incarnate Word. John Paul II calls her the most perfect disciple, inasmuch as she, more than anyone else, may be said to have heard the word of God and faithfully obeyed it. She consented to the Word at the moment of the incarnation, accepted Jesus' mysterious vocation to do the Father's will, walked with him in his public life, and stood by his side even at the cross.

In his words from the cross Jesus indicated that Mary was to have a maternal relationship to the faithful, represented by the Beloved Disciple. As she was the mother of Christ's physical body, she was appropriately designated to be the mother also of the Church, the Mystical Body of Christ. The apostles gathered with Mary to pray for the descent of the Holy Spirit, the event that John Paul II regards as the birthday of the Church.

Ecclesiology

The mystery of fruitful obedience, first accomplished in Jesus and in Mary, is subsequently realized in the Church, which becomes fruitful by its bridal relationship to Christ, who loved it and gave himself up to make it holy. The Church's obedience does not constrict the personal growth of its members but opens up a path whereby they can be led to the fullness of life that is to be found only in Christ. The Church, marked by receptivity and obedience, has a Marian character leading to life and holiness. Like Mary, the Church is virgin, bride, and mother.

John Paul II understands the Church in personalist terms. It is a living reality constituted by persons who come to themselves by discovering and affirming their own identity. It is a communion of persons, a community of disciples. The community itself is not a merely human fellowship. It is humanity brought into a higher and more consciously experienced union with Christ through the Holy Spirit, or rather through the inhabitation of all three divine persons. Thus, the pope is favorable to what might be called the *communio* model of the Church which emerged at Vatican II. As already indicated, he understands the council's interpersonal presentation of the Church as People of God as marking a vital stage in the Church's progressive self-realization. More than ever before, the members of the Church are called upon to internalize their faith by free and conscious adherence. They can enrich their own faith by prayerful reflection, faithful discipleship, and candid dialogue with other believers and with nonbelievers.

The interior grace of the Holy Spirit is not reserved to those who are formally members of the Church. God in his providence makes it possible for every human being to be associated in a salvific way with Christ and the Paschal mystery. Christians of other communions, adherents of other religions, and nonreligious persons of good will can be related in a variety of salvific ways to Christ the Redeemer. This orientation opens up a multiplicity of potential relationships to the Church as the Body of Christ, which serves as his instrument for the redemption of all.

As a reconciled and reconciling community, the Church is called to be a "sacrament of unity." Among the sins of the members of the Church, John Paul II singles out for special reprobation those that are directed against unity. It is a scandal that Christians fail to love one another and that some accept their divisions with complacency. The pope therefore attaches a high priority to ecumenism, the form of the apostolate that seeks to repair the damage done by sins against unity.

The Church has a visible aspect insofar as it becomes historically tangible in the creedal, societal, and sacramental structures with which it has been endowed. As a sacrament of Christ in the world, the Church participates in his threefold office as prophet, priest, and king. As prophet it teaches and bears witness; as priest, it sanctifies, and as king it orders human life in accordance with the will of Christ. As the "social subject of responsibility for divine truth," the Church has been endowed by its founder with the gift of infallibility (RH 19). The institutional aspects of the Church, for John Paul II, are subordinate to its character as graced community.

Sacraments

John Paul II recognizes baptism as the fundamental sacrament of incorporation into the Church, binding together all the members in a single body. He has written extensively about several other sacraments, including the Eucharist, penance, marriage, and ordination. The Eucharist for him is the sacrament that most perfectly expresses and accomplishes the union that exists among the members of the Church, binding them together in Christ, who continually builds up the Church through the Paschal mystery. The sacrament of penance, for this pope, constitutes a personal encounter with the crucified Christ, who utters through the priest the words of forgiveness, healing, and reconciliation. It belongs to the personal character of the sacrament that it be administered, as far as circumstances admit, to individual penitents rather than groups.

Matrimony, as treated by John Paul II, is the sacrament that most evidently manifests the nuptial union between Christ and the Church. The permanent, loving union between Christ and the Church provides the model for Christian marriage. The sexual union of husband and wife expresses their total mutual self-giving within the nuptial covenant. The Christian family, Wojtyła maintains, is a church in miniature, an *ecclesia domestica*. Like the Church itself, the family represents the fruitfulness of love.

Priesthood and Consecrated Life

Priesthood in the Church is conferred in a general way upon all the members, including the laity, through baptism and confirmation, and in a special way upon certain ministers through ordination. All Christians are called to participate in Christ's threefold office as prophet, priest, and king, because they must bear witness to Christ, share in his consecration, and order their lives according to his example and precepts.

Participation in the threefold office takes on a special quality in the case of those ordained as bishops or presbyters, since they are called to maintain the Church in the unity and truth that come from Christ. The sacred ministers act in the name of the Church when they offer prayers and sacrifices on its behalf. Sharing in Christ's role as head and bridegroom, they act in his name with regard to the faithful. Bishops and presbyters are called to proclaim the word of God with authority, to administer the sacraments, to bring about the eucharistic sacrifice, and to govern the People of God as its appointed shepherds. Since these sacred functions are reserved to the ordained, there should be no blurring of the distinction between them and the laity. The general priesthood of the faithful and the ministerial priesthood of the ordained are distinct in kind.

The consecrated life, for John Paul II, stands at the very heart of the Church as a decisive element in her mission. It particularly manifests the striving of the whole Church as Bride toward deeper union with her one Spouse.

Hierarchical Office

The ministerial priesthood is exercised on the highest level by the bishops, who are gathered about the successor of Peter as the center of their unity. For John Paul II the unity among the bishops is brought about by means of primacy and collegiality, neither of which can be properly exercised except in combination with the other. Through a variety of councils, synods of bishops, and meetings of episcopal conferences the bishops build up their solidarity with one another and with Rome as the center of unity. By means of their hierarchical communion with one another they manifest and strengthen the communion among their respective churches. By collegial activity the bishops also assist the pope in exercising his primatial office. He, for his part, is called to strengthen them in fidelity and unity.

To prevent an unwholesome clericalism it should always be kept in mind that the hierarchical leadership has an essentially servant character. Its purpose is to assist all the members of the Church to carry out their particular calling. The hierarchy exists not for its own sake but for the sake of the whole Church; not to lord it over the laity but to perform a necessary service on their behalf. All the ministry of the ordained is intended to build up the Church in holiness, the ultimate purpose of the Church. Those who hold priestly office cannot effectively perform their tasks unless they excel in personal holiness.

Mission and Dialogue

Like Jesus himself, the Church is sent into the world to accomplish God's saving work. It is always in a state of mission. Every Christian has a share in the missionary responsibility of the whole Church, in accordance with the particular state of life and vocation of each individual.

The mission of the Church may be studied under two headings, evangelization and humanization. In the thinking of John Paul II these two are in the last analysis inseparable. They are two sides of the same coin. The world cannot achieve unity and peace except in the truth, which is most fully disclosed in the person of Jesus Christ. Humanity cannot achieve its God-given goal except by personal transformation in Christ, by sharing in his holiness. Conscious of this, John Paul II dares to challenge the world not to be afraid, but to open up its doors courageously to Jesus Christ.

Mission must also be understood in relation to dialogue. Conscious of the dignity of the human person and of the workings of grace among all peoples, John Paul II calls attention to what Vatican II, following some early church fathers, called "seeds of the Word" and "rays of divine truth" in the various religions and ideologies. Dialogue seeks to identify these seeds and bring them to maturity.

As a personalist, John Paul II profits from the dialogic philosophy of Jewish philosophers such as Martin Buber, Abraham Heschel, and Emmanuel Lévinas. In dialogue, he holds, we give witness to our own convictions while listening respectfully to the testimony of others. Dialogue, therefore, is inseparable from missionary proclamation.

Evangelization

By evangelization John Paul II, like Paul VI, means the whole process of bringing the world into a conscious and explicit adherence to Christ as redeemer, in whom alone creation can achieve its fulfillment. The principal agent of evangelization, as Paul VI had already said, is the Holy Spirit. Bishops and priests have a responsibility to stimulate and direct the evangelizing efforts of the whole Church. The laity are called to evangelize by bearing witness to Christ and by transforming the temporal order according to the norms and ideals of the gospel. Large portions of humanity, the pope observes, are still in need of primary evangelization; they have not as yet heard the call of Christ and the gospel. In many parts of the world today there is need for reevangelization, since the faith of earlier generations has not been effectively passed on.

Humanization

Multitudes of persons, although endowed with human nature from their conception, are caught in situations in which they are unable to develop their basic human powers. The world is full of starving, uncared-for children, and adults who live in political fear or economic destitution. Sharing in the compassion of Jesus, the Church is called to a role of leadership in building what Paul VI called "a civilization of love." This involves work for peace, for solidarity among peoples and nations, for justice and human rights. Throughout the centuries, and perhaps especially under John Paul II, the Church has been an outstanding champion of the poor, the weak, the elderly, the unborn, and the newly born. The grace of Christ, mediated by the Church, gives hope for a human fulfillment beyond all that this world can offer.

In a broader sense of the word, biblical revelation calls for the "humanization" of the world itself, as the environment of human activity. The vocation to "subdue the earth" (Gen. 1:28) does not authorize us to exploit and pollute the earth, the seas, and the atmosphere in irresponsible ways, but gives us the mandate to make the world what Vatican II calls "a dwelling worthy of the whole human family" (GS 57).

Politics and Economics

The Church as such does not have specific programs for the organization of human society, but it does have a body of social teaching that articulates the basic principles. For John Paul II the first essential would seem to be the rights of the individual person, which are sacred and inviolable. The state is under a solemn obligation to protect the God-given rights of the citizens, including the freedom of conscience and of religion. Individuals perfect themselves by seeking truth and moral integrity in community, serving one another. Authentic community is threatened today by currents of utilitarianism and collectivism that would treat persons as mere means. John Paul II is on guard against institutions and programs that would subordinate the good of human subjects to political power, economic development, or technological progress, pursued for their own sakes.

The goal of social action is to bring about a community of love, in which the members freely participate in the realization of a common good that redounds to the benefit of the members themselves. The idea of participation, as set forth in *The Acting Person*, excludes individualism, which undermines community, and "totalism," which simply absorbs the individual into the anonymous mass. Individualism leads to anarchy and totalism to coercion. In place of both, Wojtyła proposes the ideal of persons in solidarity.[6]

To translate these general principles into concrete programs is properly the task of the laity, who are called to involve themselves in the spheres of politics, business, and the secular professions. Seeking to avoid clericalism, John Paul II

---

[6] These aspects of the pope's social thought are well explained in Rocco Buttiglione, *Karol Wojtyła: The Thought of the Man Who Became Pope John Paul II* (Grand Rapids, Mich.: Eerdmans, 1997), 168–76.

wants to give scope to the Catholic laity to be creative in their initiatives and to enter into voluntary collaborative arrangements with other persons of good will. The laity are called to see to it that the gospel has its leavening impact on the spheres of culture, law, and politics. The leadership of the Church must remind the laity of their responsibility to bring the gospel to bear on the new worlds of science and communication that are in such rapid flux today. These spheres are what John Paul II calls the "Areopagi," or cultural centers, of the modern world.

Theology in Relation to
Philosophy and the Sciences

John Paul II has shown a sustained interest in the relationships between faith and reason. Philosophical inquiry, he believes, can discover intimations of the divine mystery and thus dispose sincere inquirers to receive and welcome revelation. The dynamism of reason is fulfilled by faith, which in turn makes use of philosophical reason to understand what it believes.

Wojtyła speaks with high esteem of the contributions of science to the development of human understanding and technological proficiency. In his addresses to the Pontifical Academy of Sciences and to university professors he has repeatedly insisted on the need for a lively dialogue between science and theology. Speaking as a personalist, he pleads with scientists to take account of philosophical and ethical values to prevent their achievements from being used against the human good.

John Paul II holds up Albert the Great as an example of a theologian who embraced and mastered the scientific knowledge of his day. In the Counter-Reformation, he believes, the proper distinction between the orders of knowledge was blurred, with the result that Galileo was erroneously condemned. Anxious to prevent any recurrence of such errors, he has expressed openness to the theory of evolution and to various cosmological hypotheses, provided that these are not linked to materialist or reductionist philosophy. As a former professor, the pope envisages Catholic universities as places where the various disciplines may fruitfully interact, to the benefit of all, including theology. Theology, in its turn, can remind scientists of the primacy of the moral and spiritual over the technical and material aspects of life.

Critique of Cultures

In the pope's vision, the gospel cannot take hold of individual persons and societies except by being incarnated, so to speak, in cultures. Western European culture, in spite of its past and present greatness, no longer suffices for a world Church. From every cultural sector, including the younger churches of Asia and

Africa, come distinctive contributions that show forth the manifold riches of Christ the Redeemer. By implanting itself in various cultures, the gospel preserves, elevates, and purifies them all, supplementing whatever may be lacking in each of them individually. By a connatural tendency culture reaches out to the true, the good, and the beautiful. Since these properties are most perfectly realized in God, culture itself has a religious dimension and an affinity with the truth of revelation.

In some of his recent writings the pope makes a broad contrast between two cultures—a culture of life and a culture of death. Since Jesus came into the world in order that men and women might have life and have it more abundantly, Christianity is committed to a culture of life. But in many countries, not excluding prosperous societies such as our own, the pope sees alarming symptoms of degeneration and decay. He finds a falling away from truth and a disregard of God's creative plan. Forgetful of permanent and transcendent truth, people are turning more and more to the quest for utility, convenience, and personal pleasure. Economism tends to reduce the value of persons to their ability to serve the needs of the marketplace. In a consumerist culture, primacy is given to entertainment, gadgets, and luxury items. People seek freedom without responsibility, even to the extent of falling into hedonism.

Following Paul VI, John Paul II is convinced of the Church's present call to evangelize not only individuals but cultures themselves. In this apostolate the Church and its representatives must not fear to become signs of contradiction. The faithful following of Christ is not intended to be a path of ease and popularity. Inspired by the example of Christ and the martyrs, Christians must be prepared for rejection, even to the point of the cross.

Grounds for Hope

John Paul II, however, gives no warrant for discouragement. With his eyes fixed on Christ and the Holy Spirit, he is convinced that the divine Lord of history is in control. Even in the midst of poverty and oppression, many are reaching out—he says—for the meaning of life. Increasing numbers are disposed to hear the message of the gospel, provided that it be authentically proclaimed to them. Even before being accepted in its fullness, the gospel exerts a beneficial influence on the ideas and values that are shaping the world of our day. Movements for peace, justice, human rights, and protection of the environment are basically sound. A large patrimony of truth and holiness survives in Protestant and Orthodox Christianity. The seeds of the word of God and the rays of divine truth that are present in secular humanism and in the many religions of the world are sources of encouragement.

In the hope of achieving greater unity in the truth, the pope returns to the theme of dialogue. Vatican II and Paul VI summoned the Catholic Church to dialogue with other churches, with world religions, and with those who have no religious belief. Such dialogue, John Paul II insists, must not be aimed at weak pragmatic compromises but at unity in the fullness of truth.

The Coming Jubilee

The teaching of John Paul II manifests a lively consciousness of the present situation of Christianity. Defining his pontificate in relation to the coming of the third millennium, he strives to prepare the Church and the world for the great jubilee that is at hand. Like every Advent, the closing years of the twentieth century should be a time for prayerful examination of conscience and repentance for past errors. Conscious of their own failures, past and present, Catholics should beg forgiveness of those whom they have injured. Looking forward in hope, they must renew their confidence in the Holy Spirit, who made the womb of the Blessed Virgin fruitful at the moment of the incarnation, and in the Father of Mercies, who gave his only Son for our redemption. The arrival of the year 2000, properly celebrated, will provide an auspicious occasion for a renewal of the Church, a new outburst of apostolic energy, and a more universal adherence to Christ as the way, the truth, and the life.

Conclusion

This final summary, which restates themes more fully explained in the preceding chapters, may be warranted because of the breadth and complexity of the teaching of John Paul II. He has written so voluminously on so many topics that it is easy to lose sight of the unity and coherence of his thought. His theological vision reaches back to the origins of revealed religion and outward to the furthest reaches of human communication. While making himself the faithful guardian of the deposit of faith, this pope shows an astonishing openness to dialogue with other churches, other religions, and the secular worlds of science and technology. Guided by his philosophical studies and his experience of the Second Vatican Council, he has forged a Christocentric humanism and a dynamic personalism capable of encountering and respectfully challenging all opposing ideologies and spiritual movements. The Catholic Church and, I submit, the world at large have been greatly blessed by the intellectual leadership of this brilliant, energetic, and prayerful successor of Peter.

Index